To: Dr. Tania Orzynski
with many thanks for
your help and care.

Leonard Mafutz

01/07/10

ISBN: 978-1-4349-0310-5

Printed in the United States of America

First Printing

For more information or to order additional books,
please contact:
Dorrance Publishing Co., Inc.
701 Smithfield Street
Pittsburgh, Pennsylvania 15222
U.S.A.
1-800-788-7654
www.dorrancebookstore.com

From Russia
with Tales and Confessions
to Discovering America

by

Leonid Heifets

DORRANCE PUBLISHING CO., INC.
PITTSBURGH, PENNSYLVANIA 15222

In memory of my parents and many dear friends

FOREWORD

The chapters of this book were passed around to family and friends for first impressions as our father was writing it. While the book was taking shape, we discovered a striking similarity with the spirit of Jonathan Swift's *Gulliver's Travels*. Gulliver provided a calm and "objective" view of events and characters that he had encountered during his travels to exotic fictitious countries. His biting satire and parody of life in Europe during the seventeenth century turned out to be more effective than direct criticism.

From Russia with Tales and Confessions to Discovering America could be called the fifth book of Gulliver's travels befitting the descriptions of Soviet absurd realities. The descriptions in this book in a way culminate the insanity and satire of Soviet existence over the last two generations. Soviet scientific history could indeed rival in absurdity the Laputian Academy on many occasions. The reader will easily recognize trails of Liliputians, Brobdingnags, Houynhnms, Yahoos, and Laputian scientists all meshed together in this entertaining, yet sad and instructive, narrative. "Gulliver" is a Soviet scientist trying to make sense of his career in such a bizarre and twisted society reminiscent of the civilizations described in the Swift's novel. The author of this book, our father, lived a life full of struggle in the Soviet Union, and we, his sons, had an opportunity to witness many of the events described in the book.

Although the book contains many autobiographical elements, the focus is on other people and events, which may be of interest to a Western reader not quite familiar with life in various parts of the former Soviet Union. Life in the Far North of Russia; interactions with tribes of the Caucasus Mountains; work in various former Soviet republics including Uzbekistan, Kyrgyzstan, Tajikistan, and Kazakhstan; and especially his membership in the Soviet medical expeditions to Central Africa in 1960 and 1962: all these activities gave him an opportunity to witness and describe diverse situations and people. Such stories are contrary to mainstream stereotypes of Russia and Russians. It was a struggle for survival, a struggle against the authorities on issues related to the bacteriological warfare program, and a struggle to implement modern scientific methods for objective assessment of the vaccines' efficacy.

This uncharacteristically calm narration of the past of the Soviet Union is due to a long, twenty-nine year period of living in the United States. That period of time in the U.S. can be compared to the wanderings of Jews in the Sinai. Jews leaving Egypt were not ready to become a free nation the moment they fled the oppression. Similarly, it took the author some time to free his mind completely from Soviet influence. Professional experience in the U.S. during these years provided an opportunity to objectively compare and analyze various social and professional issues in both countries.

Therefore, the events and interactions described in this book are far beyond historical interest related to the former Soviet Union, but may also serve as a source of many lessons to be used in modern times wherever a reader may be.

Michael Heifets and Herman Heifets

CONTENTS

Introduction ix

Chapter One. The Taste of Bread 1

Chapter Two. Uzbekistan, Young Man's Dilemmas,
    and Stark Realities 26

Chapter Three. Moscow, New Horizons,
    and New Challenges (1945–1950) 50

Chapter Four. Northern Exposure, Soviet Style (1950–1957) . .69

Chapter Five. A 20-year Journey through
    the Post-Stalin Era (1957–1978) 95

Chapter Six. Russian "Shaman" in Africa 133

Chapter Seven. *Homo Sovieticus* 174

Chapter Eight. Dangerous Assignment 192

Chapter Nine. Under the Sword of Damocles 207

Chapter Ten. Code Name "Green Eggs Project"
    and Escape from Russia 224

Chapter Eleven. "Discovering" America, First Impressions .249

Chapter Twelve. Thirty Years Later, More "Discoveries" 272

INTRODUCTION

One must know the past to be successful in the present and in the future. Many lessons can be learned from the history of the Soviet Union, a country that has ceased to exist. Scholars have published many books and articles on this subject, but there can never be enough detailed accounts of the personal experiences of those who lived there. The perceptions of these people broaden and enrich our knowledge of the truth about the Soviet Union and will help in understanding that society as well as other countries with similar social tendencies.

Recollections of the people and events of my life have sparked my memory and have given life to this project. My life has taken me to the ends of the earth, and the stories in this book wander from the Far North of Russia, to desolate Siberia in the east, away to the little-known Central Asian Republics, up to the heights of the Caucasus region, and down to the jungles in Africa. Woven into the fabric of some of these stories are the extraordinary and colorful people I met while living in Russia.

Although my stories took place in Russia, I can neither suggest to the reader a comprehensive description of life in Russia, nor can I provide a comprehensive description of the typical or average Soviet citizen. In Soviet folklore, they were known as *Homo Sovieticus*, a stereotype developed out of the conditions of the system. One of the characteristics of such a "species" was based on the complete separation of deeds, words, and thoughts as a tool for survival in that society.

I hope that these stories and episodes and the descriptions of the individuals involved will contribute to a better understanding of life, particularly the life of a medical scientist with humble beginnings, struggling under the dominance of a totalitarian regime. This is not just a story of the past. Similar situations still exist in other countries. Some of these stories may be of special interest to people involved in research activities because science, due to the applications of new discoveries, has always been and always will be dual in nature, with dual implications—good and evil. Choice and balance between these two options largely depends on the ethics and morals of a society. Therefore, the political systems of countries have the final decision with regard to the preferred direction of research in any discipline, including biomedical sciences.

Science is no longer viewed as an Ivory Tower, but a young person entering scientific research traditionally does so with the noble desire to make life better for mankind. This noble endeavor of young scientists will inevitably come into conflict with the social systems of some regimes. Often, these governments do not allow scientists their independence in research, but rather have different (and often sinister) plans for their educated young people. It is not easy to preserve your integrity under these conflicting circumstances. Nevertheless, it is possible! I hope that, in this regard, my experiences will help some young scientists develop their own way of preserving their integrity and honesty. These survival tips are useful even in the free world where the negative elements of human nature may still redirect any pure and noble scientific intentions.

After reading some of my stories, one of my advisors commented that I had a tendency to go against the stream rather than to compromise so that I might get along with other people and circumstances. He asked, "Is that because of the environment you lived in, or is it just your character?" I answered, "Perhaps it is both. In any society, and not only within the climate of a totalitarian regime, people face a dilemma—whether to please everybody and just be a 'nice' person or to express counter-cultural positions, opinions, or beliefs. This choice presents itself whether establishing social standing, creating a personal life, or writing scientific reports."

It is quite common for people to try to be like everybody else and to act according to what is expected by the majority. There are certain benefits to this choice, but the price can be very high if you lose your identity. To preserve your identity may not be easy, but it makes you stronger through self-respect and respect from others. Most of the time I chose the second option, and not only because of my stubbornness, but also because I learned that my stands in research based on principles and honesty would often puzzle my opponents, help me win allies and sympathizers, and earn respect from both sides.

A human life is like a river with no return. Some people choose to swim with the current of this river without realizing that, though this seems to be the easier way, they may face treacherous rocks and dangerous white water. Swimming upstream, against the current, is much more difficult, but it can be less dangerous and even more efficient, if you have enough energy and determination to make it. One cannot succeed in such a venture alone, without help and support from others. I was blessed with a large number of loyal friends, both back in Russia and now in the U.S. and around the world. Friendships with many of them developed throughout my lifetime, but in some cases within short periods of interaction. It was based on a readiness to be available when needed and to come forward at difficult times, especially in Russia. I would like to express my deep thanks to all of them, including many individuals whose names are not mentioned in this book. The memory of some dear friends who are not with us anymore will always be in my heart and mind, and I hope that some stories included in the book may serve as my expression of gratitude to them.

In conclusion, I would like to take an opportunity to express my appreciation to my friends and family for their encouragement and support given to me while I was pulling from my memory the many almost-forgotten episodes and writing them here. This project would not be possible without advice and editorial help from my friends Janice Clotfelter, Rev. Catheryne Queen, Ken Clare, and

Dr. Henry Milgrom. I thank you all, and I hope that this product to which you have all contributed so much time and emotions will not be a disappointment when it is complete.

July, 2008

CHAPTER ONE

The Taste of Bread

"Blessed are you, Lord our G-D, King of the universe,
who brings forth bread from the earth."
From the Shabbat Blessing (Ha Motzi)

1. Roots, Belarus
2. From Jewish History of Belarus
3. Belarus after the October Revolution
4. Parents
5. Some Childhood Memories
6. School Years
7. At the German Invasion
8. The Taste of Bread
9. About Cossacks
10. Xenophobia

Fig. 1. "Taste of Bread": soldiers in a military train at a small railroad station in Central Russia in 1941. *Drawing by Edward Tabachnik*

Fig. 2. Remnants of the past Pale of Settlement in Belarus central square in a Jewish settlement (*Shtettle*) converted on a Sunday into a market as viewed in 1930s.
Drawing by Edward Tabachnik

Fig. 3. Family photographs taken in Kolyshki, Vitebsk
District of Belarus, left to right, top to bottom:
- Shlomo-David Heifets (1911);
- Golda Mindlin, wife of Herman Mindlin (1928);
- Luba Mindlin, daughter of Golda and Herman (1923); and
- Luba Mindlin married to Boris Heifets (1925).

Fig. 4. From the Cossacks' history in Siberia (I took these photographs in July, 2007):
Three photographs are of houses and a church in a Cossacks' settlement/village of 18-19th century, preserved near lake Baikal in Siberia.
Model of a wooden fortress (*ostrog*) displayed in the Blagoveshchensk Museum representing the period of initial conquest of Siberia in 16-17th centuries, when the Cossacks had to protect themselves from the local tribes (Tartars, Kangalas, Tungus, Buriats, and others).

1. Roots, Belarus

The place was the Governmental University Medical School in the city of Minsk, the capital in the Soviet Republic of Belarus. It was 1923 and only five years after the 1917 October Revolution. My father, Boris Heifets, a second-year medical student, was nervously awaiting his meeting with the dean. He was twenty years old and had just recently lost his beloved mother (Leah bat Aharon, 1860–1923). In due time, Boris was called before the dean. He sat quietly while the dean perused documents that Boris knew contained information that could have a ruinous impact on his future.

He had just returned from his mother's funeral in his hometown of Kolyshky, where he began attending the local synagogue, which, by the new Communist standards, was unacceptable activity for a university student. Someone noticed that Boris was visiting the synagogue and reported it to the medical school. Just as he expected, the dean confronted him about it. Boris explained that he was very attached to his mother and that her death had been a terrible blow to him, and, further, that his father and other relatives living in town told him that to properly mourn his mother's passing he should attend the synagogue. Boris politely told the dean that he did it just to comfort his father, but he himself did not believe in God. He also stated that he was loyal to the Communist ideology and did not intend to have anything to do with religion in his future life. The dean took a fatherly approach to Boris's admission and told him he knew that he was a good boy and, therefore, he would not be expelled from the medical school.

From that day forward, almost until the end of his life, Boris kept his word. He never crossed the threshold of a synagogue again, and he never spoke of God to his children. This must have caused him psychological suffering throughout his life. I had no knowledge of this until he was dying from heart failure at the age of sixty-eight. He knew precisely the day he was going to die, and a few days before it happened he requested to speak with a neighbor, a man in his late eighties named Roovim, who was known as an observant Jew. He and my father had a long conversation behind the closed door. The day my father died, Roovim came to our house and told me my father's last wish: He wanted me to organize his funeral according to the Jewish religious rules. He also wanted me to read *Kaddish* every day for a year and then every year on the anniversary date of his death. The man gave me the text of this prayer, which my father had transliterated into Russian letters. I was shocked, impressed, and in spite of how difficult it was in Moscow to fulfill it, I followed his request. This episode brought me closer to the Jewish religious ideology and observance, and I came to believe that in this observance I was compensating for the gap in my father's life that he would have wanted me to fill. I cherish this handwritten *Kaddish* page, which is the only item I inherited from my father. It is also my sign of *tshuva*, the return to the religious values.

2. From Jewish History of Belarus

Until 1992, Belarus was one of the Soviet Republics. Historically, it was part of Poland, a country captured by the Russian Empire through partitions of Poland at the end of the eighteenth and beginning of the nineteenth century. For many years, the Polish people, and in particular the aristocracy, tried to regain their independence from Russia and staged a series of military rebellions and insurgencies. Poland had a substantial Jewish population (about 20%), and most of the Polish Jews were sympathetic to the Polish resistance rather than to the Russian occupation.

My uncle Isaiah-Joseph told me the legend of one of our ancestors who was involved in the Polish resistance against the Russians. His name was Hirsh Heifets, and he lived in what was then the small town of Minsk. Hirsh was relatively wealthy and made a business of transporting people between cities and villages; therefore, he owned coaches and horses. The story goes that Hirsh modified his passenger coaches with hidden compartments to conceal arms and ammunition, which he delivered to the Polish rebel camps in the forest. From time to time, Russian Army officers would hire Hirsh to take them by stagecoach to various places; however, the officers frequently failed to arrive at their intended destination, ending up instead amongst the rebels in the forest. When the Russian authorities learned of these nefarious activities, the famous outlaw Hirsh disappeared into the forest. Wives of the Russian Army officers would sometimes threaten their children with, "Be quiet or Heifets is going to come." Eventually, Hirsh was captured by the Russians and hanged in the central square of Minsk, as my uncle told me.

With the acquisition of Poland, the Russian Empire suddenly possessed a large Jewish population, about 1.2 million, according to the records of 1815. To contain the Jews within the conquered territories, the Russian Empress Catherine II (Catherine the Great), established in 1795 the Pale of Jewish Settlement in the newly acquired territories, enforced later by her decree of 1815. The Pale of Settlement was the only area of the Russian Empire where Jews were allowed to live. They were not allowed to enter Russia proper and could not live in the cities, even those within the Pale. One of the restrictions imposed on the Jews during the reign of Alexander III was a 3% legally enforced enrollment limitation for acceptance to the Russian universities outside the Pale. Jews were neither allowed to possess land nor to be directly involved in agriculture. They lived in small towns, or settlements, called *shtettles* in Yiddish. These settlements were like small islands surrounded by large agricultural areas where the local peasants lived in small villages and farms. Livelihood in a *shtettle* was limited to small merchants, tailors, blacksmiths, and carpenters, and a few owned limited amounts of livestock. Only a few Jews in the Russian Empire could achieve the wealthy merchant status that allowed them to reside in large cities, including Moscow. Only a few fortunate families could afford to send their children to Western Europe for higher education. In spite of all restrictions, at the time of the October Revolution of 1917, there were about 200,000 Jewish professionals living in Russia, some educated in Russia and some abroad.

Lifestyle in the Jewish settlements was well described in books and stories by Sholom Aleichem and other famous Jewish writers. Isolation from the rest of the world and boredom with everyday life in this environment sometimes created unusual and even weird individuals—among them were some of my relatives. One such individual was my mother's cousin, Joseph Mindlin. I remember him as somewhat older than my mother, a very skinny, short man, with large eyes behind heavy glasses on a small face, always very expressive and easily agitated. He eventually became a famous actor, and in the 1940s I had a chance to see his brilliant performance in a classical stage production called *Tevye* that later became the musical known as *Fiddler on the Roof*. He had performed in many Jewish theatres in the country—as long as the Soviet authorities allowed them to exist—including the famous Jewish theater in Odessa. Growing up in an extremely poor family, Joseph, as a teenager, had many fantasies that today might be deemed sociopathic. He was always angry with the small merchants in the town whom he considered as unfairly possessing too much wealth. He developed a habit of setting fires in their shops. He was caught and reprimanded by the community but never turned over to the Russian authorities. Throughout his later life he was often called "Josele-the-arsonist."

Another unusual character was my uncle Isaiah-Joseph, known as a storyteller. I remember him as a relatively short, stocky man with dark, deep-set eyes and a penetrating expression. These qualities somehow helped him to survive in difficult times. He was a simple man without a profession. During the war with Germany, he managed to escape with his family from the advancing German Army. He settled in a rural area in the Eastern part of the Soviet Union, but he was unable to obtain a job to support his family. This area was so impoverished that the local peasants had no access to social activities, education, or medical care. According to the story Isaiah-Joseph told me after the war, he decided to fill this gap. He nurtured a rumor, started by local peasants, that he possessed the power to cure ailments, provide counseling for family problems, and even predict the future. He became know as a local shaman, a "witch doctor," and for all these services, the peasants reciprocated by giving him enough food for his family's survival. After the war, Isaiah-Joseph settled with his family in the city of Astrakhan. Once he came to visit us in Moscow because he started to feel ill. My father examined him and diagnosed a large, incurable stomach cancer, but he had difficulty telling his brother that he had only few months to live. Eventually, he asked me to write a letter to the uncle's wife. This was one of the few times my father acknowledged that he needed my communication skills.

Most Jews living in the Pale strictly observed their religion and traditions. One of those was the ingrained belief in education, which had been passed down for centuries. Beginning at age five or six, all boys had to study Hebrew to learn how to pray and to read the Torah. The same Hebrew letters were used to read and write in Yiddish, the everyday language of the Eastern European Jews. They also learned Polish, the original language of the country, subsequently replaced by Russian. As a result, almost 100% of Jewish males, and, to a lesser extent, females, were literate. By contrast, the peasant population in the surrounding villages had very limited options for education in the few schools in the rural areas, and most (at least 70–80%) were illiterate.

3. Belarus after the October Revolution

After the October Revolution of 1917, the Soviet Government lifted all restrictions imposed by the Tsarists' Imperial System on Jews. This suddenly opened up new opportunities for literate young Jews from the small towns. Therefore, it was no surprise that many young Jews like Boris took advantage of the situation and rushed to the universities. In addition, according to the new Soviet rules, preference was given to members of the poorest working-class families to seek a higher education, and Boris fit the category.

Life in Kolyshky continued after the revolution without much change until 1941, when the country was overrun and destroyed by the German invasion. When I was six or seven years old, my father and I traveled from Orsha to visit my aunts and cousins who still lived in Kolyshky, which was our birthplace. Although the purpose of our visit was to see the town and our relatives, my father had a hidden agenda. He wanted to let his relatives and everybody else know that he had attained the highest achievement according to their standards—he was a doctor. He was the only one from among the residents of the town who had made it!

This was an opportunity to observe remnants of past life in Kolyshky. It made such an impression on me that, despite my young age, I still have vivid memories of life in that town. My father told me that within the same Vitebsk district where Kolyshky is located was a tiny settlement named Lubavitch by the local peasants, because of the generosity and kindness of one of its residents. The word Lubavitch originated from the Russian word *lubov*, which means love. This generous man was Rabbi Shneur Zalman (1745–1812), the founder of one of the Hasidic movements. The Lubavitcher movement later established its headquarters in New York, and the family name became Schneerson. In a tone of important secrecy, my father told me that one of our ancestors had served as an assistant to Rabbi Shneur Zalman of Liadi. Another area within the Vitebsk district was the birthplace of the artist Marc Chagall.

In the Soviet time, Kolyshky continued to be the center of trade activities in the area. Even the Orthodox Church, which previously was obligatory by Imperial Russian standards for such settlements, continued its regular functions under the new regime. Every Sunday, the peasants from the surrounding areas went there to worship. Afterward, the central square would become a large open market filled with horse carts from which the peasants sold their agricultural produce. Little shops surrounded the square where the peasants bought clothes, boots, and other goods from the Jewish merchants and could obtain various services like blacksmith, carpentry work, etc.

4. Parents

My parents were both born and grew up in the generally very poor community of the *shtettle* and were from the poorest families. My father was the youngest child of a large family, which meant he was considered the least important among his siblings. His father, Solomon (Shlomo-David ben Haim HaLevy, 1860–1928), was a kosher chicken butcher who also taught boys, ages five to seven, to read and write. Of course, my father concealed his father's livelihood from the Soviet authorities. The religious rituals associated with butchering chickens would have been viewed negatively. My mother, Luba, also had something to conceal from the Soviet authorities. On one hand her father, Herman, was a blacksmith, which was a respected profession by the Soviet system; however, her brothers and one sister had emigrated to America before World War I began. Luba, her other sister Basia, and their mother Golda were expected to follow. They already had their documents and tickets to sail from Hamburg to America, but their plans were interrupted when war with Germany broke out in 1914. In the Soviet environment, it was unsafe to have relatives living abroad as a matter of record and this had to be kept secret. I was born into a family with many secrets, which at that time was not uncommon. While growing up I learned to keep them inside, and I learned that one should not reveal family events to the outside world, which was quite the opposite of what the schools taught in every grade.

I remember my father being a very serious person most of the time, but at times he could reveal a keen sense of humor. His life was greatly affected by his chronic heart condition, which limited his movement and kept him far from slim. My mother, Luba, was the daughter of a blacksmith, which was a service much needed by local peasants but relegated to the lowest social status in the Jewish community. Many people viewed my mother as a beautiful woman. She was slim, of average height, had dark (almost black) hair, and very soft manners. In a picture from 1922 or 1923, when she was nineteen or twenty years old, she looked very similar to Anne Frank.

Although I was born in Kolyshky, my early years were spent in Minsk, the capital of Belarus, where the university was located. After my father graduated from medical school, our family moved to the city of Orsha in the Vitebsk district of Belarus. My father was assigned to the local government clinic, where he began his medical practice and my mother became a pediatric nurse. My memories go back to the early 1930s, when I was five or six years old. My paternal grandfather, Solomon, died in 1928, before we moved to Orsha. My maternal grandmother, Golda, came from Kolyshky and lived with us until her death in 1932.

My grandmother, Golda, used to take me to the grocery market and everywhere else she went in town. After one such trip I developed a fantasy that my grandmother could fly, and that once she flew with me over the river. Perhaps I drew this fantasy from an incident when we were walking on a bridge over the river in a very strong wind. My grandmother was tightly holding my hand and the wind blew her skirt. My mother became angry when I told her that I flew over the river with my grandmother and forbade to me to speak of this nonsense. Nevertheless, I kept it in my mind and for several years often visualized her flying in my dreams. My grandmother was an extraordinarily soft person, and my mother inherited some of her soft kindness.

One remarkable side of my mother's character that is still engraved in my memory is how she would reach out to people in need. She had an unusual ability to comfort those who sought her company, but it was mostly from the contact rather than substantive help or advice. Her kindness and love were essential elements that have helped me throughout my life and in my growth and development, and it significantly influenced my character and attitude toward people. My mother's influence often balanced the harsh temperament of my father, who usually implanted in me skepticism and mistrust.

My father suffered from a heart valve deficiency. Once, when I was about eight years old, he had a recurring episode of heart failure, and he thought that he was dying. He called me to his bedside and sent my mother from the room. Then he said, "Leonia, I will tell you one very important thing that I want you to remember throughout your life. Never trust anybody on anything. Nobody! Never! Now, you can go and tell your mother to come back." I have remembered this episode throughout my life, and perhaps my father's advice did help me survive some treacherous situations in the Soviet Union. Conversely, I often try to imagine my mother's approval or disapproval of my decisions when faced with difficult dilemmas in personal or working relationships, especially when someone's well-being depends on my decision.

5. Some Childhood Memories

Our house in Orsha was on a street near a large hill developed from ruins of a medieval Polish castle and was thereby named Castle Street (*Zamkovaya Ulitsa*). Digging around the hill for old Polish coins was an adventure for the boys, while another favorite attraction was a waterfall formed by a dam that provided water for a nearby water mill. Some wild teenagers considered it a show of bravery to jump from the bridge into the waterfall, and a few died. This neighborhood has remained in my memory for many years, and nostalgic feelings often emerge in my dreams at night. It was not a prestigious area at all, and we settled there because, as a young physician, my father could not afford a house where the other doctors lived. Wild drinking parties were quite common in some nearby houses, and the people in those houses were considered low class. It was common knowledge that a nest of professional thieves lived in the house next door, but they were particularly nice to us. Some friends told us that we were living in the safest area of the city because professional thieves never robbed their own neighbors but were protective of the area where they lived.

I used to hang around with the children from these unusual families, and I learned manners and habits that were far from refined and respectable. One such habit was fighting frequently with little or no provocation just to see who was stronger and more violent. I was not physically strong, and I avoided any temptation to try to be a champion. Once, however, I became so irritated at being teased that I started a fight with one of my tormentors. Suddenly, I felt rage inside me, and I started beating him so violently that I bloodied his nose and damaged my knuckles. I won the fight, but inside I felt ashamed. I could not believe what I had done. I felt sorry for the boy, and I even felt sorry for myself. The pain in my knuckles stayed in my memory for many years, and I never again engaged in a physical fight. This shameful memory became a reminder that helped give me control over feelings of rage, even in my adult life.

Another form of entertainment among the boys was to go to the hills on the shore of the Dnieper River, where we hid in the bushes, waiting for a soldier to bring a girl. Usually it was the maid of a wealthy family. We would quietly wait until the amorous couple started making love, and then we would suddenly come out of the bushes shouting and run away.

Nearly half of the residents of Orsha were Jewish and the rest of the population was identified ethnically as Belorussian, Russian, and Polish. Yiddish was the common tongue in Orsha, even among the non-Jews. In my childhood I did not feel any different from the rest of the children my age. Although we considered ourselves ethnically Jewish, my family did not observe any religious traditions. I was never clear about the differences between people of various ethnic origins, and religion was not even an issue in our lives. Besides my ignorance of the religion, I also knew nothing of the origin and history of Jewish people.

My parents often took me with them to their work places. In addition to the time in the ambulatory clinic, my father also made house calls to patients. He was provided with a special carriage (phaeton) to travel across the city, and he often took me with him. Looking around and learning about other places was my favorite thing to do. Sometimes he would take me inside a patient's house, and I would sit quietly in a corner observing him tending to his patient.

I recall another time when I waited in the carriage and talked with the driver, who was our neighbor. This man had a beautiful daughter my age, and sometimes she would join us on those trips through the city. Her name was Genja. Those trips were especially pleasant for I had developed a friendship with her. I remember that she had golden hair with slightly red highlights, smooth alabaster skin, and a pleasant, soft manner. I enjoyed playing with her. It was such a stark contrast to being with the boys. Perhaps I felt a romantic attachment to her if one can imagine such feelings in an eight-year-old boy.

My father had a second job as a medical examiner with the city police. Once, when I was only seven, he took me on a work trip. With a team of policemen we traveled to the crime scene in a distant forest, and what I saw there made a lasting impression. My father examined the cadaver, and then the policemen dressed the body, applied make-up, and placed it under a tree. The dead man looked as if he were alive! They took photographs, and we then drove back to the city with the corpse.

My mother also took me to her job, which was quite different. We would walk to the homes of women with newborn babies after they were discharged from the hospital. Her job was to inspect the hygienic conditions of the household, to examine the baby, and give proper instructions on handling the newborn child. I did not like these visits and thought they were boring, and the babies were always crying. Nevertheless, it was another way of experiencing my mother's caring manner.

6. School Years

Most of the schools in Orsha were assigned to teach in Belorussian, with two others for Yiddish and one for Russian. I was enrolled in the Russian school. Classes were large, with thirty to forty students in each and multiple classes in each of the grades. I have unpleasant memories of my school years, especially the first two. The environment was noisy, with constant fighting among the boys and abuse from the upper-grade boys. In addition to what I had already experienced in my neighborhood, I had to learn more survival skills in this hostile environment. Teachers were unpleasant and angry most of the time, and there was continual indoctrination of the Communist ideology. They also promoted an idea that enemies of the state (called "enemies of the people") had been penetrating our socialist society and that everybody should be alerted to watch for them.

The authorities developed widely publicized stories about young "heroes" who reported anti-Government activities on their own parents. One such hero was Pavlik Morozov. They erected monuments for him after the "enemies of the people" allegedly killed him. Nevertheless, this propaganda did not gain much acceptance by the students, even of the youngest age. In addition, we hated the ones in our school who reported various "wrongdoing." It was customary for a group of boys to catch the informer outside the school and beat him up, avoiding causing any bruises on his face. To do this we covered the victim's head so he could not see who was beating him. It was called "darkness" (*tiemnaya* in Russian) and was often practiced in Russia, even by adults, particularly against the Secret Police informers.

It was fashionable among the families in my parents' circle to enroll their children in private piano lessons. I started at age twelve and enjoyed some of it and even achieved some success by performing Mozart's *Turkish March* at fifteen in a public concert; however, piano was boring, and I hated spending Sunday taking long walks to the teacher's house.

It was unusual for a teenager living in the bleak pre-war environment of the Soviet Union to be interested in reading, but I spent all my spare time reading books about adventure, science fiction, and romance. One book, *Microbe Hunters* by Paul de Kruif (1), strongly influenced my thoughts about the future. One hero of this book, a Russian microbiologist named Ilya Metchnokov, became my role model. In fact, as I learned later, in his original book published in English, Paul de Kruif (1) wrote, "Elie Metchnikoff was a Jew and was born in Southern Russia in 1845." A part of this phrase was deleted in the Russian translation that I had during my school years, and perhaps I did not care about the ethnic origin of this famous scientist, one of the first Nobel prize winners.

In contrast to these stories, daily life was dull and boring, and I craved excitement. One day, when I was twelve, I decided to run away. After school, without any preparation, I walked down the road that led to the outskirts of the city and into the surrounding forest. It was already dark, and I crawled into a small cave where I intended to spend the night. Perhaps an hour later, after a dreamy rest, I suddenly felt cold and very hungry. I did not know what to do, so I just took another three-hour walk back home. My appetite for adventure had been satisfied, but my family was in a panic. My parents and my Aunt Basia had been searching for me. After I quietly entered the house, I hid for a while in a dark atrium and listened to them talk about me, not without some satisfaction. I finally emerged, anticipating a well-deserved punishment, but everyone was so relieved to see me, they did not even reprimand me. I did not want to scare them any more with an account of the dark forest, so I said that I was just upset with many things and spent all the time sitting on a bench in the post office. There was only one sarcastic question from my aunt. "Leonia, what were you doing? Exposing your tongue to provide the visitors with moisture for their post-stamps?" The incident was over, and finally, I had gotten their attention!

The school curriculum became quite intense. It included detailed lessons in various fields of science, mathematics, history, and even foreign literature. At the same time, it was an extremely biased exercise in indoctrination, attempting to mold single, uniform views across several subjects, especially the ones that related to social and political matters. It was quite risky to ask questions, even simple, innocent ones that implied no opinion. This was not a very comfortable situation for me, especially since my father had constantly advised me not to accept things at face value. Once, during a history lesson in the eighth grade, comrade Lomako, the teacher, was talking about the ancient world, and he referred to the kingdoms of Israel and Judea. Keep in mind that the students had no knowledge of events described in the Bible and were devoid of knowledge about Jewish history, even the meaning of the names Israel and Judea. It suddenly occurred to me that the Jews living in and around the city might be more than just inhabitants of Belarus, and that they may actually have some important historical connection to people of the ancient world. I asked a question. The teacher became furious, almost violent. He said, "Yes, yes, those people in ancient Israel and Judea were your ancestors! Are you satisfied with knowing that now?" This was uttered in a barely controlled rage, which implied a strong emotion about Jews, both the ancient and contemporary. This was the very first time I learned something about my people and the first time I experienced a real outburst of anti-Semitism.

Much later, I learned that this teacher had collaborated closely with the Nazis during the German occupation of Orsha and had participated in rounding up Jews. After the war, the Soviet authorities executed Lomako as a traitor.

In 1936–38, when I was eleven and twelve years old, the country experienced one of Stalin's infamous purges. During this period about one million people were executed, and, at the end of 1939, millions were in camps. This period was later labeled in the history books as a period of Great Terror. I remember my parents whispering to each other about episodes of arrests among their acquaintances. The people most affected were usually in government or party positions. My father was not among them, but I could feel the tension, especially when there was noise from a rare passing car. The Secret Police arrests would come in the middle of the night with the terrifying "knock at the door."

Despite the awful dread and gloom of this time, the students somehow managed to have a little fun at school. Every week the teachers commanded us to tear out pages containing pictures of another "enemy of the people" from our textbooks. We had even more fun when the page could not be removed and we were instructed to cross out the picture with ink.

7. At the German Invasion

On June 22, 1941, more than three million German troops invaded the Soviet Union and began their takeover of the Western part of the country in a new, efficient, and alarmingly rapid style. Only two weeks before the war started, my father took me on a vacation to the South of Russia, leaving my mother and sister at home. We stayed in the famous resort city of Kislovodsk, which was recommended at that time for people with heart problems. When the war started, we abruptly ended our vacation and boarded a train for home; however, the Germans had advanced so fast that, in spite of our sudden departure, we could not reach our home. It was already under German control. At one of the railroad stations we were placed, along with refugees arriving from the captured region, on one of the trains directed east toward Siberia.

The trains they threw us into were not ordinary passenger trains but the type used to transport livestock and various farm goods—cattle cars. They were stuffed with refugees. Some sat on their piles of belongings, but not everyone could sit or lie down at the same time because of the cramped conditions. Families would take turns lying down to sleep so that everybody could at least obtain some rest. My father and I had the small suitcase we had taken for our vacation, so we took turns sleeping on our suitcase. This forced us to curl up very tightly to fit into the small area that we had been able to commandeer. The train trip was wretched. There were no toilets; when we reached a station (few and far apart), people would rush off the train toward the bushes to take care of their natural urges. Some were not able to wait for the stops, which led to the sickening smell of human excrement in addition to the intolerable stench of unwashed bodies. The sweltering temperature in the car heightened the mingling smells, making it quite difficult to breathe. There was no food or clean water. People were hungry, tired, thirsty, aching, and miserable. We endured these conditions for over ten days, and each day they became more unbearable.

My father became extremely depressed, not so much because of the conditions (after all, people can become accustomed to almost anything) but because he feared my mother and my six-year-old sister, Galina, had not escaped the Germans; however, as we learned later, they had actually escaped. They were forced to flee from our hometown, leaving behind all our possessions. We had no way of receiving this information during our journey, and my father fell deeper into sullen anger and despair. During this time, he would barely talk to me.

I felt very lonely and upset. I could not understand how it had happened. How was it that our "brave Red Army, the strongest army in the world," as we were told in school, was not able to prevent the German invasion? I felt anger. I felt fear. I felt sadness. I felt hatred for the Germans. With all these emotions building up in my heart, I decided that I should not go into refuge with my father; instead, I would join the Army and go fight the Germans. I started looking for an opportunity. I was only fifteen years old at the time and, therefore, much too young to qualify for induction into the Army.

At the beginning of the war, the Army developed a tradition that allowed its detachments to pick up orphaned boys of any age and provide them with shelter, food, and clothing. These boys would wear special Army uniforms and were given the unofficial name of "sons of the regiment." I wanted to become one of these sons, and luckily—or unluckily—an opportunity was soon manifested.

8. The Taste of Bread

Do you know the taste of bread sprinkled with tears and blood? Well, I do. It happened more than sixty-five years ago, but the memory of this taste remains fresh in my mind.

In 1941, the railroad system in Eastern Russia consisted of only single tracks. Therefore, at railroad junctions, trains of refugees like ours going eastward would permit the more important military trains going westward toward the war front to pass us. At one stop, I left my train and approached a military train that also had stopped. This train consisted of cattle cars as well, but it was apparent they were not as crowded as the cars of our train, and there were sleeping accommodations for the soldiers. As I approached one of the cars, I saw soldiers sitting at the opening of the car dangling their legs over the edge trying to obtain some fresh air in the summer heat. It was very hot and dusty, and the air was saturated with the smell of grease, overheated rails, and creosote from railroad ties. I stepped over the track ties toward the soldiers. I can now only imagine the scene of the past: Here was a tall and very slim boy, obviously exhausted and obviously Jewish, with dark hair and a look of determination and desperation in his brown eyes, boldly approaching the Slavic/Aryan-looking soldiers with their light features. When I recall this event, I become emotionally overwhelmed as the scene is replayed in my mind.

I approached the soldiers and said to them, "Comrades, would you take me as a son of your regiment to the front lines? I want to fight the Germans." These troops did not have any experience with "sons of regiments" because they were freshly mobilized in Siberia, and they had not yet experienced the war. They laughed and responded, "Wait a few years, until you become a man, then go fight the Germans." One soldier in particular told the rest, "Look, boys, he is probably hungry." I looked over at the soldiers and realized they were eating bread. I suddenly began salivating over the bread, despite my exhaustion and thirst. One of the soldiers broke a piece of crust off his loaf and handed it to me. The bread was very dark, nearly black, with a clay-like texture; it was not the type of bread we have now. Nevertheless, without any restraint, I voraciously ate the bread. They told me they could not take me with them, but they kindly asked me if I had any family on the train. I told them my father was on the train, and they gave me some extra bread and told me to take it to him. When I asked them to reconsider my joining them, they were adamant about not letting me and told me to return to the train.

At this point, a soldier emerged from the back of the car and said to the others, "Boys, what are you doing? Can you not see this boy is a *Zhid*?" The one who had handed me the bread asked, "Is this true that you are not a Russian but a Jew?" I responded, "I do not know." At that age, the difference between the two was still very hazy for me. Suddenly and ferociously the soldier yelled, *"Go away, Zhid!"* Two of them picked up gravel and started to throw it at me. One or two pebbles hit me in the face, and my upper lip started to bleed. I began to cry; however, I did not throw away my now dirty, tear-stained, bloody bread. I turned and ran to my cattle car and finally returned to my father. He saw my tears and blood as I handed him the bread. Still crying, I told him what happened. When I had calmed down enough, I asked him, "What does *Zhid* mean? Why did they suddenly hate me for it?"

We were sitting on the grass near the station and waiting for the train to start up again. Seeing my distress, my father could no longer ignore me and finally spoke to me. He looked at me and explained that not all people are equal members of the "perfect social environment" portrayed by the authorities. "We are not Russian; we are Jewish. We are descendants of an ancient people who came from the ancient kingdom of Israel in the Middle East." The word *Zhid* originated from the Polish language, which just meant Jew, but in Russian it became a derogatory term used by those who hated Jews. (*Zhid* is equivalent to the American *Kike*.) Self-identification was one of my first lessons. Sadly, this lesson will always be associated with other people who may hate me for who I am. Nevertheless, we ate the bread soaked with my tears and sprinkled with my blood. I will never forget this humiliating episode as a reminder of who I am and as a warning to beware of people who could defile my bread with blood and tears. My father also explained to me that the soldiers in this particular group came from an area in Siberia populated by people called Cossacks, Siberian Cossacks.

9. About Cossacks

In the fifteenth and sixteenth centuries the Cossacks were known to establish independent semi-military settlements in the south of the present-day Ukraine and Russia. Most of the population in these tough settlements consisted of runaway serfs escaping from their owners in Russia and Poland, although the original groups of Cossacks could have had a different ethnic origin, most likely Slavic. They were know as professional fighters and became famous for their horsemanship and ferocity.

In the sixteenth century, the army (rather, a band) of independent Cossacks led by their famous leader (*ataman*) Yermak (Ermak, or Yermak Timofeyevich) crossed the Ural Mountains and conquered the Tartars and other tribes in Siberia. Under leadership of Yermak's successors the Russians continued the conquest of Siberia for more than a century, and in 1646–48 reached the shores of the Pacific Ocean and the Bering Strait. Because not all these conquests were by the regular Russian Army (particularly at the beginning of the campaign), the Cossack leaders would "present" the newly obtained territories to the tsar. Over the years, the Cossacks developed a large number of settlements throughout Siberia and initiated most of the ethnic Russian population of Siberia.

In 1648–49, the Cossacks of the Ukraine, led by Bogdan Khmelnitsky, started a war for the independence of the Ukraine from Poland. Because there was no substantial number of ethnic Poles in the Ukraine, the Cossacks simply directed their violence against the Jews. The massacre was devastating. Between 100,000 and 200,000 men, women, and children were brutally murdered (out of a Jewish population of 500,000), and about 700 Jewish communities were destroyed.

During the Civil War of 1920, the gangs of Cossacks that fought against the Red Army never missed an opportunity to massacre Jews when taking over a town or a settlement. It is estimated that they committed about 800 pogroms and killed 150,000 Jews, 10% of the Jewish population of the entire Pale of Settlement. My father's lecture broadened my knowledge of Russian history well beyond the textbooks we had in school.

After almost two weeks of starving and traveling in squalid conditions, we arrived at a small village called Grebeni in the Chkalov (now Orenburg) district. Those who left the train at this station were placed in a local school or in the homes of some local peasants. One family hosted my father and me. The first food we had was a loaf of freshly baked bread and milk. This time the bread had a different taste, not so much because of its cleanliness and better quality, but because of the hospitality, empathy, and friendliness of the hostess. She felt bad for us because of our plight and our suffering, having left behind our homes and families. I will never forget her motherly touch and kindness; thank you so much, Matrena Evstigneevna, from the bottom of my heart! Thanks not only for being so kind but also for helping me to develop a balanced attitude toward people when the first impression might be negative or biased. Matrena and her family were Siberian Cossacks. The whole village of Grebeni was one of the Cossacks' settlements previously mentioned. All the people we met in the village were very kind to us, and they knew we were Jewish! Such a contrast to those soldiers in the train! After all, nothing is as simple as it seems.

10. Xenophobia

Webster's definition of this Greek word is "fear and hatred of strangers or of anything unusual or foreign." Perhaps this phenomenon has a biological basis, inherited by humans from the instinct of self-preservation in the animal world. Unlike animals, humans have a freedom of choice, and, in this case, it is either to attenuate this biological instinct or to magnify the xenophobia by giving it some intellectual justification.

The Cossack soldiers on the train were an example of those with xenophobia enhanced by an anti-Semitic indoctrination, perhaps by their families. Most of them, living in remote Siberian villages, probably never met any Jews and never learned anything about them. They did, however, see that the boy standing in front of their train car had a markedly different appearance from their own. This, together with some vulgar slurs from their clever comrade, was enough to make them nasty and violent. In sharp contrast, the people in the village of Grebeni, also Cossacks, were a wonderful example of the ability to transcend the bigoted slurs and the angry negativism. Their village was close to the large city of Chkalov, and the Jews they encountered living there were more real to them than the ugly racial propaganda and vicious legends. They knew that most of us on the train were Jewish, and they treated us with warm hospitality and kindness.

The episodes described above were my first steps over the threshold into the realm of adulthood. In addition, it was the beginning of my self-recognition as a Jew. Part of this lesson was humiliation—the humiliation of being hungry, the humiliation of being made to pay any price to satisfy man's basic needs for survival. It was also an important lesson in how to cope with humiliation and how to survive humiliation. Despite the horror of this memory, I have managed to preserve a positive outlook toward mankind. Even now, I still ask myself if there is hope that different people and different nations will be able to overcome the natural xenophobia within each of us and unite against the current surge of mass violence threatening us all. Will the various nations of the world be able to share—in peace—the major gift of heaven, the bread of our Mother Earth?

CHAPTER TWO

Uzbekistan, Young Man's Dilemmas, and Stark Realities

"The turning point in the process of growing up is when you discover the core of strength within you that survives all hurt."

Max Lerner

1. **Uzbekistan in the 1940s**
2. **Our Family in Chelek**
3. **High School Student**
4. **Medical Student in Samarkand**
5. **Bukharan Jews**
6. **People I Met**

26

Fig. 5. Uzbekistan in 1940s: a street in a small town.
Drawing by Edward Tabachnik

Fig. 6. Uzbekistan today: streets of Tashkent (I took these pictures in 2002). Left to right, top to bottom:
- **People in the street;**
- **Sculpture of Timur, founder of the Uzbek nation;**
- **Rehearsing for performance in a movie; and**
- **A folk dance by a professional performer.**

Fig. 7. Photographs of the WWII period, left to right:
- With Father at the start of the war (June, 1941);
- As a medical student in Samarkand (1943);
- Lev Hoffman in a photo from front; he was killed soon after this picture was taken (1943). On the back of the photo: "For a life-long memory to my best friend of childhood and school years"; and
- Yury Gusev, a good friend in the Samarkand Medical School (1943), killed in the war.

Fig. 8. Sweet memories, top to bottom:
- Professor Turkevitch, Chairman of the Anatomy
  Department, mentor and friend (1943);
- Suzan Rechtman, Samarkand (1943);
- With Dara Rosenfeld, Samarkand (1944); and
- With Dara, fifty-four years later, Hartford, CT (1998).

1. Uzbekistan in the 1940s

The German armies invaded the Soviet Union on June 21, 1941. When the war started, my father and I were on vacation out of our hometown of Orsha, which was captured by the Germans during the first week of the war. As a physician, my father had an obligation to check with the military authorities. He received an assignment to travel to one of the districts of Uzbekistan to assume a position as head of a hospital in the small town of Chelek, which was about fifteen miles from the city of Samarkand. We traveled to this area, and my father started his job; I was enrolled in the ninth grade of the local school.

In 1941 Uzbekistan was one of fifteen Republics of the Soviet Union and had a population of nearly twenty million residents, mostly rural. Today, the Republic of Uzbekistan, which is slightly larger than California, has a population of about twenty-seven million people consisting of Uzbeks (80%), ethnic Russians, and others. It became independent in 1991 after the disintegration of the Soviet Union.

Chelek was a small town with about ten thousand inhabitants, mostly Russian, descendants of the Cossacks. My father's hospital served the whole district around Chelek. The first impression one had of the place was hot, dry, and dusty with the temperature reaching one hundred degrees and more in the summer. The streets were dirt-packed roads, and it was common to see donkeys pulling two-wheeled carts. Occasionally a donkey rider, but seldom a horseman, would appear in the street dressed in a heavy robe (called a *chapan* and made of cotton and linen) and a turban on his head. The wind often carried the tumbleweeds throughout the town. While walking these dirt roads the smell of overcooked cottonseed oil dominated the senses, an indication that someone was lucky enough to be able to make a pilaf.

One day, I was sitting with a group of local boys in a place called *Chaihannah*, which is "house of tea" in Uzbek. As you entered the place, there were no chairs and tables but large elevated platforms. People sat on top of them with their legs crossed Indian style and their backs and elbows resting on pillows. The servers brought tea in a large, round porcelain pot and poured it into one cup. The person seated at the head of the table would then hand it to one person in the circle. Then the same cup is again filled by the head person and passed to the next person. The cup was always only partially filled, never to the brim. When you took the cup from the master of the table, you had to take it with your right hand and your left hand rested on the crease of your right arm. You had to drink the tea very slowly as a sign of respect and to not appear greedy. This was a traditional place for Uzbek men to socialize with one another by drinking green tea.

The *Chaihannah* was for men only. Uzbek custom excluded women from this type of gathering. All the men were dressed in heavy, thick cotton robes, and their heads were always covered with a small hat called a *tubiteyka*. The colors were always black and white for adults; for children, they were multicolored. The elderly people wore a heavy turban on the top of this *tubiteyka*. This showed their close affiliation with the Muslim religion. I wondered why they wore such heavy clothes in the hot climate and was told that such clothing actually protected them from the heat.

The reason for the gathering of the local boys was that they wanted to hear my story. They wanted to hear about my escape from the war and living under the attack of German bombings. Ahmed, the leader of the group, was a tall, strong boy with dark skin. He was seventeen and was about to be drafted into the army. He was not an Uzbek but a Tartar by origin, and I asked him to tell me about the country of Uzbekistan. He responded enthusiastically that he was very interested in the history of his country. He believed that his family was descended directly from Timur, a great warrior. What I learned from Ahmed about Uzbekistan and from subsequent readings went far beyond the formal history lessons that I had been taught in school.

Uzbekistan was the site of very old civilizations and, as Ahmed stated (perhaps with exaggeration), it had a history of more than three thousand years. It was influenced by many of the different people who passed through the country. In ancient times this area was a Persian province of Sogdiana, which was conquered by Alexander the Great in the fourth century. Turks from Siberia influenced the language during the sixth century. Islam was imposed on local people during the Arab invasion in the seventh and eighth century, and the territory became part of a large Arabic Khalifat (Caliphate).

In the thirteenth century, the Mongolians under Genghis Khan invaded the country, and in the fourteenth century, Timur (also Timurleng or Tamerlane), a descendent of Genghis Khan, united all the tribes in the area, conquered more territories, and transformed the country into a very powerful state. He was considered the founder of Uzbekistan although he was not an ethnic Uzbek himself. The real Uzbek tribes, remnants of the Mongolian Golden Horde, moved from the Northwest into this area only in the sixteenth century and later. There were three kingdoms that were established in the eighteenth century in Central Asia, with the capitals in Bukhara, in Kokand, and in Khiva. The Russian tsars defeated them during 1865–1873 and turned the whole Central Asian region into a Russian colony, though most of it remained under the nominal authority of the Emir of Bukhara. In 1922 Uzbekistan became a Soviet Republic.

I was fascinated by Ahmed's story and asked some of the boys to teach me the local Uzbek language. After the party, the boys suggested we go and earn some money by taking the horses of a wealthy owner to the creek to wash them. We rode six or seven horses to the outskirts of the city. This was my first experience riding a horse. There was no saddle, only a large wool blanket on the horse's back. I sat on the horse, squeezing his back with my legs so I would not fall and held the reigns tightly. The reward was arriving at an irrigation canal that had cold water. It was so refreshing to be in the cold water on such a hot day. This water was the only source of life in the whole area. It flowed from the mountains and not only fed the crop in the fields but was also for drinking. The ride back to town was easier, and I was able to observe the environment, which mostly consisted of cotton fields, fruit, and mulberry trees. I was told that the leaves of the mulberry trees were used to feed the silk worms. In the food shortages of the later war years, mulberries became the only food available for many starving refugees.

2. Our Family in Chelek

At the end of the summer of 1941 my father became very ill. His chronic heart condition worsened, and he was near death.

Frustration and despair set in; I was only fifteen, and I had no one else around. We sent letters to different agencies trying to locate my mother and sister but to no avail. My mind turned to a higher authority for the first time, and I began to silently pray in my heart. I did not know any formal prayers or blessings, but instinctively I made up my own prayers and rituals that I hoped would reach heaven and help me during that awful time.

Whether my prayers counted or not, a miracle happened and everything changed. My father began to recover, and then we received news that my mother and sister had been found alive. They joined us soon afterward, and once again we were a family. Earlier, when the Germans had advanced and approached the outskirts of Orsha, my mother took my six-year-old sister and just walked away from our hometown toward a distant railway station. They were unable to take anything with them and were among those who caught the last train to leave before the Germans moved in and captured Orsha.

Everything became better when my mother arrived in Chelek. My father was healthy enough to resume his work as the head of the hospital. He became popular among local people in Chelek and the surrounding villages, and many people requested his help as a private physician. As payment for his services, they brought us flour, chicken eggs, and, sometimes, even a chicken, so we were no longer starving. An odd thing happened when the Uzbek women from a village would come as patients to my father. Usually, a woman was accompanied by her husband, who would not let the doctor examine his wife. My father was only allowed to speak to her through the husband, who acted as mediator and interpreter. Most of the women did not speak Russian.

The spread of typhus was quite typical during those times of war and social turbulence, and in 1941 most patients who came to the hospital had typhus. The epidemic of typhus was related to the lack of hygiene, lack of bathing facilities, and the overcrowded shelters that housed the displaced. Often the people were literally covered with lice that transmitted typhus and would inadvertently be sharing their vermin with each other. I watched as the patients' clothing, crawling with lice, was placed on the ground for subsequent disinfection. It was not easy for the medical staff treating such patients and their belongings to protect themselves and avoid dangerous contact. One of the nurses who used to take care of me in addition to her work ended up contracting typhus and succumbed to it. Once I saw naked men standing in the field near a fire shaking their clothes over the fire to rid them of lice. Our family lived in the hospital building in a small two-room apartment with a separate entrance. I was able to closely observe the progression of this local contamination and the people struggling with filth and disease. The situation was, perhaps, similar to that in medieval times.

3. High School Student

In September of 1941, I started ninth grade, and I enjoyed getting back to regular life as a schoolboy. The school in Chelek was small, but we had very good teachers, some of whom had escaped from the German invasion. My small class had only twelve or thirteen students. During the years of war, and for a long period afterward, I developed an unusual intolerance to any sound of music. I could not even think about taking the music lessons that were available at school. This was probably a reaction of shock because of the war and all the hardships that I had gone through. (It would be many years, and only after I had become a doctor, that my love of music returned.) That year of school and returning to regular conditions was physically and spiritually good for me. Nevertheless, it was still wartime and our lives were to be visited by more unpleasant events.

Another episode of hostility reminded me that, as a Jew, I was still different. One day as I was walking down the street, a group of teenagers attacked me. All these boys were Cossacks (again!). They recognized me as a Jew and a stranger in this place by my appearance. They made fun of me by using derogatory terms and names, and they played "football" using me as the ball. There was no way I could fight back; there were five of them. They were not only older than I was but also physically stronger. I finally escaped them and ran to the police station only half a block away. A Russian policeman was sitting at the desk, probably a Cossack as well. I complained to him and he sarcastically replied, "Why don't you bring these bad boys here and I will talk to them?" I realized that there was no way I could count on protection from the Russian authorities. This episode, along with my previous Cossack encounter, increased my disgust for the Soviet system and, to some extent, the Russian people in general.

In addition to this painful experience during my school year, there was something entirely new. One of my schoolmates was a girl named Vera Kunkel. She was a tall blond with very white skin and blue eyes. This was probably my first serious attraction to a girl, but I am not sure I could call her my "first love." I was very eager to spend all my time after school with her. In the evenings we would go to her parents' house for tea, usually sitting outside and experiencing quite romantic feelings, enhanced by the cool breeze of the night air, and listening to the sounds of crickets around us. I soon learned that Vera was German, and, for that reason, her family had been expelled from the city of Samarkand and forced to live in Chelek. Vera's father was a physician and worked in the hospital with my father. As Vera's father told me, they were descendants of the Germans who, in 1763, had been invited by Catherine the Great to settle in the region of the lower Volga River. They belonged to the Mennonites, a religious sect that was persecuted in Germany by the predominant Lutheran Church. In 1924, the Soviet government established an Autonomous German Republic in the lower Volga River area. Those among the Germans who were suspected of not being loyal to the Soviet system were expelled to Central Asia, and mostly to Uzbekistan. Included in this group was the Kunkel family. Vera's brother was in the Soviet Army and served as an interpreter. At the time they were telling me this story, they were unaware of the Holocaust. I did not have any animosity toward this German family—after all, they were Soviet citizens, and, in my view, not any different from us.

At the end of the ninth grade, I faced the dilemma of having to decide my future education, and that decision became an important turning point for my future in general. Because there was a shortage of pupils going to tenth grade (the final grade of high school), the principal gave us the opportunity to take tenth-grade exams during the summer. I knew I would be drafted into the army the next year and decided that I did not want to join the army anymore. I do not remember being conscious of the fear of getting killed, and not because of bravery; rather, the war conditions had made me indifferent and even apathetic. I was used to living with death. It came in many letters from the frontline and from the starvation and disease all around us. It was mainly the wretched, unforgettable memory of the soldiers on the train and my dread of going through that again.

There was only one way to avoid the army, and that was to enroll in medical school. With this decision, the hot summer of 1942 in Chelek was different from the previous one of 1941. No more horse rides or spending time with the local boys. Instead, we tried to escape the heat by going into buildings with thick walls for one purpose only: to study for final exams. There were only three of us who decided to spend our summer studying for the tenth grade: Vera Kunkel, a girl named Maria Evlach, and me. At the end of summer all three of us passed the exams, received our high school diplomas, and intended to apply to the Medical School in Samarkand. Unfortunately, because Vera was German, the authorities forbid her to leave Chelek. Maria and I journeyed fifteen miles to Samarkand in a primitive one-horse cart. We met with the medical school dean a few days before the application deadline. He was very impressed with our grades, and so we were accepted. The decision to spend the summer in intensive studies probably saved my life; otherwise, I would have been sent to the war front and most likely killed.

I also think of other turning points during that year. I learned much about hate and how to deal with it. I experienced my first real attraction to a girl. Most importantly, I learned how to make important choices that had long-lasting effects.

4. Medical Student in Samarkand

Samarkand is one of the oldest cities of the world, as old as Babylon and Rome. Its 2,500-year history reflects some of the major historic events of mankind. Despite the war, concerns associated with life there, and my regimen of studies at the medical school, I took advantage of learning about the rich history of this place. While visiting one of the historic sites I met someone my age, Aron Katsenelenbogen, who was also fascinated with history. Together we visited such famous fourteenth and fifteenth century monuments as Registan, Shakh-i-Zinda Necropolis, and the Ulugbek Observatory. Aron and I became friends and met again in Moscow, and then many years later in Philadelphia. Aaron became a well-known economist and philosopher. He was on the faculty of the University of Pennsylvania. He passed away in 2005, and I miss our infrequent but most enlightening discussions which entailed a broad spectrum of subjects.

In 1942 I became a medical student at the age of sixteen. The medical school in the city of Samarkand was filled with professors of Russian origin. Most of them had escaped from the war-torn areas, and there were some who were professors and instructors from the Military Medical Academy who had been evacuated from Leningrad to Samarkand. There were only a few Uzbeks among the teachers, a situation that changed dramatically after the war. Currently, most of the faculty at the Uzbekistan universities are from the local ethnic groups, and this is also true in the other republics of Central Asia. The level of teaching in the Medical School of Samarkand was of the highest standards, and the studies were exciting. For the first year it focused on the basic knowledge of biology, chemistry, and human anatomy. In addition, we studied the Latin and Uzbek languages.

Aside from the studies, life was a challenge in other ways. The major one was hunger. It was quite common on my way to the school in the early morning hours to see corpses of people on the side of the street who had died from starvation (and typhus). Many were people from Poland who had either escaped from the Germans or were soldiers who had been captured during the previous Soviet invasion of Poland by the Russian army and sent to Siberia, where they were later released. As medical students, we were given rations through food stamps. Unfortunately, because of the extreme food shortage, even these food stamps did not always guarantee that we would get food. I started working as a technician in the department of anatomy, and my job was to prepare teaching material (different organs and tissues) for the students. There were truckloads of cadavers collected daily from around the city and delivered to our department. They were corpses of people who had no family or identity.

There were two other students who worked with me as technicians. We were assigned to an experienced technician (an Uzbek man in his early sixties) who taught us how to preserve the corpses, how to make skeletons, and how to prepare separate organs for demonstration. He told us that before the Revolution he served as an executioner in the court of the Emir of Bukhara. Obviously, he was quite familiar with death.

Our standard operating procedure was as follows. First, we would pump formaldehyde solution into the blood vessels of a corpse. Then we would place as many corpses as possible into a large tank filled with formaldehyde. The Uzbek would cover them with wooden boards and would make us jump on top of them so that he could fit more bodies into the tank. We also made skeletons. The Military Medical Academy that had evacuated from Leningrad to Samarkand shared facilities with the local Medical School. People at the academy had suddenly realized that they had the opportunity to enhance their future teaching capabilities, so they decided to put the tragic situation of so many deaths to some good use. They wanted us to make a great number of skeletons for the Academy so there would be ample teaching material when they returned to Leningrad after the war.

For our work at the Department of Anatomy, and in addition to our undependable student rations, the three of us received the most treasured payment at that time: four hundred grams of bread every day. We would often take this extra bread to the market and exchange it with the peasants for some butter or fruit. Another opportunity to get more food was in the students' kitchen, where all students had to take turns working. The only food that was available at that time was plain, boiled wheat grain and—sometimes as a luxury—ground/smashed grain. To suppress our hunger, we frequently smoked. Real tobacco or cigarettes were unavailable to us, so we used pieces of dried tobacco stem leftovers from the tobacco production plant, and we wrapped them in newspaper. Smoking these "cigarettes" before going to bed made us dizzy, and we would fall asleep easier. Despite all these problems, most of us were glad to be alive, and we were very enthusiastic about our studies. During these years I contracted tuberculosis, but it did not interrupt my studies. I survived and recovered because of new medications that my father had somehow obtained from his medical military colleagues.

During the summer breaks, we were asked to volunteer in rural areas to participate in work to control the malaria epidemic. After my second year and during the break, I volunteered to work in the area neighboring Chelek. This provided me the opportunity to stay with my parents and also experience some challenging work in the field. I was given a donkey with which to travel around a large rural area, and my assignment was to visit the peasants and look for malaria patients. When I found any, I was obligated to report the case and to make subsequent visits to the household to administer quinine to the patient. This procedure is now known as "directly observed therapy"; it means that the drug is to be administered in the presence of someone. The administration of quinine was a quite barbaric procedure. I would tightly wrap one gram of this extremely bitter powder in a piece of newspaper (the only paper available), and then put it deep into the patient's mouth and follow it with a large amount of water. Without my assistance, the patients would generally avoid taking this drug. People had orders from the authorities to obey, but I also felt that they had developed some appreciation and understanding that I was helping them. Because of my age (I was not yet eighteen), they knew that I was not a doctor. Nevertheless, they called me *kichkine doctor*, which in the Uzbek language meant "little doctor." Often they would ask me about medical problems other than malaria. For these, I had to ask my father or read the textbooks to have an answer for them at my next visit. Most of the patients were women, often left alone at home because the men were in the army. It was an expression of trust by the local Muslim population to allow me to visit a woman without the presence of a male relative. I spoke the Uzbek language well and developed good communications with these peasants and, most importantly, with the leadership of the collective farms and other authorities. For this work I was paid by the collective farms with flour and butter, which I would proudly bring to my family in Chelek.

At the beginning of my first year of medical school, I stayed in the dormitory with five or six people per room. We slept on mattresses on the floor, had limited facilities outside the building, and, basically, had no appropriate place to do our homework. My father would visit me in Samarkand from time to time, and, after learning of the uncomfortable condition in the dormitory, he rented a place for me in a private home. He would also bring me bread he had earned from his practice as a private physician.

A near-tragic episode occurred during one of my father's trips. There was no public transportation between the cities and towns at that time. Some truck drivers would pick up passengers for a fee and take them along, but this was an illegal enterprise and the drivers were afraid of being stopped and punished. Sometimes these trucks full of people were stopped by the military patrols looking for deserters or conscription evaders. My father was riding in one of these trucks on his way from Samarkand to Chelek. A military patrol tried to stop the truck for inspection, but the driver attempted to escape and drove away. The patrol started shooting at the truck, and my father was the only passenger wounded. He was taken to the hospital with a deep wound in his back. Given the condition of his heart, I did not think he was going to survive. I went to the hospital, but they would not allow visitors. I told one of my teachers, who also worked at the Medical Military Academy, about my father's conditions and my fear of his contracting an infection common for this type of wound. He sympathized with me and obtained penicillin (a rarity at the time) from his military colleagues. I went to the hospital to give the drug to my father's physicians.

The hospitals were off-limits at that time, and the guards would not let me in; neither would they let me speak to anyone in authority. I had no other choice, so I climbed over the wall and ran toward the building where my father was kept. I ran fast and the guards could not catch me. When I delivered the penicillin to the quite surprised attending physician, I was proud that my mission had been accomplished, and it did not matter that I was arrested by the military guards. This was the only arrest I have ever experienced in my life. I was soon released, and my father recovered shortly afterward, and only a deep scar on his back was a reminder of the episode. Shortly afterward, he got a new job as a physician in a large clinic in Samarkand, and our family moved from Chelek. I joined them in a rented place in the Eastern Quarter of the Old City, an area of Samarkand that was populated by Bukharan Jews.

5. Bukharan Jews

The first impression we had when settled in the Eastern Quarter of Samarkand was that, unlike the Ashkenazi Jews of the European part of the Soviet Union, the Bukharan Jews remained closely attached to the Jewish religion and observances. This presented me with the opportunity to learn about Judaism and the Jewish traditions.

Bukharan Jews are descendants of the Israelites who came to Central Asia more than two thousand years ago from the Babylonian Exile. They had been ruled by the Persian Empire since 135 BC and adopted a version of Pharsi as their spoken language. Most of them lived in Dushanbe (Tajikistan), Bukhara, Samarkand, Tashkent, and Kokand (Uzbekistan). The Europeans called them "Bukharan Jews" in their published reports because since the sixteenth century almost all of them had been subjects of the Bukharan Emirs. They developed their own unique culture and traditions because for centuries they had been isolated from the rest of the world and from other Jewish communities. Yosef Maman, a Jewish scholar from Morocco, visited this area in 1793 and became their spiritual leader. He "updated" the Bukharan Jews on the changes in Jewish traditions that had occurred over the centuries and, in particular, he introduced the traditions of the Sephardic (Spanish) Jews. Since then, the Bukharan Jews are often called Sephardic Jews, although they are not direct descendants of the Spanish Jews. Like any other group of Jews, throughout their history the Bukharan Jews experienced periods of persecution intermittent with periods of prosperity. Since the establishment of the Soviet regime in Uzbekistan and Tajikistan, they felt less oppressed than under the tsars, and they did not experience any interference with observance of their religious practices.

Our new friends from among the Bukharan Jews invited us to participate in the Passover celebration (Sephardic style), which was my very first experience of this type. It was also the first time I ever attended a ritual circumcision. The Bukharan Jews adopted the Muslim tradition of circumcision for boys at the age of thirteen, and the boy who was celebrating this occasion was proudly standing at the table while this procedure was done. When our friends discovered my total ignorance of Jewish religion and traditions, they politely tried to introduce the basics to me.

The houses and the walls surrounding the homes in the Eastern Quarter were built from clay mixed with straw, similar to the adobe material in New Mexico. The streets, not wide enough for a car, were very narrow and were sometimes suitable for pedestrians only. Each house consisted of four buildings that formed a square, with windows and doors that only looked inside the yard. After entering through a heavy gate, a visitor would usually see a small pond in the middle of the yard, most likely with a large tree, a wooden platform, and the entryways of the four buildings. They were one- or two-story structures. We rented space in one of these buildings (really just one large room), while the owners occupied the rest of their house. They were very hospitable, and they helped us as well as many other families who had evacuated from the war zone. They helped us to adjust to the local conditions and connected us with their community. My father became their favorite physician, and he developed many friendships that lasted long after the war. Their children, who now live in the United States and Canada, located my sister in Toronto and told her that their families had named their children Boris in memory and honor of my father. I will always cherish the memories of these warm and kind people in my heart.

6. People I Met

During the first year of medical school, I had a friend named Yuri Gusev who was about five years older than me. He came to the school after being wounded in the war. He was very tall, slim, with very dark hair and a constant sadness in his dark eyes. He assumed a somewhat fatherly approach toward me by protecting me from constant trouble. Once we went to the open market, and I was attracted to a crooked card game. I lost all my money. Afterward, Yuri, who had silently observed my involvement, told me that he had anticipated what would happen but did not stop me because I needed to learn a lesson for the future—to not become involved in gambling. Besides his physical wounds, Yuri was psychologically affected by the war. He refused to talk about his war experience and even became angry when I asked if he had experienced killing Germans. My Uncle Misha was another person

43

badly wounded in the war who also came to Samarkand. Like Yuri, he was quite displeased when I asked him the question about killing Germans. Perhaps the experience of killing another human left a painful psychological scar on both men. Yuri was very upset with what he considered the far too comfortable life we were living and our total unawareness of the terrible conditions and the great number of lives lost at the front lines of the war. I think that his life was dominated by general depression and disappointment in life. As a result, forgetting about the health problems from his serious wounds, Yuri quit school at the end of the second year and went back to war. I never heard from him again and, most likely, he was killed. Many close friends and relatives were killed. One of them, Lev Hoffman, who was my childhood friend and schoolmate, sent me a picture of himself as a soldier that was taken just before he was killed.

A new close friend in Uzbekistan was Hamid Mansurov. We not only studied together, but we shared many hungry times together. We also dated the same beautiful Uzbek girl, who later became Hamid's wife. Hamid was a handsome man, much taller than most of the men of Central Asia, with slightly Mongoloid facial features. He was very talented and had a great sense of humor. We often spoke about politics, which at that time was quite dangerous, and we learned we could trust each other as we struggled to find enough food.

Once Hamid invited me to visit his uncle for dinner. I thought Hamid was an orphan from a Tajik family that had been displaced into Uzbekistan, and I was surprised to learn that his uncle was living in Samarkand. We approached the gate of heavily armored wood and knocked with the clapper. A servant opened the gate and ushered us into a large estate surrounded by high walls. Hamid's uncle was Sadreddin Aini, the famous Tajik poet and writer who, for some reason, chose to live in Samarkand rather than Tajikistan. Perhaps he was in his late fifties, but he appeared to be a much older man, with deep wrinkles in his face and a full white beard. He wore a large white turban and a robe, the typical attire for that region. He spoke Russian fluently and graciously welcomed me as a friend of "his Hamid." There was an air of mystery and secrecy in that place. It was probably because of his aristocratic roots and extreme wealth, which were very rare in the Soviet Union, especially in a time of war. For Hamid to take me to meet his enigmatic uncle was a strong expression of trust.

Clearly, Aini was not a typical Soviet writer, and his status was a mystery to me. Many years later, I learned that he lived a double life, which was typical for some Soviet celebrities. Conversely, he was educated in a *madrassa* as a Muslim cleric, but on the outside he pretended to be a Soviet loyalist. He became a member of the Communist Party and was recognized as a first-class writer and eventually became the President of Tajikistan's Academy of Science.

At that time, I had a chance to witness him in his personal setting without knowledge of Aini's skillful maneuvers for surviving the purges of Stalin. After washing our hands (and feet), we were invited outside to the "table," which sat on a wooden platform covered with carpet and a large canopy next to a small pond. We sat on the floor surrounded with comfortable pillows. The main course was pilaf, which we ate with our fingers (a special skill required by local etiquette), leaving our palms dry. The conversation was mainly about our studies, and Aini asked many questions about my family. After dinner Aini lifted his hands and said a blessing in Arabic. Hamid explained to me later that it was for our friendship and safety. Was he not only a poet, but a cleric as well? I was honored to meet the famous Aini, but, most importantly, we had a great dinner of pilaf and other local delicacies. What could have been better for perpetually hungry students?

Neither starvation and sickness nor the depression of the war could stop us from being young and acting accordingly. We knew that our optimism and good spirit helped us to survive. We even managed to have parties, usually sponsored by the Chairman of the Department of Anatomy, Professor Turkevitch. He was a popular teacher with the ability to make his lectures quite interesting, even on such a boring subject as anatomy. He had an unusual ability to reach the students on a personal level, and he had a great sense of humor. This tall, slim man in his sixties had a head full of reddish hair, which he never combed. His facial features indicated that he was an alcoholic. Turkevitch was a descendant of Polish aristocracy and often told us stories about his family's past. We learned that after Russia conquered Poland at the beginning of nineteenth century, many Polish aristocrats rebelled against Russia, for which they were exiled to Siberia and Central Asia. Turkevitch's father was not a part of the rebellion. Actually, he was a secret agent for the tsar. He was sent to Russia along with other aristocrats (as a cover) with a peculiar special assignment from the Russian government. The assignment was to promote the ideas of ethnic and religious intolerance, including anti-Semitism, as a tool against potential social disturbances among the local population. The professor said that he felt a moral obligation to tell us about it because he had special sympathy for the three of us working in his department —and because all three of us were Jewish.

Unfortunately this beloved mentor's alcoholism was severe. Sometimes the local students who knew his weakness would deliver huge canisters of wine made in their villages in the hope of improving their grades. The generous supply of wine gave us an opportunity to have strange drinking parties in his house. It was rather bizarre to have these parties while the world around us was in shambles and while we had so little food (other than the local villagers' gift of dried fruit).

One of my fellow students, Misha Yanyshevsky, was a refugee from Romania and often tried to show his superior worldliness and sophistication in contrast to the rest of us poor Soviet bumpkins. He was also fluent in several languages. I disliked his arrogance and cynicism, but I was also jealous of his skill with French and the facile charm he could use in social situations. Being quite shy at the time, I picked up a few of Misha's skills, but not enough to get very far. Turkevitch was in his sixties at that time, and his wife, who was an associate professor in his department, was fifteen to twenty years younger than he. She was very attractive and was quite interested in young men. At one of our parties at their house she expressed a definite interest in Misha. He was two or three years older than me, short, and not particularly masculine, but obviously had some experience with women. The Turkevitch's house had many rooms, which accommodated many people after the late evening drinking parties. On one such night Turkevitch suddenly woke up from his chair, started wandering around the house, and eventually found his wife and Misha sleeping together in one of the bedrooms. When Misha awoke from his drunken stupor, Turkevitch patted him on the head and said, "Oh, do not worry; go back to sleep. Everything is okay." Oddly, this episode did not affect the relationships within this happy family or their relationships with the students.

The hardship of life did not stop me from being romantic and falling in love with Suzie Rechtman, an attractive, petite blond and a very serious medical student. The relationship was rather superficial. We studied together, walked the streets in the evenings, and sometimes exchanged innocent kisses. Suzie and I had to pass a test in the Uzbek language. I appreciated the opportunity to learn this simple and interesting language and became quite good at it. The instructor was very nice to me, and I passed the exam with an A. Then Suzie wanted me to take her test for her. I did not want to ruin our relationship, and an opportunity for adventure was tempting. So I placed my picture into Suzie's certificate and went to the same elderly instructor who had given me the exam a week before. I bravely assumed the name Suzie, which was not a name commonly known to this Uzbek man, and I expected that he would not know that it was a woman's name. I went up to him and said, "Hello, my name is Suzie Rechtman." He became only slightly suspicious and asked me if I had already passed the test and had come to repeat the test to get a better score. Then we proceeded with the test. He told me that my pronunciation was not always correct and gave me a B. With this "victory" I went to Suzie, but instead of being grateful, she became angry with me and said that she could not believe that I got an A for myself and only a B for her. Obviously there was a touch of cold calculation in her persona and a tendency toward pragmatic use of people. I realized that this was the end of our relationship, and I realized for the first time that not every beautiful girl in this world had a warm, friendly disposition.

During the third year of school, I met Dara Rosenfeld, a second-year student. This relationship became very serious. We were both very much in love and often spoke of the possibility of our future together. She was very attractive, with golden hair, white skin, and blue eyes. She was my height and statuesque. We read poetry together, and she even wrote some; she was a warm and kind person. Dara and her younger sister, Nonna, lived with their

mother in a very small rented place. Her father was a political prisoner, and the family had very limited resources. I spent almost
every evening with Dara and during the day could not wait for the
next evening's date. Perhaps we were destined to be together, but
circumstances simply would not permit that to happen.

In May of 1945 the war with Germany ended. After finishing
my third year of school, I decided to transfer to a medical school
that would improve my professional future. I had good grades and
a letter of recommendation from the dean, so I moved to Moscow.
It was not an easy venture, but with help from some distant relatives who had the necessary connections, I managed. I settled there
by renting a "corner" from an elderly lady. This was a bed, slightly separated from the rest of her small room in a communal apartment. Within a year my family also came to Moscow. My father
purchased a house in one of Moscow's suburbs, and I joined the
family. In 1946, during summer break, Dara came to Moscow on
her way to Ukraine to visit her relatives, with the hope of moving
her family there. We had a wonderful reunion. We went to the theater and stayed in the apartment of some distant relatives while
they were out of town. When she left, we decided to meet again on
her way back from Ukraine to Samarkand to decide our future.
Unfortunately, that did not happen; because of some unbelievable
confusion with the train schedules, I missed meeting her at the
railroad station. She felt that it was intentional, became angry, and
then left for Samarkand. She would not answer my letters, and I
lost touch with her.

Many years later, in the 1960s, I learned that Dara was living in
Leningrad. I met her there on my way to a scientific conference.
She had become an ophthalmologist, married a navy physician,
and was in her last month of pregnancy. Even pregnant, she still
had the same beauty. That was the last time I would see her, or so
I thought. Many years later, I received a call in my office in Denver,
Colorado. A man speaking in Russian was trying to learn if I was
the same person who was a medical student in Samarkand during
the war. After he was satisfied with my answer, he said, "Here is
somebody who wants to talk to you." It was the sweet vibrating
voice from the past—a voice I recognized instantly—Dara! The call
was from Hartford, Connecticut, and the caller was Dara's second

husband, Simeon. He was so impressed with the story of Dara's past romance with me that, after their emigration to the United States, they both decided to find me. More than fifty years after the event in Samarkand, I visited them in Hartford. It was strange, but very pleasant. We had both aged, but Dara's voice had not changed at all, and her character was still the same—full of sweetness and kindness. Her husband and I became friends. Simeon is now writing and publishing Russian poetry, and I translated some of it into English to be included in his books. We still communicate from time to time.

That was the story of my first serious romantic attraction, which happened when I was nineteen. Reminiscence brought back a mixture of memories about the complexity of life at that time. It compels me to remember my survival in that disjointed time in Russia during and after the war and my efforts to succeed in my future life.

CHAPTER THREE

Moscow, New Horizons, and New Challenges (1945–50)

"It is a jungle out there."
R. Kipling

1. Life in Post-war Moscow
2. Anti-Semitism
3. Becoming a Medical Professional
4. Veronika Michaleva
5. Darwinism and Religion
6. Out of Moscow

Fig. 9. Moscow, Red Square. Victory Parade in 1945. About 57,000 German prisoners of war were taken through the Moscow streets. Soviet soldiers are throwing the Nazi banners at the foot of Lenin's Mausoleum.
Drawing by Edward Tabachnik

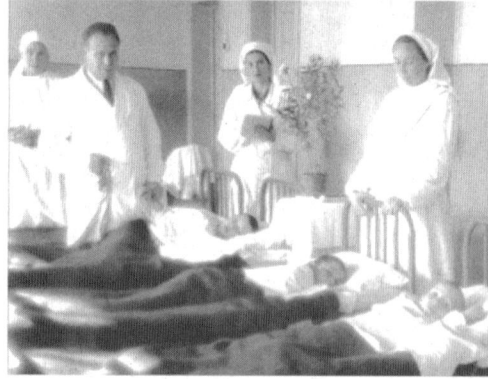 

Fig. 10. In Moscow after the war (left to right):
- My family survived and re-united (1945);
- My mother, Luba, in Moscow after the wa;r
- Father making rounds of his patients in a small Children's Hospital in a Moscow'suburb;
- My mother in Pabrade (Litvenia) visiting her sister Basia's family.

Fig.11. Bright sides of life during the dark years of
Stalin's era, top to bottom:
- Class of forensic medicine (heating failed in the
  building and we are wearing warm clothes);
- With two friends, Yury Yudin and Rouben
  Chilingorian;
- Official bosses at the post-graduate School of
  Epidemiology: general T.E. Boldyrev, Chairman of
  the Department; and
- N.E. Geffen, Associate Professor of the
  Department of Epidemiology.

Fig. 12. Current reflections of Stalin's era (left to right):
- Memorial at Ural Mountains in the Sverdlovsk District (Oblast) to the victims of Stalin's terror (I took this and two other pictures in 2003);
- A part of the Memorial with names of victims;
- An official border between Europe and Asia near the Memorial (with my friend and colleague Dr. Michael Iseman): and
- Birobidjan railway station (signs in Russian and Yiddish) of the so-called Autonomous Jewish District at the Far East of Russia. I took this picture in 2007.

1. Life in Post-war Moscow

In 1945 after the war, our family settled in the suburb of Moscow called Chuhlinka, which by train was only fifteen minutes from Moscow. My father took a job as the head of a small children's hospital for infectious diseases and soon became very popular with the local community. Contrary to Soviet rules, many officials wanted him to serve as their private physician when their children were sick. My sister was enrolled in school, my mother took care of the family, and I was busy with an intense clinical program in medical school. My father purchased half of a log house, to which we added another room. The carpenter hired for the addition allowed me to work as his helper during the summer, and I learned some useful skills in timber construction. We were happy to resume a normal and peaceful life after four years of upheaval caused by the war. At the same time, Stalin's new strategy for the political and economical environment created tension in everyone's life. The post-war period of severe restraints and unspeakable terror lasted until Stalin's death in March of 1953.

I stayed in Moscow to attend the last two years of medical school (1945–47) and then three years (1947–50) of graduate training (fellowship) in epidemiology and microbiology of infectious diseases. Despite the less-than-favorable environment for an intellectual and professional life, I was pleased with the opportunity to study in one of the best medical schools. (It is rated by the U.S. Kaplan's system as the fourth best out of ninety-nine medical schools in the world.) I was optimistic about my future and dreamed of reaching new horizons in medical research. This unjustified optimism may have grown out of the euphoria of simply surviving the war and almost recovering from tuberculosis; however, the realities of the Soviet world could not be long ignored. Even now, the horror and utter despair of what lay ahead defies comprehension. The lofty and noble idea that humankind should be respected, and even revered, was torn asunder by Stalin's savagery and his icy disregard for all human feeling.

During the war (1941–45) ten million soldiers and ten million civilians were killed, totaling more than 10% of the population of the country. A large part of the country was in ruins and the government's restoration efforts enormously drained the resources.

Everything was in short supply, especially food. The overriding problem, however, was the oppressive political climate created by Stalin's regime, with its pervasive control over individual lives and behavior that even extended to our thoughts. Stalin sought total control and demanded complete submission from everyone. Millions of people were arrested and sent to the Gulag system for slow extermination in its slave labor camps. By the end of 1950, there were approximately 2.6 million people imprisoned in this system. It is estimated that at least eighteen or twenty million Soviet citizens were victims of Stalin's reign of terror during the purges of the thirties, forties, and fifties.

After the war with Germany ended in 1945, the Soviet system used forced labor from several categories of prisoners. Among these groups were the German Prisoners of War (POW), a small proportion of whom survived the camps and later went back to Germany. Another group, called "displaced persons," were former Soviet soldiers taken prisoner by the Germans and forcibly sent back to the Soviet Union from Europe by the British and other Western allies. Finally, there were those who were arrested for various excuses just to fulfill the quota demanded of each regional state security office (NKVD, MGB, and under other titles that were predecessors of the KGB).

In 2003, under the provisions of collaborative research with some Russian scientists, I traveled to the Swerdlovsk District (Sverdlovsk Oblast). While visiting an area located near the Ural Mountains, I learned of brutal executions that frequently occurred in that area during Stalin's reign. Trains often moved convicted political prisoners from Moscow to camps in the Far Eastern part of the country. Sometimes, when the train reached the Ural Mountains, a message from Moscow to the local state security administration would arrive indicating that because of the "severity of anti-Soviet activities" committed by the prisoners, the Tribunal had changed the sentences from imprisonment to death for everyone on the train. The reason for the abrupt change was simple: The Gulag system was overcrowded. This area, close to the Europe/Asia divide, seemed unobtrusive and a good place for these mass atrocities. After the fall of the Soviet Union, a large monument was erected to honor the thousands of innocent souls who were brutally executed in his area. Sadly, only a few hundred names are inscribed on the monument. The others could not be identified.

On August 6, 1945, the first American nuclear bomb was dropped on Japan. Stalin had appointed Lavrenty Beria, who was supervising the Secret Police, Security and Intelligence services, to run a program with the code name of "Task Number 1." It was aimed at developing a Russian nuclear bomb. After the defeat of Japan, under Beria's supervision, Russia adopted advances already made by Japan in its bacteriological warfare program for development of all forms of weapons of mass destruction. These activities required mobilization of all available scientific and economic resources, as well as intensified spy activities abroad and an intensified internal "witch hunt." Another important event of that period was Churchill's famous "Iron Curtain" speech in Fulton, Missouri in 1946, which marked the beginning of the Cold War.

In 1949 the country celebrated Stalin's seventieth birthday. This occasion became the dominant event of the state, involving every aspect of social and cultural life. It marked the peak of Stalin's cult. At the same time, series of campaigns were initiated to seize control of all establishments connected with science and culture. All fields of intellectual endeavor were inundated with an intense regimen of Communist Party indoctrination. Weekly ideological seminars were mandatory for everyone in the workplace. The Party bosses, including Stalin and his entourage, became self-appointed experts in literature, linguistics, music, art, physics, biology, agriculture, medicine, and other fields. The Party issued official declarations and critiques in all these fields. Stalin wrote a book on linguistics in addition to his rewrite of the Communist Party's history. These and other publications became mandatory study material for everyone. One of his associates, Zhdanov, launched a terror campaign named "Zhdanovshchina" against writers and journalists and subsequently followed with an attack against music composers. One of Stalin's favorite merchants of terror was Trofim Lysenko, an ignorant "agricultural expert." He led a campaign against genetics and geneticists that often resulted in imprisonment of those who diverged from the Stalin-imposed mandates. It is hard to identify a science, or any other intellectual discipline, that was spared Party indoctrination.

2. Anti-Semitism

In 1947 the establishment of the state of Israel was among the events that influenced the post-war social climate in the Soviet Union. Arrival of Israeli Ambassador Golda Meir to Moscow in 1948 stirred up a wave of self-awareness and cultural consciousness among the Russian Jews, particularly when Mrs. Meir visited the Choral Synagogue during the Jewish New Year. Jews became the only national group with a foreign-based homeland that were placed under suspicion of potential divided loyalties. These momentous events triggered intensified government-sponsored anti-Semitism that included discrimination in the workplace, dismissal from high-ranking positions, limited admittance to the universities, and closure of Jewish theaters. An anti-Zionist propaganda campaign against Israel saturated the media, followed by attacks against prominent intellectuals of Jewish origin, especially those involved in Russian literature, journalism, music, theater, cinema, education, and science.

In fact, the escalation of anti-Semitism in the Soviet Union had its roots long before the establishment of the state of Israel. In 1942, despite the critical war situation, the Communist Party leadership found time for meetings of its Central Committee to address the national policy in art, literature, theater, cinematography, and journalism. The bottom line of these meetings was to promote ethnic Russian personnel for leading positions and to eradicate Jewish influence in these areas. Many Jewish army officers who were wounded on the line secretly told their families and friends stories about anti-Jewish statements coming from the Commissars and the denial of medals and recognitions of bravery to the Jewish soldiers and officers when submitted by the lower command to the higher army hierarchy for approval.

Nevertheless, the first official statistics regarding the ethnic origin of those awarded recognition for bravery indicated that Jews had a fourth place, after Russians and the Ukranian Belorussians.[2] In later publications, Jews were not listed at all, being included as "the others." I remember that in high school history textbooks the number of Jews awarded with Hero of Soviet Union (the highest award for bravery) was 170, third place after the Russians and the Ukranians. This number was dropped to 117 in the next year's edition, and later, no Jews were listed at all. Eventually, particularly after the war, a policy was established to deny Jews any role in the war efforts. The official propaganda also denied the exclusive (compared with other ethnic groups) suffering of Jews in the territories captured by the German Army, including denial of the Holocaust.

The detailed analyses of anti-Semitism in the Soviet Union and other East European Communist regimes have been addressed in a number of publications, particularly in the review by Amur Weiner [3] and in the book by Jan T. Gross.[4]

It is well known that at the beginning of the twentieth century, Marxist ideology appealed to many young nonreligious Russian Jews and to many other groups suffering from social inequalities and harsh realities. Not surprisingly, many Jews supported the 1917 October Revolution and became visible in the leadership of the new regime. The situation changed thereafter, particularly under Stalin's reign. To give credit to only himself for the establishment of the Soviet Union, Stalin staged purges to eliminate many of his former comrades, including many Jews among them. The same attitude applied to his views on any field of Soviet life; this was enhanced during the war by an excuse for confronting the German propaganda on the leading role of Jews in the Soviet Union that may have appealed to negative feelings toward the Communist regime by a certain part of the Russian population.

What was the reason to continue this line after the war? Was it to enhance Russian nationalism? Was it to divert the attention of the population from the harsh reality of life after the war, the failing economy, and repressions? Perhaps it was all of these, plus Stalin's growing ego and the need for targets for the brutality that was embedded in his pathological mind. Recent publications have revealed that in 1947, a secret directive from the Security establishment recommended to its subordinates to consider "persons of Jewish nationality" enemies of the Soviet Union and subjects of accusations and arrests for anti-Soviet nationalist activities and

American espionage. On December 1, 1952, at the meeting of the Central Committee of the Party, Stalin declared, "Every Jew is a potential spy for the United States." This declaration, although not published at that time, became a directive for the Party system and Security organizations.

In 1942, under Party approval, a Jewish Anti-Fascist Committee (JAFC) was organized with the goal of appealing to the Jewish communities around the world for financial support of the Soviet war efforts, and it was very efficient! After the war, in 1946, the Security Police searched the JAFC office and declared that they found documents indicating that this organization was affiliated with America and Zionism. In January of 1948 Stalin ordered Abakumov, Minister of State Security, to kill the Chairman of JAFC, the prominent actor and theater director Solomon Mikhoels. It was staged as a car accident. Other members of the committee were arrested and sentenced to death in the court. Thus the JAFC was eliminated.

The anti-Jewish campaign of 1949 was called the fight against "rotten cosmopolitans" and "Zionism." Any mention or complaint about anti-Semitism was deemed anti-Soviet propaganda and was cause for imprisonment. At the same time, criminal "cases" were brought against prominent Jewish professionals. Usually, the newspapers did not mention the ethnic origin of the accused, but the predominance of Jewish names could not go unnoticed.

The anti-Jewish campaign culminated in 1951–52 with a case against the "Jewish Medical Conspiracy," known later as the "Doctor's Plot." On January 13, 1953, *Pravda*, the leading newspaper, published a headline article, "Vicious Spies and Killers under the Mask of Academic Physicians." The article accused a group of nine prominent physicians (six of them Jewish) of being recruited by American Intelligence as members of an international Jewish Zionist organization conspiring to murder high-ranking Soviet officials.

Stalin died on March 5, 1953, the day before the trial was to begin. A month later, *Pravda* announced the doctors had been found innocent and were released from prison. It was later discovered that Stalin had planned to organize pogroms (violent attacks on Jews) around the country and then coerce Jewish leaders to publicly beg for protection. This protection would be achieved by shipping all Jews to Siberia.

In anticipation of the "Killers in White Coats" trial, the campaign then focused on Jewish medical professionals—doctors, dentists, and nurses. It was staged by the media and often accused these professionals of attempting to poison their patients. Many were fired from their jobs. My father was also targeted, but then he was suddenly called to attend to the sick child of a local Party chairman in the suburb of Chuhlinka. It was a bit of luck that postponed his firing until Stalin's death reversed the situation. I was also on the verge of being fired from my job at the medical school in Arkhangelsk. Stalin's death was a miracle for millions of us in the Soviet world.

3. Becoming a Medical Professional

Under the conditions of life described above, my fourth and fifth years at the Moscow Medical School in 1946–47 were spent covering every aspect of medicine, including patient treatment, surgery, various other procedures, and intensive work at the hospitals during the summer. Initially I was interested in becoming a surgeon and volunteered to assist in numerous surgeries; however, I eventually decided against surgery. I was somewhat shocked at the primitive general anesthesia procedures at the time, which sometimes resulted in the patient dying during surgery. Instead I began to focus on the epidemiology of infectious diseases. I began spending extra time in the hospital with adult patients who had infectious diseases and at the Department of Epidemiology. At that time, there were no internship or residency programs, but some departments had Ph.D. fellowship programs. Epidemiology was one of them.

Usually, along with their MD diplomas, graduates were given a work assignment as practicing physicians in various places around the country. Only the graduates who received a diploma with honors (A students) were eligible to apply for a fellowship, and I was one of the lucky ones. I was accepted for the three-year program in the Department of Epidemiology.

Two of my close colleagues also managed to get their positions in Moscow. One of them, Rouben Chilingorian, was an Armenian.

Rouben got his job as a medical administrator through his connections with the representatives of Armenian Republic in Moscow. My other colleague, Igor Yudin, was a close friend with whom I spent a lot of time preparing for the exams, as well as leisure time. Igor possessed rather patrician features along with blond hair and blue eyes. I remember him as somewhat pedantic with a keen eye for detail. His father's family had some aristocratic roots, and he was the nephew of Dr. Sergey Yudin, a famous surgeon. Igor's father once shared a secret with me. In the past he had been close to the Imperial Court of Nicolas II and was the appointed manufacturer of ornamental epaulets for the military uniforms. Igor's famous uncle was the key to the continued survival and prosperity of the family. It is how Igor received his fellowship in surgery. He remained in Moscow for the rest of his life working as a surgeon at different institutions. He specialized in proctology and became one of Mr. Brezhnev's personal physicians.

Igor secretly confided in me that the proctology assignment had been directed for him. I recall him saying, "Leonid, I'm a doctor of asses," and he proceeded to show me a book filled with his photographs relating to his particular field of proctology. Igor's professional position was the source of many jokes between two old friends. At the same time, the job provided a good basis for Igor's prosperous life in Moscow. Before he was married and while he was in fellowship training, Igor did not have much time for social activities or to engage in a relationship with women. Fortuitously though, there was a woman who lived upstairs in the same building, and she and Igor engaged in a noncommited physical relationship. After emigration, I lost contact with Igor and my other colleagues and students.

My fellowship in the epidemiology of infectious diseases included training with patients and in microbial diagnoses procedures; however, the primary task was to prepare and defend my dissertation for the Candidate of Medical Science degree, which is the equivalent of a Ph.D. in the U.S. The Department of Epidemiology did not have its own laboratory for work with pathogens, and General Boldyrev, the chairman of the department (and also the chief epidemiologist of the Soviet Army), assigned me to perform this work at a military research institute. Because of the growing shroud of secrecy at that place and also because I lacked the right status level to be among the military scientists, this arrangement did not fare well. To further my research, I was transferred to the Metchnikov Institute for Vaccines and Sera. The topic of my studies included analysis and optimizing the cultivation of *Salmonella typhi* (typhoid bacteria) and other related bacteria in large volumes of a liquid medium in special tanks as part of manufacturing vaccines against typhoid fever and other enteric infections. Dr. Alexandra Naumovna Zamuchovskaya, my advisor for these studies, was a most knowledgeable expert in the field and the head of the production department. The research was successful. I published a paper in a leading Russian journal and presented the dissertation. Although the main findings had already been published, the administration issued a secrecy assignment to the dissertation that required defense of my thesis to be set up for an audience authorized for classified materials. Naturally, this delayed the process. The defense finally took place in 1952, two years after my graduation from the fellowship program. Another obstacle was that during my last year of fellowship, the medical school handling my thesis was targeted for punishment because of "political inappropriateness" of some faculty members. As a result, the school was banished from Moscow and became the Riazan Medical School. After resolving these bureaucratic problems, I graduated from the fellowship. I was given an assignment by the Ministry of Health as an assistant professor of microbiology at the medical school in the Far Northern city of Arkhangelsk, a position that I assumed in December of 1950.

In spite of the difficulties of life and brutal political environment, the three years of my fellowship turned out to be one of the most exciting periods of my life. One of my early dreams had come true. I became a scientist in the desirable field of medicine and successfully accomplished an interesting research project. Also, life in Moscow, even with political indoctrinations and repression, was filled with opportunities and excitements. One was going to theaters for fine performances, as I was particularly interested in ballet and opera performances at the famous Bolshoy Theater. The Moscow Conservatory was another attraction, and my interest in classical music was revived. It was also an opportunity to meet interesting people, provided one observed caution in group conversations. There were always informants around who would report any remark that diverged (or seemed to) from the required political attitude. People tried to live normal lives in spite of the tense environment and constant danger.

4. Veronika Michaleva

It was during this period that I met Veronika Vasilievna Michaleva, a young microbiologist from an agricultural research institute. Veronika came to Moscow from Vologda, a Northern city famous for its dairy products. Her assignment to the fellowship in Moscow came from the industrial dairy institution in Vologda. Perhaps she was not a beauty by some standards, but her attractiveness was in her soft, pleasant manners, her kindness, and her attentiveness. It was a pleasure to spend hours conversing with her on a variety of topics, including microbiology, theater, and art, and listening to her unusual opinions and expressions tempered with a soft Northern accent much different from the Moscovites. We fell in love and dated for two years. We visited theaters, museums, and concerts. Thanks to Veronika and lectures by the famous Russian musician-educator Kobalevsky that we attended together, I developed a taste for classical music, mainly inspired by our romantic involvement. Many of our dates were in her friends' apartment when they were not at home. Ironically, it was located in a small street almost across from a mansion that was a residence of Lavrenti Beria, Stalin's associate in charge of Security and Secret Police structures (*Lavrushinsky Pereulok*). Perhaps the secret service guards patrolling the street at the walls surrounding the mansion already knew why we were sneaking into the nearby apartment building and that we presented no security risk to their boss. Nevertheless, as I later learned more about Beria, these interludes were risky. But we were naïve and had little choice.

Our beautiful relationship ended over disagreements on the political situation, particularly the rising anti-Semitism in 1949. Veronika did not perceive any problems, but I certainly did. I suddenly realized that a non-Jewish person's view could be less attuned to it, regardless of how intelligent and caring they may be.

We ended our relationship, and I decided I would never again date a non-Jewish person and certainly would not consider marrying one.

Many years later I met Veronika at a scientific meeting. We were happy to see each other, and she told me that she was married, after all, to a nice Jewish man. She told me that soon after we broke up, she realized I had been right about the rising anti-Semitism, but it was too late since I had already left Moscow for Arkhangelsk. She confessed that she cherished the sweet memories of our past romance and even mentioned that she felt that our time together had helped make her the woman that she was. I realized with regret that in the circumstances of our lives and my perception of events I had missed an opportunity to be with a wonderful person. Unfortunately this was neither the first, nor the last time...

5. Darwinism and Religion

In 1948, the Department of Marxism-Leninism of our medical school organized a mandatory course of seminars and workshops for all Ph.D. candidates in biology and medicine at every Moscow medical institution. The purpose of this year-long event was to ensure that all research was in compliance with the Communist ideology. Passing a final exam on the subject of Marxism-Leninism was a requirement for submission of any Ph.D. dissertation. Moreover, each candidate was given a topic for an essay presentation at one of the workshops.

My assignment was on "Critical Analyses of Darwin's Theory of Evolution." I read Darwin's books, particularly *Origin of the Species*, along with Russian and foreign scientific papers. Perhaps this was much more than expected; the usual approach was to read the recent papers about Darwin's books and not the books themselves. That way, the politically correct view would be regurgitated. I gave a forty-five-minute presentation at one of the workshops and submitted the handwritten, twenty-page essay to the chairman of the Marxism-Leninism Department. Unlike other similar workshops, this time the chairman did not initiate any discussion. He simply adjourned the meeting and invited me into his office.

In his office he asked me if I believed in God. "Are you religious?" he asked. The question seemed ridiculous, and I responded,

65

"Of course not! I do not know anything about religion! Why are you asking me about it?" It was an honest response. He said he believed me but told me that the way my essay was written cast doubt on Darwin's theory of evolution.

In fact, when I prepared it, I initially had no doubts about the theory of evolution. I presented well-known examples of selection of the fittest as a driving force in evolution. But these examples were related to evolution *within* the species. Darwin's theory was very logical with regard to evolution *among* the species, and I referred to his original suggestion that such an event was still a theory which required evidence to be found in the form of intermediate organisms. These were "missing links," as Darwin put it, in the chain of evolution to be found either by fossil excavations or by experiments. What angered my mentor was that I suggested that Darwin's theory was still a hypothesis instead of embracing the politically correct assertion of Neo-Darwinism—that the theory was now a scientific fact. He said, "If you do not accept Darwin's theory of evolution as the only explanation of the origin of the species, then logically you believe in the alternative, the theory of creation." I emphatically denied that suggestion. After realizing that I was honest in my response (or maybe to avoid complications), he said, "I believe that you are going to be a good scientist, and I am not going to destroy your life by forwarding your essay to the administration. Instead, I will pretend I never saw it. I would also suggest that you never get involved in speculations about Darwinism. You need to just focus on your experimental research." With these words, he tore the manuscript into small pieces and threw it into the wastebasket. Thank you, Mr. Melentiev, for your kind counsel and wisdom! I followed your advice and never wrote or spoke again about Darwinism as long as I lived in the Soviet Union.

But what can stop me now? From time to time I discuss the validity of Darwin's theory with biologists and philosophers, gleaning from them a broad range of opinions. The question is not whether evolution takes place, but whether it is really a driving force in the transformation of one species into another. Is there new evidence today that the genetic barrier between species can be crossed over? Is it possible by artificial inbreeding even between

two close species to create a hybrid that would have l
ducibility than the parent species (a requirement to be
according to Darwin's theory)? The answers to thes(
remains "no." So far, no fossils, no inbreeding experi.
any modern molecular biology has shown the possibilit
ing a barrier between two species, no matter how close the species
may be. That leaves the defenders of the theory of evolution with
fear expressed in the form of a question by Huxley, the Neo-
Darwinist. "What is the alternative if you do not accept the theory
of evolution as an explanation of the origin of the species?" On the
other hand, modern opponents of Darwin's theory, like Phillip
Johnson in *Darwin on Trial*, assert that the theory of evolution has
no more proof than the theory of creation, and, therefore,
Darwinism should be viewed just as another religion based on
beliefs rather than on reproducible facts.[5] Some religious fundamentalists exclude not only studies of Darwinism, but also of modern biology in general from the curriculum of religious schools.
The history of debate around biological science versus religion
began with the ridiculous "Monkey Trial" in the 1920s and continues today. It is generally based on ignorant suggestions from both
sides and confirms the eight-hundred-year-old statement by
Maimonides: "Those who see a controversy between religion and
science have ignorance of religion, or science, or both."

6. Out of Moscow

In spite of the overall suppressive climate of life in Moscow, the
five-year period of my life in Moscow was quite productive. I
received my MD, and I also received training in infectious diseases with an emphasis on microbiology and epidemiology. I
completed my Ph.D. dissertation, and I was eagerly preparing to
continue the interesting research at the Metchnikov Institute for
Vaccines and Sera. The Institute requested that the Ministry of
Health arrange for me to be assigned to that institution; unfortunately, the ministry turned it down and, instead, assigned me to
the Medical School in Arkhangelsk. A friend at the ministry told
me that this decision was part of the anti-Jewish politics that esca-
lated at that time.

Those five years also taught me many survival skills, both literally and professionally. I learned techniques for pursuing my goals in the atmosphere of a hostile totalitarian regime. I learned to deal with anti-Semitic sentiments in general, as well as those specifically directed toward me. Despite all this, I learned how to remain optimistic. The key was to find a point of balance between a relationship with the system and preserving one's dignity and honesty. Those skills probably enabled me to survive the rest of my years in the Soviet Union. Cultural terror continued unabated when I moved from Moscow to Arkhangelsk, and the future was most uncertain. My horizons were much cloudier than five years before when I came to Moscow. Battles for survival lay ahead.

CHAPTER FOUR

Northern Exposure, Soviet Style (1950–57)

"Every hour was filled with shock and surprise....
No lazy, sun-kissed life was this, with nothing to do but
loaf and be bored.
Here was neither peace, nor rest, nor a moment's safety."
Jack London, *The Call of the Wild*

1. **Arkhangelsk**
2. **Life in the North**
3. **Job at the Medical School**
4. **Investigating Outbreaks**
5. **Politics in Personal Life**
6. **The End of "Northern Exposure"**

**Fig. 13. At the Plesetsk railway station:
the starting point to one of the Gulag Archipelago areas.**
Drawing by Edward Tabachnik

Fig. 14. In Arkhangelsk (left to right):
- I am an assistant professor in the Department of Microbiology at the age of twenty-five (1951);
- Becoming more mature (no moustache anymore) at the Northern Dvina River (1955);
- Writing a scientific paper; and
- Associate professor at the Infectious Diseases Department (1956) with friends Dr. Vera Koroleva (at the far left) and Dr. Tatiana Kamolikova (next to me at the right).

Fig. 15. In Akhangelsk (left to right, top to bottom):
- Prof Matochkin with the target of his attacks, Dr. Josef Serebrenikov;
- Prof. M. V. Pickel, a family friend and a pediatrician to our children (picture was taken in 1990s after her retirement);
- Prof Grishanina, Department of Microbiology; and
- With Sima on Northern Dvina River, March 1955.

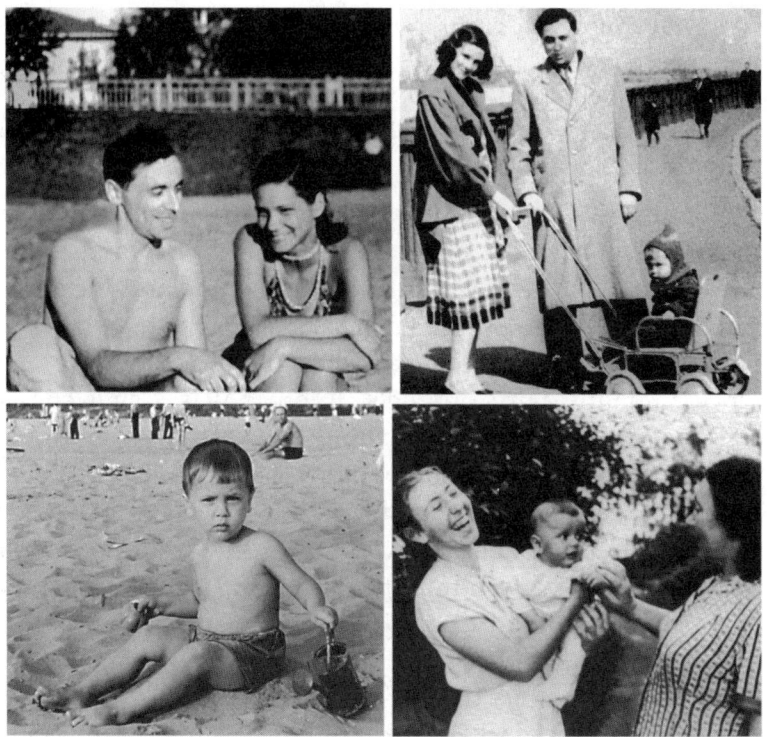

Fig. 16. Life in Arkhangelsk after Stalin's death (left to right):
- With Sima at the beach of N. Dvina River (1954);
- With Sima and Michael at the boardwalk (1955);
- Michael at the beach of Northern Dvina(1957); and
- We brought Michael to Moscow during the summer vacations. He is with my cousin Galia (from Pabrade, Litvenia) and my mother Luba.

1. Arkhangelsk

After graduation from the fellowship in epidemiology of infectious diseases at the Moscow Medical School, I received an assignment from the Ministry of Health as Assistant Professor in the Department of Microbiology at the Medical School in Arkhangelsk. In December 1950, I moved to this northern city where I lived for more than seven years.

Arkhangelsk is located at the same latitude as Fairbanks, Alaska. Traveling directly north from Moscow to Arkhangelsk by train took almost twenty hours and was quite an experience. The areas through which the railroad passed were flat and gloomy with forests only at the beginning; it was swampland for most of the journey. Unlike many other areas of Russia there were not many significant stops. One was the city of Vologda, a place known for quality dairy products. Another was a sinister place called Plesetsk. Before approaching Plesetsk the conductors walked through the cars closing window shades and warning the passengers not to open them and look out. Once I was overcome with curiosity and violated the warning. I saw a group of about twenty or twenty-five men from the last car of the train surrounded by a group of military guards and German shepherds being escorted across a ditch on a small footbridge. They remained with their backs to the train until it pulled away from the station. Plesetsk was one of the entry points to the "islands" of the "Gulag Archipelago." What I saw was just another group of prisoners being taken there from Moscow. The scenario at this station was always the same with each trip to Arkhangelsk. In the future I wisely refrained from making further dangerous attempts to observe this horrid ritual.

Arriving at Arkhangelsk was a challenge; the railroad station was on the left bank of the Northern Dvina River, and the city was on the right bank. There was no bridge at that time, and passengers were transported on small steamboats during the warmer months. In the cold months they crossed the frozen river by sled. Upon arrival, my initial impression was that most of the city's buildings were only two-story wooden structures, and most of the walkways were boardwalks. During the winter there was almost no daylight, and it was cloudy most of the time; however, for enduring nearly total darkness, one is rewarded by the incomparably beautiful and mysterious Northern Lights. Moreover, in summer there is almost no darkness. Sunrise and sunset occur almost in the same spot on the northern horizon, allowing approximately two hours with the sun down but with the light of dusk remaining below the horizon.

The history of Arkhangelsk goes back to the sixteenth century when Tsar Ivan the Terrible encouraged merchants from England and Holland to bring their goods to Russia through the White Sea and the estuary of the Northern Dvina River. To further boost development of the city, Peter the Great ordered construction of a shipyard in 1693. After a long period of decline, the city began to develop again at the end of the nineteenth century when a railroad to Moscow was completed and timber became a significant export commodity. Today Arkhangelsk is a timber and fishing center with its port open year-round, thanks to modern icebreaking technology. The population of the city currently is about 350,000, but in 1950 when I arrived there, it was only 250,000. It is the capital of the large Arkhangelsk *Oblast* (region), which is more than 587,400 square kilometers (larger than France) and has a population of about 1.5 million. Some inhabitants of the northern areas of the Oblast are descendants of Pomors, ethnic Russian explorers who settled the area before the twelfth century. Included in the Oblast at that time was the Autonomous *Okrug* (district) of Nenetsia, a large area of 170,000 square kilometers, with only 55,000 people, including nearly 6,000 Pomors and 7,000 Nentsy. The Nentsy are an indigenous people related to the Samoyedic linguistic group of ancient nomads who lived in this tundra area and also in parts of Siberia.

Another unusual part of the Oblast was the archipelago (mainly two large islands) called *Novaya Zemlya*, which is one of the extreme northern points of Europe, located in the Arctic Ocean between the Barents and Kara Seas. These islands were known as a place of exile for political prisoners and were also used for thermonuclear and atmospheric tests, especially during the time I lived in Arkhangelsk. From Arkhangelsk one can access another group of islands, although they are not a part of the Arkhangelsk Oblast; these are the *Soiovetsky Islands* (or *Solovky*, as the Russians call them). These islands are located in an eastern part of the White Sea (in the Onega gulf) about 150 kilometers south of the Arctic Circle. They were famous for some historic monuments, such as the Russian Orthodox Monastery, which had a large sixteenth-century cathedral and a system of canals built by monks. Also, it was the place of one of the first labor camps for political prisoners (1923–1939) and a starting point for the Gulag Archipelago. Solovky is now an important attraction for Western tourists via Russia or Norway.

2. Life in the North

The appointment as an assistant professor in the Department of Microbiology of the medical school was my first official job after graduating from the fellowship. I also received my first housing accommodation: a room in an apartment that I shared with a married couple (they had two rooms; I had one). They were also assistant professors, but in other departments of the school. On one hand, I was quite proud of achieving independence at the age of twenty-five; but on the other hand, I felt as though I had been expelled from the convenient environment of Moscow and consigned to this strange place where I did not know anyone.

Life in Arkhangelsk during the winter months was quite depressing, somewhat because of the cold, wet climate but more because of the perpetual darkness. The sun appeared on the horizon for a couple of hours, shedding faint light behind heavy clouds. The only source of light by which to live and work was artificial. Life for everyone was routine, without much social activity in the city. It was basically going to work in the morning and rushing home at night. Conversely, beginning in late May and more so in June and July, people enjoyed the twenty-four-hour-long days, when the sun was below the horizon for only a few hours after sunset while still reflecting light in the broad Northern Dvina River. The weather was warm, and people spent many hours enjoying each other's company on the banks of the river. It was the main gathering place during those long days.

Entertainment consisted of a theater that showed mediocre performances, two movie theaters, and some dances at the army officers' club. Because there were only these few establishments, people would have small parties with heavy drinking and a small variety of food. Grocery stores always had bread and dairy products, including cheese and a type of yogurt called kefiir, but there was no meat or poultry. The only available fish was salted cod in barrels. There were no green vegetables or fruits, and even the supply of potatoes was sparse and unreliable. The quality of the drinking water was a serious problem because it came from swampy areas and was known to be deficient in some microelements. The poor quality of the water, along with an insufficient supply of fruits and vegetables, was considered the main cause of prevalent tooth-loss among the Arkhangelsk children.

The only place to get a decent meal was at the Poliarny restaurant in the Intourist Hotel. The Poliarny was where only those who could afford the prices gathered. I felt quite lonely, but the income from my assistant professor's salary allowed me to enjoy these social activities. Some of the late-night-drinking parties were with the actors from the theater who needed to unwind from their evening performances. They were a loose and somewhat bizarre group of people who were always seeking excitement and love affairs. One of my drinking partners was Nikolay Ikonnikov, a military man. (I believe he was either a captain or a major.) He was the husband of my colleague at the Department of Microbiology, Dr. Veshchezerova. Usually on Saturday we would spend late hours drinking, discussing women, family relations, and life in general. Inevitably, we greeted the morning with a terrible hangover. Nikolay often complained about the dullness of his life. He was being faithful to his wife but was clearly looking for adventure. Sometimes, in a shy way, he would ask my advice on how to start an affair and keep it discreet. Drinking with Nikolay was a typical part of my superficial social existence during my first year in Arkhangelsk. Then, fortunately, I started to meet people who were more interesting and of some intellectual depth.

Maria Vladimirovna Pickel, who was fifteen years my senior, was a popular pediatrician and an associate professor at the medical school. She was mature and a very sophisticated woman who became my trusted friend. During that time, at approximately age forty-five, she married Dr. Alexander Grigorievitch Margolin, who had also become my friend. He was a widower, a well-known neurologist, and a faculty member of the medical school. Margolin's son, George, who became a prominent surgeon, is now a professor at the Arkhangelsk Medical School, and Margolin's daughter immigrated to Israel with her family.

Maria's life history and survival was a remarkable story. Her father was of German descent and had been a pediatrician at the Imperial Court of Nicolas II. Before the October Revolution, the Pickel family lived in Gatchina, a famous suburb of St. Petersburg and the place where many people who were associated with the tsar's court resided. After the Revolution, perhaps in the 1930s, the members of the Pickel family, along with other Gatchina residents, were exiled to various places, mostly in Siberia. Maria, her father, and one of her sisters came to Arkhangelsk.

The members of this large family suffered several misfortunes, including tuberculosis. Throughout her life, Maria took care of all her siblings and their children. I only met some of them in Arkhangelsk, where two of her nieces lived at that time. Being of German descent and having a German last name during World War II was sufficient reason, in addition to her Tsarist-connected past, for Maria to end up in the Gulag. What saved her was the fact that she was a brilliant pediatrician who was constantly in demand by high-ranking local authorities. She is now ninety-six years old (2007), retired from her professorship at the medical school, and living in Arkhangelsk, where she keeps busy translating books of German poetry into Russian and publishing them.

Maria and I spent memorable evenings sitting on a wooden floor in a warm corner of my future wife's apartment and discussing a wide range of topics, including political matters that one would only dare discuss with a very trusted friend. She would compare the faculty and the whole setting at our medical school to Heinrich Heine's satirical presentation of the German professors in his book *The Harz Journey*. Knowing Dr. Pickel and spending time with her was an important "intellectual window" in our life, which was mostly monotonous, punctuated occasionally by danger and fear. Dr. Pickel was the pediatrician who eventually provided medical attention for our sons, Michael and Herman (born in 1955 and 1957, respectively), until we moved from Arkhangelsk to Moscow. We sorely missed her excellent care of our sons long after we moved, and we missed the pleasure of her conversation and the glow of her brilliant intellect.

There were many civilians and military personnel (mostly Jewish) who had recently transferred from Moscow and Leningrad to work in Arkhangelsk. Perhaps this was not an accident but rather a reflection of the politics of the Soviet Union. These people were representatives of the country's intellectual elite, who mostly managed to survive in spite of the depressing political climate and persecution. The faculty did not always welcome such bright personalities among the newcomers. Many of the faculty members were "homegrown" people who came from local peasant families with limited cultural backgrounds. They were traditionally suspicious of big-city people. To assimilate into this society one had to hide one's originality and novel ideas and pretend to be simple and ordinary, without special talents or achievements. Not everyone was suited to this role, so newcomers were closely watched for signs of any inappropriate behavior or beliefs.

One newcomer, Professor Mazhbitz, became the Chairman of the Department of Obstetrics and Gynecology. Dr. Mazhbitz was very bright and outspoken, with a certain level of arrogance that was reinforced by the admiration of his influential patients. He came from Leningrad, where he had a prominent job at the medical school. Dr. Mazhbitz loved giving public lectures, and he never missed an opportunity to give a presentation at scientific conferences at the medical school. His presentations were extraordinary and in sharp contract to the usual dull reports. He used examples from many different fields, embellished by interesting slides. It was a true joy to listen to his lectures. Naturally, his style irritated several of the less sophisticated faculty members. In their resentment and jealousy, they looked for excuses to penalize him. One of these discomfited individuals was the mediocre Professor Matochkin, Chairman of the Anatomy Department. He avoided controversy in his job; after all, his "patients" were silent. He was of the lowest imaginable intellect and reminded me of characters in plays by the famous Russian dramatist Alexander Ostrovsky— generally wealthy nineteenth-century merchants, semi-literate, who hated anything Western. Professor Matochkin's short, stocky build, typical of nineteenth-century Russia but unusual in the Soviet Union of the 1950s, was a caricature of this type. He hated Mazhbitz at first glance. Although Matochkin always targeted Jewish professionals, I can't be certain he was anti-Semitic; however, he was clearly xenophobic toward anyone outside his environment and provincial culture. Finally the opportunity arose to put Mazhbitz in his place, and Matochkin seized it. Mazhbitz, in one of his scientific presentation, kept referring to "my department" and "my laboratory" and Matochkin immediately created a scandal. He claimed that such terminology portrayed a mentality foreign to a socialist society where all departments and laboratories belonged to the school and to the people. The administration took these vulgar arguments seriously and arranged a series of official discussions. In the end, Mazhbitz had to apologize for his unintentional use of offensive phrases.

A more serious scandal arose against Dr. Josef (Yosif) Serebrenikov, an assistant professor at the Department of Pathophysiology. He and his wife Tamara were transferred from a medical school in another city and were my neighbors in the same apartment. Tamara's father had been Chairman of the Pathophysiology Department in their previous workplace, and that was used as a rationale for Serebrenikov's transfer to Arkhangelsk. They were a strange, childless couple with no desire to extend their family in the future. They were completely focused on their professional careers and continued with the research they had started at the previous medical school. During one of Josef's presentations, someone noticed Tamara's father's name, rather than Josef's, at the bottom of some slides documenting the experiments. That was sufficient reason to accuse Serebrenikov of plagiarism, and then, later, falsification of results. It did not matter that Josef explained that the preliminary results were from a joint study in the past (a common practice in modern research) and that he had a special letter supporting his explanation from his previous mentor (Tamara's father). Some faculty members, with Matochkin in the lead, simply rejected the explanation. The scandal never ended, and eventually the couple had to move from Arkhangelsk. Many years later I met Serebrenikov in Moscow; he and Tamara were divorced, and he was working as a physician in a private clinic.

There were many other episodes like those with Mazhbitz and Serebrenikov, but somehow life went on, and people tried to extract as much as possible from the limited opportunities in professional and social life. In such a close society as Arkhangelsk everybody's life was an open book, and it gave me the opportunity to closely observe life and its surrounding events. For some inexplicable reason, people (generally women) often chose me as their confidante, and I gleaned a lot of inside information. Even now some of it fascinates me.

Professor V., one of the most decent faculty members and a well-known expert in organic chemistry, was a tall, slim man in his late fifties. He survived his two previous wives, both of whom were much younger than he. When I met him, he was married for the third time and, again, to a very young woman who was a former student of the school. This wife also died while I still lived in Arkhangelsk. Mysteriously, all three women died from various types of cancer. Despite such misfortune, Dr. V. remained a joyful man who was adored by his students. During the time his last wife was still alive, a fifth-year female student, one of the top graduates, approached Dr. V. with an unusual request. In addition to being unattractive, she was also handicapped by deformities in her hips and could barely walk. She knew that her chances of getting married were nil, but she wanted to have a child. She wanted to have a child by Dr. V. She knew well that he was very loyal to his wife and suggested that she would ask her permission for such an affair. She also promised that she would leave the city without any subsequent tie or obligation to Dr. V.'s family. Her wish was granted, and she became pregnant; only few people knew about this. From then on, no one ever knew where she moved after graduation.

I will call her Elsa A. She was an assistant professor, quite an attractive and sexy woman in her early thirties. Early in the war, while still a fifth-year medical student, she married an independent young man named Boris D. who was soon mobilized to the army and sent to the front. Soon after, close to the time of graduation from medical school, Elsa began an affair with a prominent professor. Such events were quite common at that time, although society considered such behavior a betrayal of the soldier fighting the war. The situation was different in this case because Elsa and

Professor Vladimir K., a divorced man, started living together as husband and wife although they never formally married. Elsa even wrote a letter to Boris about the situation, suggesting that they get divorced upon his return.

One could only imagine Boris's distress. He wrote back condemning Elsa's betrayal and stated that perhaps he would not survive the war to see her again. The probability of death at the front was very high. In fact, although he was severely wounded, he survived, and years later he came to Arkhangelsk to formalize the divorce with Elsa. By the time Boris arrived in Arkhangelsk, the professor had moved to another city to take a more prominent job, married another woman there, and some years later had died. The peculiar fact in this story is that Elsa gave birth to a daughter, and it was unclear who the child's father was, Boris or Vladimir. Most likely it was Boris, considering the timing of the girl's birth after Boris's departure to the front. Although she wasn't formally married to Vladimir, Elsa, with the help of her friends, succeeded in arranging a birth certificate for her daughter listing Vladimir as the father. At the time I lived in Arkhangelsk, Boris arrived from Moscow to formalize his divorce from Elsa but did not know, and was not told, that he might have a daughter. Elsa's mother was of German descent, which provided Elsa the opportunity to emigrate to Germany with her daughter in the 1980s. The relationship between the daughter and mother was quite peculiar, similar to a phenomenon described by Dianne Fossey in one of her observations of gorillas, when a full-grown child refused to be separated from the mother and remained fully dependent on the mother's activities. Elsa's daughter was quite lazy, could not keep a job, and was economically dependent on her mother. After emigration, under the pretense of taking care of her aging mother, she stayed with Elsa, still fully dependent on financial assistance provided to Elsa by the government. Only a few people knew about these events. One can learn a lot of hidden secrets from female friends...

Boris Anatolievich Kantorovich (R.A. Kantorovich, as listed in his publications) was a virologist from the Leningrad Institute for Microbiology assigned to work in the Arkhangelsk Microbiology

Institute. Boris was a talented scientist with an interest in the epidemiology of rabies, particularly in the historic evolution of rabies and its connection with a similar illness affecting polar foxes. The opportunity to study polar foxes in their natural habitant was the formal reason for Boris' transfer to Arkhangelsk, but the real reason was much more complex. It was common knowledge that his superior at the Institute in Leningrad had a love affair with Boris's wife. Just as it had been between the baron and his subjects in the feudal setting during the middle ages, simply because of the boss's rank and connections, he was exempt from officially proclaimed moral and ethical standards! Boris could barely hide his frustration and anger. He became extremely cynical in his relationships with women. It seemed as though he wanted to make them all suffer for his wife's indiscretion. He changed his sexual partners with unbelievable frequency, showing a preference for married women. Once his wife came from Leningrad to celebrate New Year's Eve with him, and Boris, knowing that she was coming, immediately left town the day before. He headed north to spend New Year's Eve with the polar foxes.

Eventually he divorced his wife and got a new job in Moscow, where he married a very young woman with whom he had a son. We continued to see each other in Moscow, but I noticed that, despite his new and seemingly successful marriage, he had not abandoned his habit of seeking sexual trysts.

Boris spent a lot of time in the tundra of the Nenetsk District tracing epidemics of rabies-like infections among the polar foxes. This involved many short trips in light planes of Polar Aviation. Quite often he had to remain for days in small airfields when snowstorms prevented departures. He shared a number of stories with me about life with the Polar Aviation pilots. He obviously embellished some of these stories to impress the audience, especially the women. Sometimes he took stories from Russian folklore and presented them as personal experience. He called one such story "True Russian Roulette." To be sure that the listeners had not heard it before he would ask first, "Did you hear about the true Russian roulette?" If not, he would proceed:

"A group of pilots was stuck at an airfield for more than a week. There was little to do so they drank spirits, had sex with the woman who kept the place, and played cards. The days passed and the weather showed no signs of improving. Boredom set in. Suddenly one of the pilots said, 'Boys, let's play roulette.' I knew well what that meant so I lay down in the upper bunk, pretending I was drunk and asleep. There was a table in the middle of the room with a hole in the center, indicating that true Russian roulette had been played there before. Strings, with loops at the lower ends, one for each player, were placed through the hole. The woman definitely knew her role; she crawled under the table and put the loops on each player's penis. Each player put ten rubles on the table and pulled one of the strings trying to guess to whom the string was attached. If he was right the winnings were his, but if he guessed wrong he lost his money and had to wait for the next sitting. The catch was that if he pulled the string too lightly the man attached to it would not wince. Therefore, the string had to be pulled hard enough to cause pain to the unfortunate man on the other end, revealing the victim and winning the money."

Some may have heard this story before—borrowed from Russian folklore and adapted to the Polar setting—but were reluctant to confront his plagiarism. Boris was a highly educated, well-recognized virologist and possessed extensive knowledge of English, rare at that time. It was sad to see how the pain of his first marriage turned him bitter and cynical. Boris died in Moscow in the 1980s from some mysterious neurological illness, officially stated as multiple sclerosis. Recently (in 2007) I met Dr. Botvinkin, a prominent Russian expert on rabies who had just come back from an international conference on rabies in Paris. He had known Boris in the past and told me that Kantorovitch is now internationally recognized as a pioneer in studying the epidemiology of rabies among wild animals, particularly the transmission of a rabies-like infection from lemmings to polar foxes with the potential to infect humans.

3. Job at the Medical School

The Medical School in Arkhangelsk (listed on the Internet today as the Northern State Medical University) was established in 1932. When I arrived in December of 1950, it was housed in an old, dilapidated building with many of the supporting hospitals in old, timber, barrack-style structures. On my first day I was called to the personnel department to fill out a questionnaire and write an autobiography. Many times during my first year I was asked to repeat the same procedure under the pretence that previously written documents had been lost. But as throughout most of the USSR, the personnel department was run by the regional security/secret police office (known after 1953 as KGB). It was clear that they were looking for discrepancies in my various presentations. I actually had to memorize most of the first document just to stay consistent about my life's details and avoid raising their suspicion.

My daily work schedule included laboratory training of three groups of students. One group was from 8 AM to 10 AM, and the second group was from 10 AM to noon, followed by an interval of two hours, and then the last group was from 2 PM to 4 PM. Each group consisted of fifteen to twenty second-year medical students. They were admitted to medical school after graduation from high school and had no previous training in microbiology. There was no pre-med requirement in Russia at that time; therefore, training in medical microbiology, both lectures and laboratory exercises, were held at the very beginning. It was quite tedious to repeat each exercise three times a day, especially to immature students with little cultural and educational background. Besides two technicians and myself, there were only two other individuals in the department, an assistant professor by the name of Veshchezerova and a chairperson, Professor Grishanina, who was a self-centered, elderly woman with obsolete knowledge of microbiology. My only interesting challenge was to deliver lectures that were allowed only occasionally by the chair. There was no time for the research required by my job description. This dull existence continued for a few years, and I started hating all teaching activities. But then, after much delay, something new emerged.

I received my Ph.D. in 1953 and was offered a position as an associate professor in the Department of Infectious Diseases. Beginning in 1954, my new responsibilities included delivering a course of lectures in epidemiology, running specialized classes for the fourth-year students, and giving care to the hospital patients as a staff physician. That was interesting work, and I started to develop skills in lecturing and speeches.

The graduates of the Arkhangelsk Medical School received a military rank as reserve Naval Medical Corps officers. This required some special training during the five-year period of studies. My job within this program was to teach military epidemiology, and, therefore, I had to attend special training with the Northern Fleet each year. Training took place at Northern Navy bases, particularly at the Poliarny base, and I had the opportunity to visit all types of warships, including submarines. Part of our training was the drafting of operational procedures in preparation for possible nuclear, chemical, and bacteriological attacks. We studied secret files on the details of the Nautilus, the first American atomic submarine, and our general feeling was that the Soviet Navy was preparing for military conflict with the U.S.

Additional duties as an epidemiologist included assisting the Arkhangelsk Regional Department of Health in analyses of any outbreaks of infectious diseases occurring in the Oblast. During these years I developed investigational skills while working to decipher several mysterious outbreaks and formulate infection control measures. These skills became quite helpful later when I was requested to collaborate with the Ministry of Health in Moscow. As an epidemiologist (before moving to Moscow), I was invited by the Moscow Metchnokov Institute for Vaccines and Sera to participate in a multi-site field trial. We were evaluating the efficacy of a typhoid vaccine by organizing a field study in Arkchangelsk, and this project eventually paved the road for my transfer to Moscow in 1957.

4. Investigating Outbreaks

Among the many infectious disease outbreaks I worked with when in Arkhangelsk, there were two that give a portrait of the general conditions at that time.

The first was an outbreak of dysentery, occurring in a small town south of Arkhangelsk. To my surprise, it was mostly populated by Volga German families who had been deported in 1941 from the German Autonomous District that had existed at the lower Volga River. In the 1950s these families were still waiting for permission to return to their homes. They were required to register at the local police station every week and were not permitted to travel outside the area. For more than twelve years they lived in abject poverty without decent jobs. Goats and chickens became their source of food. Since their status was close to imprisonment, the authorities had organized a place where food was served once a day.

My investigation included bacteriological testing of patients and those in contact with them. It took place in a primitive, temporary laboratory, but it revealed that the source of infection was one of the German settlers temporarily appointed as a cook and server; it turned out that he was a chronic carrier of the dysentery bacteria. I left there sensing that these malnourished and badly mistreated townspeople would have to wait even longer for their release.

The second incident, an outbreak of hepatitis (jaundice), occurred in the Far North area above the Polar Circle in a village called Oxino. This was in the previously mentioned Nenetsk National District. Pomors, the inhabitants of the village, were descendants of those who had settled in the Far North many years ago, possibly before the Mongolian invasion. Most of their livelihood was fishing and hunting, but they also raised cows, pigs, and chickens. Each house was two stories, the upper level being the family quarters and the lower level for the animals. This arrangement appeared to be very useful during the long cold winters. It provided shelter for the livestock and provided the living quarters above with additional warmth from the animals' body heat.

When visiting these houses, the first impression was a very strong odor that did not come from the animals below but from within the upper level living quarters. The source was a large barrel filled with salmon. As the residents laughingly watched our reaction, they explained that they put the fish in the barrel and watched it day-by-day until it began to produce fluorescent light (from phosphorus-metabolizing bacteria), and then they added salt. To us, the smell was unbearable, but the local residents said the smell, bad or good, was a matter of one's perception and habits. They were quick to point out that some of the cheeses many city people love to eat smelled much worse.

Another interesting habit of the Pomors was their taste for raw, frozen fish and reindeer meat. With a sharp knife, very thin slices of either one of these frozen delicacies were cut, salted, and eaten while still frozen. This frozen fare was usually consumed after coming in from the extreme cold and having a drink that was 95% spirits. It was the only alcohol available in the stores and the green bottles were labeled "Drinking Spiritus, 95%." Alcohol was limited because all supplies to this area had to be delivered in small cargo planes, and regular bottles of vodka (40%) would explode in the freezing temperatures. Drinking 95% alcohol required certain skills. One had to hold one's breath while swallowing the drink and follow it immediately with water. Then one would eat the thin-sliced hors d'oeuvre of frozen fish or meat that was made just before the drink. I became adept at drinking 95% spirits, a skill that subsequently became useful on several occasions in my life; however, I never ate the raw fish. Fresh water fish are the source of *Diphilabotrium latum,* a very common parasite that can affect both humans and animals. It was actually common to see dogs running in the street with a few yards of this long worm protruding from their anus. In humans the parasite causes severe anemia, and local people were affected quite often.

The nature, origin, and epidemiology of the outbreak of jaundice in Oxino were unclear. My colleague, the virologist Boris Kantorovich from the Arkhangelsk Microbiology Institute, and I went to investigate the outbreak. We visited every single household in an effort to establish the connections among the people and obtain diagnostic samples (blood and urine) and to analyze the whole environment. We organized a laboratory in one of the houses using the top of a traditional Russian brick stove as a source of heat for our primitive incubator. It was winter, and there was neither daylight nor a regular supply of electricity. Therefore, when a tractor generated electricity for a few hours for the movie in the local cinema club, we could perform the microscopy on the samples. We practiced this ritual every evening while sitting with our microscope behind the screen and close to the source of electricity.

This outbreak of hepatitis occurred in December 1955 through January 1956 and affected seventy-four people. We discovered a close association, in most of these cases, with drinking water that was obtained from a small, abandoned reservoir. In contrast, there were hardly any cases in the majority of the population who used water from other sources. Our laboratory testing of water samples confirmed that there was high fecal contamination of the water in the suspected reservoir. The epidemic ended after the implementation of proper measures. Unlike many other occasions, we were actually permitted to publish our report about this unusual outbreak (cited in *PubMed* as Kheifets LB et al., *Voprosy Virusology*, 1956, 21 (5), 84–88, in Russian). We were grateful to the people of Oxino for their cooperation and their willingness to participate in the laboratory testing and even more so for their hospitality.

5. Politics in Personal Life

I met my future wife Sima (Seraphima) in 1951, a year after I arrived at Arkhangelsk. She grew up in Arkhangelsk and was a graduate from the Arkhangelsk Medical School, where she also obtained a Ph.D. and worked as an assistant professor at the Department of Physiology. Our mutual attraction was instant when we met. This led us to conduct some joint research experiments, which was an obvious excuse to see each other. Sima had a six-year-old daughter named Olga. Olga's father, an actor, had moved to another city and started a separate life, so our relationship was complicated from the start since, in the eyes of the community, she was still a married woman. My involvement was also viewed as inappropriate according to the ethical standards at the school (which seemed somewhat hypocritical to me). Another obstacle in our relationship was Sima's mother, Faya, who was exceedingly protective of Olga. She feared that eventually Sima might consider marrying me, a poor stranger with no wealth and an uncertain future.

Faya had an unusual personal history. She was married to a Latvian man named Otto, who converted to Judaism (including circumcision) so he could marry Faya. He was a member of the famous Latvian Red Guards in support of the Soviet regime. When the anti-revolutionary forces overthrew the Soviet regime in Latvia in 1920, Faya and Otto escaped to Switzerland, and later, through Paris, Faya came back to Russia. Otto had died abroad from tuberculosis. During the time of the purges of 1936–38, her time spent abroad was sufficient reason for the Soviet authorities to accuse Faya of being a foreign spy. For this she spent some time in prison.

Miraculously, she survived and was later released. Sima was born in Switzerland and was listed as Jewish on her internal passport. Nevertheless, everyone thought of her as Latvian because of her last name (Apsit) and her father's name, Otto.

Despite all the obstacles, Sima and I continued our relationship, and she generally spent nights at my place, to the amusement of my neighbors. Moreover, we started appearing together in public and going to dances at the officers' club. This was minimally tolerated by some of the school's administration; then the situation suddenly became quite dramatic.

It was 1953, and the newspapers' publications about the infamous "Doctor's Plot" and "Jewish conspiracy" were on everyone's mind. At the end of February, a team of site-visit inspectors came to investigate the performance and effectiveness of the faculty. Not surprisingly, only Jewish faculty members were called in for an interview. It was like a court-martial scene in some movies. The inspection committee was seated behind a table covered with green fabric, and the person being interviewed was seated facing the committee. Here are some excerpts from the interview by the chairman of the committee:

Ch: Please state your full name.
I: Leonid Borisovitch Heifets.
Ch: That means that your father's name is Boris? What is his full name?
I: My father's name is Boris Solomonivitch Heifets.
Ch: Apparently, you are lying to us, because your father's name is not Boris Solomonovitch but Boris Shlemovitch, as it is spelled out on his passport.
I: But it is the same, Solomonovitch or Shlemovitch. Both words originated from his father's name, Slema in Yiddish or Solomon in Russian. Everybody calls my father Boris Solomonovitch, and I disagree with your statement that I am lying. I am not lying on this or anything else.
Ch: We will be the judges of that. You are not married, but you live with a married woman and even appear publicly together, for example going to the

dancing club. Do you think that such behavior is appropriate for a faculty member who is teaching young people and supposed to serve as a model of good ethical standards for them?

I: First of all, the 'woman' you mentioned is a faculty member here, and I conduct joint research with her, which requires spending some time together. Besides, we are friends, and share interests in many things, such as poetry. I do not live with her. We have separate places, but we often visit each other to talk and read poetry. I do not believe that any of your informers can testify to anything else. *(I was outraged and used quite a vulgar expression by saying, "None of your informers can say that he was holding a candle to see that we were in bed together," which outraged the members of the Committee.)* Besides, the 'woman' has been separated from her husband for a long period of time, and we are planning to get married when circumstances permit. I do not think that anything in my behavior is inappropriate.

Ch: We will judge that as well. What are your plans for the future?

I: I plan to continue to teach microbiology and conduct some related research.

Ch: That is if we decide that you should continue your employment at this school.

In a few days after this interview the whole situation changed. A miracle happened: Stalin died on March fifth, and the Committee did not finish their business and was recalled when the news of Stalin's death was announced.

The country was in mourning, and many Soviet citizens mourned Stalin's death, but it was hard for me, as well as many others, to hide our joy over his sudden death. The country entered into a new era—we hoped—without the terror, and we started looking around in expectation for changes in our lives. With such hopes for our future, Sima and I decided to get married.

Our first son, Michael, was born on February 11, 1955, and two years later, on January 27, 1957, we had our second son, Herman. There were no parties or celebrations for these great occasions, just visiting the municipal office for registration. Also, of course, no religious ceremonies of any kind!

There was a memorable episode at the registration of Michael's birth. At one of the early spring weekends, Sima and I went skiing across the Northern Dvina River, and we came back in the late afternoon. We suddenly realized that there was less than an hour before the closure of the municipal office. Michael was almost two months old, and we did not want to miss the deadline required for the registration of a child. We rushed to the office in our skiing outfits just in time. The official there was a very nice lady, a neighbor of mine. She took our passports (internal passports were required throughout the Soviet Union) and was surprised that Sima was listed as Jewish. As a good neighbor and a friend she quietly suggested that she could enter the mother (Sima) as Latvian. In doing so, at age eighteen when receiving his passport, Michael would have an opportunity to list his nationality as Russian because his parents were of "mixed nationality" (Jewish and Latvian). Such things were common; Sima's daughter was listed as Russian. But I categorically rejected this offer stating that my son would have to share the future with me. Sima's mother criticized my lack of practicality while Sima herself took a neutral position. Subsequently, no questions were asked later when Herman was born.

I was proud to become a father and developed quite a passionate attitude toward the children, being sometimes overwhelmed with fear for their health and future. Whenever they had an episode of illness, I felt completely devastated. Once when Michael was less than a year old, he developed pneumonia. Thanks to the care of our good friend Dr. Pickel, we felt optimistic about the outcome. She suggested that for better recovery it would be useful to have Michael sleep in a more vertical position. I followed this literally, taking him in my hands with his head on my right shoulder, and walked around the apartment like this the whole night. Michael slept peacefully, the fever started going down, and in the morning he was almost recovered. It was a great feeling to be able to contribute physically to my son's recovery, and for many years afterward I remembered feeling Michael's warmth on my shoulder.

It was hard to settle into our family life. I had only one room in an apartment that belonged to the medical school, and Sima lived with her mother and Olga in two rooms of a communal apartment shared with another family. Making an exchange was practically impossible. There were times when Sima and our boys would spend time in my room, and in the morning on her way to work she would drop the boys off with her mother. Then she would collect them in the evening after work.

Life in the North was difficult, and the future was full of uncertainty, even after Stalin's death. At the same time, we learned that survival in the most difficult situations depends on the ability to preserve an optimistic outlook for the future and not to miss any new opportunities that may emerge.

6.   The End of "Northern Exposure"

Our situation changed at the end of 1957 when I received a job offer at the Metchnikov Research Institute for Vaccines and Sera. After almost eight years spent in Arkhangelsk, a new beginning in Moscow held the promise of opportunities both for my personal life and my professional growth. One encouraging factor was a strong change in the political climate of the country, which was beginning to recover from decades of Stalin's terror. People were being released from the Gulag and criticism of Stalin's cult was in the air. Optimism was strong; however, subsequent events did not really satisfy these hopeful expectations.

Social life and the general conditions of life were always subject to dramatic changes throughout the history of the Soviet Union, and people were cautious in their perception of the so-called post-Stalin era of thaw, which did not last very long. Under these conditions of Soviet reality, life in the North was a valuable lesson in coping with reality and finding niches for professional growth, as well as in personal happiness. The Soviet-style "Northern Exposure" was quite different from the classical *Northern Exposure* known to the American readers and viewers for addressing some exotic interactions. Although my life in the

North of Russia also had many exotic elements, my experience was dominated by specific environmental political challenges. After the experience I gained during my "Northern Exposure," I was ready for new challenges and was properly "armed" for further survival in the Soviet Union.

CHAPTER FIVE

A 20-year Journey through the Post-Stalin Era (1957–78)

"The policy of Russia is changeless. Its methods, its tactics, its maneuvers may change, but the polar star of its policy, world domination, is a fixed star."

Karl Marx

1. At the Workplace during the "Post-Stalin Thaw"
2. Taking Advantage of the "Post-Stalin Thaw"
3. Under the Shadow of Dark Years
4. In Kazakhstan
5. In Kyrgyzstan
6. In Caucasus Mountains and Other Places
7. Family

Fig. 17. From Moscow history: public execution at the Red Square near a site called *Lobnoye Miesto,* **with St. Basil cathedral in the background. On September 30, 1698 Peter the Great (on the horse) ordered an execution of 201 rebellious guards form detachment called** *Streltsy.* **In 1881 Vasily Surikov created a painting commemorating this episode (it is now in the public domain). Here is a different interpretation of the event.** *Drawing by Edward Tabachnik.*

Fig. 18. Return to Moscow (left to right, top to bottom):
- Michael and Herman (1961);
- With my sister, Galia;
- Michael and Herman are growing up (1962); and
- Aunt Basia with her husband Misha and their grandson Aliosha (Pabrade, Litvania).

Fig. 19. Through the post-Stalin era (top to bottom):
- Dr. A. P. Muzychenko, director of the Moscow Metchnikov Institute for Vaccines and Sera (1956), a former Soviet secret agent in Austria and France;
- Dr. I. F. Mikhailov, war hero, director of the Moscow Metchnikov Institute until 1969;
- I am with T. G. Bencianova and L. A. Levina at the Congress in Moscow (1966); and
- With the Tashkent team (left to right): M.L. Kuzminova, M. Z. Leitman, and L. A. Slavina (1964).

Fig. 20. Visiting Central Asian Republics (left to right):
- Dr. L.V. Salmin with a group of Uzbek children in Tashkent (1961);
- Dr. E.A. Pavlova in a street of Ashkhabad (Turkmenistan, 1962);
- In Turkmenistan, camels represented important commodities - transportation, milk, wool, meat; and
- Turkmen people in the streets of Ashkhabad.

Fig. 21. In the Caucasus Mountains at high passes (left to right, top to bottom):
- With Herman (1970);
- On a glacier with Mars (1960s);
- With Mars; and
- With Michael (1960).

Fig. 22. Traveling in a canoe on the Kabozha River with Dr. Michael Karachunsky and Herman (1975)

1. At the Workplace during the "Post-Stalin Thaw"

In 1994, Little, Brown and Co. published a book entitled *Special Tasks* containing memoirs of a former Soviet super-spy, General Pavel Sudoplatov, who during thirty years of Stalin's reign was in charge of a special elite unit called the Administration for Special Tasks. According to Sudoplatov, it was "responsible for sabotage, kidnapping and assassinations" outside the Soviet Union. One of the familiar names I found in this book was Andrei Pavlovitch Muzychenko, who is referred to as a good friend of Sudoplatov and as a former Soviet secret agent in Austria and France.

I knew Dr. A.P. Muzychenko quite well. He was the director of the Moscow Metchnikov Institute for Vaccines and Sera, at that time a well-known research institution engaged in the development and manufacturing of various vaccines and anti-sera (anti-serums). As such, Muzychenko played an important role in several events during my employment there, until his death in 1961 or 1962.

I remember him as a stocky man with a noticeably large head and a lot of curly hair. He had a constant sarcastic smile on his face, particularly when conducting conversations with faculty members in the manner of an inquisitor. Muzychenko walked with a limp and used to tell us, among other spy stories, that the French security police tortured him and damaged his leg. He also talked about his work as a Soviet intelligence resident in Spain during the civil war there and how he helped the Spanish Republican forces in their war against Franco's fascists. He claimed that he was a liaison (perhaps he meant courier) to the head of the Communist Party in Spain, Dolores Ibarruri (Passionaria). Someone at the institute learned that it was actually his wife who was the Soviet agent in Spain and that Andrei was only her assistant. No one knew the truth. Muzychenko definitely had close connections with the KGB during his directorship at the Metchnikov Institute. He was not really a scientist, but rather an administrator and manager. Nevertheless, he had a talent for quickly determining the scientific value of complex research projects and the scientific status of those around him. He did not hesitate to confront faculty members with sharply skeptical and even insulting comments about their work.

Many on the faculty viewed him as undereducated and therefore not worthy of respect. One peculiar example was when he demanded that most of the requisitions for important laboratory supplies be submitted for his signature, especially requisitions for experimental animals. This administrative style, now referred to as micro-management and, most recently, nano-management, is a growing trend in U.S. medical institutions. Several signatures are often required on minor documents in order to serve the ambition and job security of people in the management chain. By current standards Muzychenko's demands would probably not seem unreasonable. He was simply trying to impress on the faculty that they depended on his decisions. Of course, he did not always read the requisitions very carefully. Encouraged by some arrogant "old-timers," Victor Zuev, a young research fellow, decided to have some fun. On a requisition for experimental animals he wrote "ten white elephants" assuming that Muzychenko would not catch the substitution of elephants for mice. As predicted, he failed to notice the "elephants." But the director of the animal facility came to him with a straight face and said, "Dr. Muzychenko, you signed a requisition for ten white elephants. Where do you expect me to get them?" That was an expensive joke; Victor Zuev was fired. Perhaps it could serve as a survival tip for young scientists who may be tempted to chide their superiors in the bureaucracy.

What particularly irritated Muzychenko was that some of the scientists were unable to explain their research projects in laymen's language—projects that required his funding approval. Fortunately I'd been able to develop and refine plain-language scientific explanatory skills while teaching in the Arkhangelsk Medical School for seven years. Now these skills were suddenly quite valuable, and I used them to the fullest in my job interview with Muzychenko.

Moscow Metchnikov Institute needed an epidemiologist with field experience to study the efficacy of vaccines that were being developed or manufactured by the institute. Because I had participated in a multicenter trial with one of the vaccines in Arkhangelsk and because several faculty members knew me from previous training during my fellowship, some of them decided that I should be offered the job. I turned down the initial offer for junior faculty member. Afterward, Dr. M. I. Khazanov, the Chairman of Epidemiology, arranged an interview with Muzychenko to consider me for a position of senior faculty member. In response to his question of my research plans, I explained to him the idea of controlled double-blind field trials, an idea that had just started appearing in Western scientific literature. Muzychenko was impressed, and he commented on the objectivity of such trials with the statement, "Yes, you cannot trust anybody, and the system of coding the vaccines and placebo should resolve the problem." So in spite of some faculty objections that I was too young (thirty-one), and that my epidemiology experience was confined to one geographic area, I joined the senior faculty at this most prestigious institution.

In 1957, when I began my work in Moscow, most impressions of the political situation in the country were that Russia was becoming more civil and less oppressive than in the past; some Russian authors referred to that period as the "Post-Stalin Thaw" or "The Spring." In February of 1956, Khrushchev denounced Stalin's personality cult. The media began publishing critical reports about his dictatorship and the system of forced labor camps and executions. In 1962, *Novy Mir* (*New World*), one of the leading Soviet magazines, published Solzhenitsyn's novel *One Day in the Life of Ivan Denisovich*, which depicted the brutality of the forced labor camps, later labeled by him "Gulag Archipelago." Gulag was actually a Russian acronym for "Main Directorate for Corrective Labor Camps." After Khrushchev's speech there was mass rehabilitation of political prisoners from the Gulag Archipelago. Although the Gulag system was officially closed on January 25, 1960, it was estimated that eighteen to twenty million people had been imprisoned in those camps during Stalin's reign. Detailed analyses of the system can be found in Anne Appelbaum's *Gulag*, in which the number of deaths in the camps (as documented by the Gulag administration) was 1.6 million.[6] This was in addition to approximately 800,000 executions during the Great Terror years (1936–38). The actual number of deaths in the Gulag and beyond remain unknown. After Khrushchev's 1956 speech, everyone thought that this horror was over and that nothing like this would ever happen again. But the welcome period of "thaw" did not last long. Although the Gulag Archipelago was abolished, political freedom was sharply curtailed during the dark years of the late 1960s and 1970s.

2. Taking Advantage of the "Post-Stalin Thaw"

After Khrushchev's speech, the impression was that the horrible events of Stalin's era were past and from then on things would be different. The political climate of the late 1950s and early 1960s gave hope for new life and an opportunity to do things differently. Many of my colleagues started thinking that the time was right to implement some of the methods and achievements of Western science. One such achievement was a system for objective evaluation of medications, therapies, and prophylactic agents. That system was based on controlled field trials studies, which included the distribution of subjects (patients, vaccine recipients, etc.) into comparable, randomly selected groups. The system included the use of a placebo or standard treatment for the control group, with coding of the medications and placebo at the time of application and sealing the code until the end of the observation. These were the double-blind protocols that had become the accepted model for testing disease treatment or prevention around the world.

I worked at the Metchnikov Institute from 1957 to 1969 as head of a department in charge of evaluating the effectiveness of various vaccines in field trials and in the related laboratory research. From the beginning of my employment I developed a methodology of double-blind controlled field trials adjusted for Soviet conditions. I organized trials that included more than one million participants. Publications on this development were recognized from the very beginning of the program and also became known to international experts. The situation was quite promising as a new direction of productive research to establish a good basis for selecting quality vaccines for the Soviet population! It was also an important boost for my professional career. In my first year I established my laboratory and was promoted to head of the unit.

The concept of drawing conclusions outside the control of the bureaucracy, based completely on judgments made by the scientists, was quite foreign to the mentality of the Soviet system and even to many of its medical scientists. For educational purposes I had to organize a series of meetings at different levels of administration, along with presentations to groups of scientists. In the spirit of criticizing the mentality of the past, the suggestion to use the principles of double-blind trials to evaluate the efficacy of vaccines was well-received by my colleagues and approved by the Ministry of Health. To achieve these ideas I needed open-minded and creative associates in my laboratory in Moscow, as well as at the field trial sites. All my colleagues deserve full credit for the success of the program. They also became my caring and loyal friends with whom I spent most of my time. We jocularly called ourselves the "gang," having departed from the approach that had been based merely on retrospective observations.

The underlying reason for calling ourselves a gang was that most of us did not fit the stereotype of *Homo Sovieticus*. The gang members were L.A. Levina, L.V. Salmin, T.G. Bencianova, E.A. Pavlova (Moscow), M.Z. Leitman, M.L. Kuzminova, A.M. Slavina, E.Y. Melnik (Uzbekistan), and A.V. Vasilieva (Turkmenistan). Two of these remarkable individuals, Ludmila Abramovna Levina and Leonid Vitalievitch Salmin, are no longer with us, and I am honored to present their stories here. Only one person from our team is still working in the field of vaccine development in Moscow— Tatiana Grigorievna Bencianova—and her story is also included below.

Ludmila Abramovna Levina was a graduate of the fellowship program at the Metchnokov Institute, and she had a Ph.D. degree in microbiology and immunology. She was a single young woman who was committed to research and not interested in building her personal life, and she realized that my laboratory would open up an opportunity for her to do modern research. Her father had been a high-ranking expert in artillery development and was executed in 1937, along with 35,000 other military officers who were killed or imprisoned for "suspicion of treason." (Stalin's paranoia that the military was plotting against him was actually based on a letter forged by German intelligence!) Because of her father's history, Ludmila was particularly pleased with the rehabilitation of victims of Stalin's terror and was especially optimistic regarding new opportunities in research.

Dr. Levina became the most important contributor to our team's effort. She guided and supervised all experimental work within the laboratory and participated in our field work. Our success in conducting the field trials would have been impossible without her participation. The main element of her character was extreme honesty and straightforwardness on any issue, without deviation or compromise. That was extremely atypical in the Soviet Union when survival became a difficult task. She did not hesitate to express her opinion publicly on a number of controversial issues, particularly when our institute was in opposition to some decisions by the Ministry of Health.

We became close and trusted friends. Once, knowing my influence, her mother asked me to try to convince Ludmila to change her mind about getting married, as there were a number of suitors seeking her attention. It took me a while, but I finally succeeded, and she married Solomon Yurovsky, a prominent expert in aerodynamics who worked in the aircraft industry. I knew his first wife, a beautiful woman who was a pathologist and worked at one of the Microbiology Institutes. She had died from breast cancer after a heroic battle against this dreaded disease, which metastasized in her brain. Ironically, many years later, Ludmila faced the same situation. It was surely a painful tragedy for Solomon to lose both women in this way.

Ludmila and her husband continued to communicate with me after I applied for emigration, an act of bravery on their part. Moreover, Ludmila insisted on corresponding with me even after I left the country, despite the fact that Solomon was under a strict security regimen in his aircraft industry job. She was the only one I corresponded with when I arrived in the U.S., and her letters were a source of great support for me in my new life.

Much later, in 1987, after I had been living in the U.S. for nine years, Gorbachev's introduction of *glasnost* and *perestroika* had begun a kind of liberal awakening in the Soviet Union. This step toward openness created new opportunities. Ludmila gave a detailed interview to a Russian newspaper about my fight against the Deputy Minister of Health, Burgasov. Even under *glasnost*, this interview could have easily stirred up trouble. Again, Ludmila's courage was clear considering that she still worked at Metchnikov

Institute. After her husband retired, I invited both of them for a visit to the U.S. We visited the Grand Canyon, New Mexico, and most of Colorado. They enjoyed the trip very much, but they were not yet emotionally ready for emigration. It wasn't until 1996 that Ludmila and Solomon finally moved to the U.S. They settled in Pawtucket, Rhode Island, where I often visited them. After a few happy years in the U.S., Ludmila died in 2002 from disseminated cancer. Time passes, but the empty feeling in my heart caused by Ludmila's death does not go away.

Leonid Vitalievitch Salmin joined my laboratory in 1958 after returning to Moscow from Norilsk, where he worked as a physician for three years after graduation from medical school. We developed a relationship beyond our official job interactions, and I had the opportunity to meet his parents and his brother. Sometimes we met at their home or went fishing in the rivers and lakes outside of Moscow. The Salmin family represented the best of the Russian people—not too sophisticated (Leonid was the only one who had been to a university), but with very clear ideas about political and cultural events. They also had a great love for Russia and concerns about her future. They were critical of the Soviet system and showed high tolerance and understanding toward other ethnic groups.

Salmin and I used to travel together. We often shared a hotel room and had many interesting discussions not only about our professional work, but also about the political situation and different cultural events. Once, in the city of Ashkhabad in Turkmenistan, after spending the day in a preschool where we vaccinated the children, Salmin became outraged and even started cursing in language that was quite unusual for this refined and delicate man. The rage was triggered by Communist Party propaganda on the walls in the nursery school room—Lenin's portrait, some nursery rhymes in his name, and children's verses lauding the great Communist Party. Salmin actually considered these things criminal acts against humanity, and he was a member of the Communist Party who later worked at the party's Central Committee!

Leonid's hobby was Alexander Pushkin. He collected all the publications he could find by and about Pushkin. I learned much more about the life and creativity of this great Russian poet from conversations with Leonid than from all I had ever read. I've always admired Pushkin and I possess a treasure—a farewell gift from Salmin—a rare, complete 1937 edition of Pushkin's works printed in one volume on very thin paper. He pointed out a few unusual and little-known facts that might have even been too dangerous to discuss at that time. One strange item was that under Stalin, the most important experts on Pushkin were assassinated— Gessen in 1937, Modzilevsky in 1948, and Tomashevsky in 1957. No one has ever solved these mysteries, but recently someone suggested that eliminating them might have been related to the "discovery" that Pushkin was possibly a direct ancestor of Leon Trotsky, Stalin's sworn enemy. Also, Pushkin was known to be the great-grandson of the famous general Abraham Hannibal (of Ethiopian Royal origin), who fought for Peter the Great. Later, it was suspected that Pushkin may not have actually been physically related to General Hannibal, and, in some of his portraits, his Negroid features were forged to fit this version of his origin. In the Soviet Union, and to some extent in contemporary Russia, any "dirty stories" about canonized personalities like Pushkin were suppressed, and any doubts about his noble origin would be strongly spurned. These unpopular hypotheses recently arose in Russian periodicals, starting with publications by Alexander Latsis in 1996 (*Ring A*, 1996, No. 2. and *Noy*, 1996, No.19).

In addition to the official mandate from the Ministry of Health in Moscow, we often had to obtain authorization from the local health administration for mass vaccinations. Leonid knew the mentality of Soviet administrators and suggested a smart angle on how to be convincing at meetings with the local authorities in Central Asia. In his scenario he would be the main presenter, and I would sit there silently. I would adopt the rather judgmental posture of one granting final approval and confirmation. If the local boss suggested an inappropriate alternative for us, Salmin would say, "No, no, that would not meet Dr. Heifets' approval." At that moment, everybody in the room would turn to me, and I would nod in agreement with Salmin that it was inappropriate. He also suggested that I assume an attitude of importance, of one who was not to be bothered with details. This was far from easy for me. Beyond the psychological effects, another important and serious part of this game was to show these regional bosses that we cared about the welfare of the local people (which was very true) and to show them evidence that our concern was genuine. My knowledge of the local culture, respect for their ethnic traditions, and some knowledge of the Uzbek language, was also helpful.

For two months in the spring and fall every year, I would send my colleagues to several cities in Central Asia with various work-related assignments. Two colleagues, Leonid Salmin and Elena Arkadievna Pavlova, were assigned to conduct our trial in the city of Ashkhabad in Turkmenistan. Dr. Pavlova was married, and her husband had spent significant time in Afganistan. I had a sense that their marriage was troubled, and perhaps it was on the brink of failure when Pavlova went to Ashkhabad. During my visit to Ashkhabad I learned that, after working together for a month, Salmin and Pavlova had fallen in love and were living together. Their union was later formalized in Moscow and turned out to be a happy marriage, another instance in which I have had the fleeting temerity to take a small crumb of self-congratulation. It was the perfect combination of Salmin's soft, gentle nature and the strong practicality of Pavlova.

When the Ministry of Health closed my laboratory, Salmin was offered a job in the Central Committee of the Communist Party supervising activities of the Ministry of Health in the field of preventive medicine. Given Salmin's character, it is hard to imagine him in a more ill-fitting position. But perhaps someone at the top thought that Salmin's gentle nature would avoid interference with the Ministry's decisions. Also, they may have thought that since I trained him he now had equal knowledge and experience, but would be less troublesome than a difficult-to-manage Jew. In spite of certain standards at his new job, Salmin never stopped communicating with me, even after I applied for emigration. In fact, that is when he gave me his farewell gift of the rare Pushkin edition.

After I left the country, Salmin became Deputy Director of the Institute for the Control of the Bacteriological Preparations (equivalent to the FDA in the U.S.) but retired shortly aftward. These high-ranking positions were hardly compatible with his character. The last time I saw him and Elena was in 2003 (twenty-five years after my emigration) when I visited Moscow to attend a scientific conference. Salmin and Pavlova came to visit me at the apartment of Tatiana Grigorievna Bencianova. It was a warm reunion in which we all expressed how much we missed Ludmila Levina (who had passed away the previous year in the U.S.) It was also an occasion where we could have spent many more hours reminiscing and reflecting on memories of productive research and true friendship. A year later, Leonid Salmin died suddenly in his apartment, perhaps from a stroke. He is truly missed by his wife, his son, and his many friends. For me, it is another painful loss of a great friend. His memory shall forever remain with me.

Tatiana Grigorievna Bencianova was the youngest member of our gang, and she is now the only one of the group who is still working with vaccines in Moscow. I first met Tatiana in 1961. She was a graduate from the Teaching School with a degree equivalent to our bachelor's degree. She came seeking employment in research in my laboratory at the Moscow Mechnikov Institute for Vaccines and Sera. Tatiana was a petite, young Jewish woman who displayed a high intellect, was quite knowledgeable in immunology, and expressed an interest in vaccine development. I was immediately impressed with her and decided that I wanted to employ her; however, I would have to overcome some obstacles, typical for that system, in hiring a person like Tatiana to the junior faculty position. One problem was that Tatiana was a graduate of a teachers' school (not from a biomedical university, as required at our institution) and was supposed to take a teaching position somewhere else. Another problem was more serious. According to some unofficial rules, it was undesirable to employ too many Jews in the institution or in one of its departments. In addition to myself, there were others who were Jewish in my lab. It was clear that I would have to develop a plan to circumvent the system. Of course, practicing deceit was second nature to me. It was the only way to survive and achieve even limited success.

Tatiana's personal background was surprisingly remarkable. Sometime in the 1820s or 1830s, her great-grandfather was drafted into the Cantonist Battalion. Jewish boys as young as twelve were drafted, although a youngster could have been younger, perhaps even eight or nine. During the reign of Nicolas I, the term of military service was twenty-five years! That is, after a young boy had reached the status as an adult soldier. Further, the young conscripts were forced to convert to Christianity and often were baptized against their will. Tatiana's great-grandfather complied with the rules put before him and eventually become an officer, rising to the rank of General. He was so successful in interacting with people that he was appointed as General Governor of one of the large districts in Siberia. After age sixty-five he retired, returned to his shtettle in Belarus, and converted back to Judaism.

I decided to play a certain game around Tatiana's story of being a great-granddaughter of the former Governor in Siberia to ensure her employment in my lab. To hire someone to a junior faculty position, I just needed a signature/approval of one person with a rank equivalent to a Deputy Director of the institute. Vsevolod (Seva) Ivanov, Ph.D. whose title when translated into English sounds like "scientific secretary," was a tall, slim, energetic man in his thirties, with light features and a face that would fit the Nazi's infamous description of an Aryian—not very typical for most of the Russians. The type of relationship I had with him is not quite familiar to a Western reader. Very often Seva and I had to attend various banquets, at which everybody was supposed to drink. Sometimes, pretending to be drunk (being drunk was appreciated by the group), I would talk to Seva in the distinctive style of a drunk Russian, which is not taken seriously afterward. I complimented his job performance but also, as a "friend" (a common term used after a good drink), I would say: "You know, Seva, your appearance reminds me of one of my relatives. Do you have any Jews among your ancestors?" That was pure fantasy and intentionally insulting. Seva was obviously shocked, but would not show it; he just denied it with laughter—such a strange suggestion from a drunk "friend" who cannot see that his features are like that of a nobleman. Seva was known as an anti-Semite, and I was taking hidden revenge by talking to him in such a tone. We both knew that I was not his friend, but my purpose was to puzzle him and to leave him with a question on how to deal with me.

One day I went to Seva's office with Tatiana's file and application. I made a typo on purpose in her last name in the prepared documents for Seva to sign. It said Vencianova instead of Bencianova. The letters V and B in the Russian alphabet are very similar. The Russian V looks like an English B, and the Russian B is open in its upper circle. Bencianova is a typical Jewish name (from Ben Zion), while Vencianova is a Russian nobility name. I said, "Seva, I have a good candidate for the vacant position, but there is a problem in her origin. It seems that she is from nobility, and she admitted that her great-grandfather was a Governor in Siberia during the Tsars. So, I need your advice on how to deal with an obstacle to hire her." This statement amused him and completely distracted his attention from the papers in the file. He said, "Leonid, I appreciate your concern, but you are not familiar with our current political standards. You should know that only a long time ago were we concerned with the aristocrats, but not anymore." He signed the application, after which I corrected the V into B and submitted the file to the personnel department. Tatiana Bencianova became one of the most productive employees in my laboratory, received her Ph.D., and became one of the prominent experts in vaccine evaluation after my departure from Russia. She is now in charge of a section at the Tarasevitch Control Institute, controlling quality vaccine production, a section similar to that at the FDA in the U.S.

3. Under the Shadow of Dark Years

Along with the optimism inspired by Khrushchev's famous speech of 1956, one should have been aware of some alarming events that occurred simultaneously. One such event was the 1956 invasion of Hungary by Soviet troops to crush a revolt. Then in 1957, the Soviet Union launched its first spacecraft, the Sputnik. Thus began the "space race" with the U.S. An escalation in the development of nuclear weapons and intercontinental missiles began in 1958 and 1959. By that time, the controversy and discontent in the U.S. caused by McCarthyism was winding down. The enmity between the U.S. and Soviet Union fluctuated and was reflected in meetings between the leaders of both countries, but also in the downing of the American U-2 spy plane over the Soviet Union in 1960 and in the Cuban missile crisis of 1962.

In 1964, Brezhnev replaced Khrushchev and abruptly reverted to a different direction of Soviet policy and strategy. The KGB became more powerful in controlling all aspects of intellectual life and suppressing any type of freedom movement. Solzhenitsyn's books were forbidden, and he was expelled from the country. Sakharov, the "father of the Russian H-bomb," was in exile from Moscow because of his anti-war statements. The invasion of Czechoslovakia in 1968 is remembered as a part of this era, which established the Brezhnev doctrine of the right of Communist countries to intervene in other Communist states where a threat to the international Communist system might be discerned. Conversely, in 1974 a remarkable step in the Soviet Union took place with regard to emigration policy. This change eventually opened the gates for Jewish emigration in exchange for better trade status with the U.S.

After a period of "spring," and in spite of Brezhnev's suppression, the Russian people became hungry for truth and more tired of restrictions in literature, art, and music by the government. In response to these needs, some people began to reproduce novels, stories, and other documents by Russian authors, either on copy machines (to which official access was limited) or by typewriter. These activities eventually became folklore and were known as *Samizdat*, an acronym in Russian for "self-production." Discovery in one's home of such materials (labeled as anti-Soviet propaganda) was cause for arrest and imprisonment. To avoid being reported by an informer or some accidental slip, people developed special protocols for sharing the information. My good friend Dr. Ludmila Levina became one of those who risked handling distribution of illegal materials, and she included me in the circle of recipients. Ludmilla would surreptitiously let me know she had something for me to read by calling to say that she and her husband were expecting me for evening tea. I would then rush to their apartment, take the manuscript home to read overnight, and give it back early the next morning. Sometimes, I had to read the material on the spot without leaving her apartment. In addition to reading forbidden materials, we listened to short-wave radio outside the city where the jamming was less effective. Ingenuity and deception were the ways in which many people were kept both culturally and politically informed.

Life for professional people underwent changes as well. On a personal level, my initial success with modernizing the evaluation of vaccines led to a reaction against the "bourgeois ideology" in the methodology of double-blind controlled trials. This opposition was motivated by the omnipresent bureaucratic jealousy of success, particularly when we received a grant from the World Health Organization (WHO) and published our reports in the *WHO Bulletin*. On the international level, such accomplishments were unique for the Soviet Union. Initially, the scientific community paid little attention to the comments of some traditional Soviet scientists who always opposed anything that smacked of Western influence; however, that changed in 1965 with the appointment of my sworn enemy P.N. Burgasov to the position of Deputy Minister of Health. The related events are described in Chapter 8 ("Dangerous Assignment") and Chapter 9 ("Under the Sword of Damocles"). As a result of this opposition, my laboratory at the Metchnikov Institute was closed in 1968. In 1969 I began a new job and a new career as a microbiologist in the Central Institute for Tuberculosis, where I remained until my emigration in 1978.

During the late 1960s and early 1970s the future of both the country and my personal life was uncertain, and I finally decided to seriously pursue the possibility of emigrating from the Soviet Union. As was then the case for many others, it was a hard decision to make. In a general climate of political oppression and the return of government-sponsored anti-Semitism in particular, I was even more concerned about the future and the physical safety of my children.

Historically, the Jews of Russia were given equal rights after the October Revolution of 1917, and they became loyal citizens of the Soviet Union. Most of them embraced the Communist ideology and the new system. They were well-educated and made great contributions to industry, science, medicine, military development, and even abandoned religious affiliation to a much greater extent than the ethnic Russians. Until the end of World War II they were no more or no less targets of repression by the system than any other ethnic group; however, after the end of the war in 1945, Stalin began to encourage Russian nationalism as a tool to maintain his dictatorship. As often was the case throughout history, Jews were selected as convenient whipping boys for nurturing nationalistic sentiments. Many believed that this practice had ceased with the death of Stalin. During Brezhnev's era, in an economically stagnated country, with the Cold War and plans to expand the country by military means, another wave of anti-Semitism emerged as a tool to boost Russian patriotism. Partially suppressed memories of anti-Semitism (personal and collective) re-emerged for me, as well as in the minds of many other Jews. This growing anti-Semitism was also fueled by the failures of Soviet client Arab countries in their wars of 1956, 1967, and 1973–74 against Israel. Also, less well-known was the dramatic failure of Russian military technology used by the Arab countries against the American-based technology used by Israel. Again and again, most often indirectly, Jews were reminded of their second-class status. It was only natural that the establishment of the state of Israel promoted the idea of emigration to a country where one would be viewed as equal. Initially, I could not decide on where, or how, to emigrate. The predominant thought was that it did not matter. It became more and more apparent that we just had to get out!

The major obstacle for my emigration plan was the fact that I had a secret clearance in my job at the Metchnikov Institute. The policy of emigration administration was to send inquiries about an applicant to employers where the individual had been employed during the last ten years. I still held a valid security clearance and that meant that I would be refused. The only solution was to find a job without clearance for the next ten years and then apply for emigration. The TB Institute provided that opportunity for me. I decided not to waste any time during those years and worked hard to become an expert in the new field. Even after the clearance expired, there was no guarantee of permission to emigrate. Among the dangers of applying for emigration was being dismissed from your job, thus being labeled as a "parasite," followed by social ostracism and possible imprisonment. Ten years gave me a lot of time to develop and implement a plan to avoid these traps, a plan that succeeded. This is detailed in Chapter 10 ("Code Name 'Green Eggs Project' and Escape from Russia").

I remained employed until I received permission to emigrate. During my years at the TB Institute I worked as a microbiologist and resisted any attempts by the administration to involve me in epidemiological analysis, which had secret security issues. I did a number of research projects and studied foreign scientific literature. I took an additional job at the Information Institute preparing abstracts on tuberculosis in Russian from foreign scientific journals. This was my weekend job: preparing abstracts from English publications and also from European and Japanese journals. I took English lessons, some Hebrew, and even lessons in Japanese with my son, Herman. This helped prepare me for my future work in the U.S. and improved my English. It was a very busy time, relieved only by occasional business trips and short hiking vacations.

4. In Kazakhstan

My jobs in Moscow between 1957 and 1978, especially at the Metchnikov Institute, required a lot of traveling. Besides trips to Africa in 1960 and 1962 (Chapter 6), I traveled mostly to Central Asia to organize and supervise controlled field trials with vaccines and also to investigate various outbreaks of infectious diseases. One of the aerosolized typhoid vaccine field trials was organized in Tajikistan (Chapter 8). Trials mostly with typhoid vaccines were conducted in Uzbekistan, Turkmenistan, and Kazakhstan. One six-arm trial with five vaccines and a placebo was supported by a grant from the World Health Organization. The results of these trials were published in Russian scientific journals and in the *Bulletin of the World Health Organization.*

Besides the extensive field trials, I also traveled to Central Asia to investigate infectious disease outbreaks. Some of them were remarkable in regards to the unusual environment, the odd circumstances, and the measures implemented for controlling them.

In Tashkent and other Uzbekistan cities there was a high incidence of typhoid fever with high mortality. It occurred every year and peaked at the end of summer and during the fall. It affected mostly school children, and it was my conclusion that these systematic outbreaks were related to and transmitted through the irrigation system, which was also the main source of drinking water. The irrigation system was contaminated from the outhouses scattered throughout the cities. These were often very close to the irrigation canals. Water from the mountains was quite clean as it flowed into the narrow canals that ran through the city; however, there was an increased concentration of contaminants where the canals narrowed, and these were the areas with the highest morbidity rates. I published these results in a special article and monograph. Because of the secrecy codes, the names of the places, such as Tashkent, were encrypted in my publications. Moreover, only relative-rate comparisons, rather than actual case numbers, were allowed for publications. The Ministry of Health of Uzbekistan gave me an award for this discovery and for my help in implementing the control measures.

The Academy of Medical Science organized an investigative expedition for an encephalitis outbreak that occurred in the city of Leninogorsk located in Altai Mountains in the Ust-Kamenogorsk District of Kazakhstan. I was the epidemiologist of the group, while other members of the expedition were assigned to patient examination, specimens collection for subsequent virology and toxicology studies in Moscow, and collecting ticks from the environment and testing them as potential vectors of the encephalitis virus. Because the source was unknown, the Kazakhstan health authorities panicked and quarantined the city. It was surrounded by military troops. Government officials from Moscow got involved because Leninogorsk was a strategic source of important colored metals, and quarantine was hindering the flow of these materials to the industrial facilities in other parts of the country.

Initially, I joined our team's neurologist in examining the patients who were diagnosed with encephalitis. One oddity we encountered was that there were no severe cases of encephalitis. All the patients diagnosed by the local physicians were symptomatic for *nistagmus* (side-to-side rapid eye movement), an important sign that the brain was affected. It did not cause any significant discomfort to the patients, and most of the patients did not have any other symptoms except for some that previously had a low-grade fever and/or cold symptoms for a few days. The neurologist seriously doubted that the diagnosis of encephalitis was sufficiently justified in the patients he examined. He suspected that *nistagmus* was the result of an unknown toxic effect on the brain resulting in encephalopathy.

Most of the city's residents were involved in mining and ore processing, which included purification of the metals and other elements extracted from the ore. I could find no correlation between the prevalence of the illness and the mining and ore processing. Furthermore, there was no correlation found between the cases and differences in the water supply. The only connection I detected was between the location of the cases in relation to the mine and refining factory along with the predominant wind direction in the narrow canyon where the city was located. It was clear to me that the cases of encephalopathy were related to emissions from the ore refinery. Under the regimen of state secrecy, we never received any information on the details of the production, the filtration system, or on the components of the emissions. Therefore, I could not confirm my theory and was not able to find out what elements in the emissions may have caused the encephalopathy.

Our most important finding was that the contact investigation firmly excluded the possibility of transmission from person to person. Based on this, I suggested the quarantine be lifted. This recommendation outraged the local health authorities and Kazakhstan's most important academicians. They threatened me with personal responsibility in case the epidemic spread beyond Leninogorsk. One of them even asked, "Aren't you afraid of ending up as one of the miners in this or in an even less pleasant place (meaning the uranium mines) if you are wrong and the illness is contagious?" When we returned to Moscow and reported to the Academy, the decision was made to lift the quarantine. I was quite confident with my conclusion and did not wait to be arrested and sent to uranium mines in the Gulag Archipelago. They had already been dismantled anyway.

5. In Kyrgyzstan

I visited Kyrgyzstan on several occasions while collaborating with the scientists of the Microbiology Institute (Dr. Finkel's group) in developing the lyophilized medium for cultivation of the tubercle bacilli. On one occasion, I visited this area with an expedition from the TB Institute to investigate and to inspect their control program. This was an opportunity to learn about a most beautiful and exotic place, its people, history, and customs. At the time, Kyrgyzstan was one of the fifteen republics of the Soviet Union. Only later, in

1991, with the fall of the Soviet Union, did it finally achieve independence. Kyrgyzstan borders China, Uzbekistan, Kazakhstan, and Tajikistan, with most of its territory dominated by the high, snowy Tien-Shan Mountains. The population is less than five million and only half of them are Kyrgyz, with approximately 25% Russians and Ukrainians. The tribes of Kyrgyz originated in Mongolia, then formed a large state (*khanate*) in Siberia and migrated to the area of present-day Kyrgyzstan during the sixth century.

From centuries of interaction with other nations, these historically nomadic people absorbed many signs and features of other cultures. One is a Turkic-type language that is close to the Uzbek language. Also, at least formally, the Kyrgyz people are Sunni Muslim. They are not strictly observant, but heavily influenced by more ancient tribal beliefs. I saw expressions of this eclecticism at a large cemetery near the capital city of Frunze (now Bishkek). Many gravestones had combined symbols of three religions; the Muslim crescent, pagan deer horns, and the Communist Red Star. There are other signs of mixed beliefs in some traditions. One was the "protocol" for installing a new Khan (leader) of a tribe or a village, which included human sacrifice, obviously beyond the requirements of Islam. One would not find any reference to this tradition in modern publications, but a prominent Kyrgyz writer, Tolengen Kasymbekov, described it very vividly in his book *Slomaniy Metch* (*Broken Sword*). The tradition was openly practiced at least until the end of the nineteenth century.

In preparation for the sacrifice, village women would make a huge rug of pure white felt. The new Khan would stand on the rug. Then an innocent boy would meet his fate on the rug, which became red with his blood. This culminated with the men of the village lifting the rug with the Khan standing on it. After placing the rug back on the ground a big celebration would ensue to honor the power of the new Khan. This tribal ritual was unofficially observed for many years. I was told that some of the tribes actually performed it for new Khans until 1924. Then the Bolsheviks brutally used war and famine to break all people's resistance, and the country officially became part of the Russian Soviet Federated Socialist Republic.

While visiting Kyrgyzstan and Kazakhstan, I had a chance to witness more innocent rituals such as culinary traditions that may not be fully appreciated by a Western traveler. It is important to stress that the main thing is not just the food itself but rather the expression of hospitality demonstrated by the Kyrgyz people. They were willing to sacrifice their last possession (for example, the last sheep) to honor a guest. Kyrgyz people were known to greet even an occasional visitor to their felt tent (called a yurt) with a beverage called *kumys*. Kumys is fermented mare's milk that contains some alcohol due to the high content of carbohydrates. It is naturally carbonated and is always cold and refreshing when poured from a sack made of lambskin. Fermentation takes place when the sack is placed on a horse's back, and sometimes provided cool comfort to the rider. Kumys is a clean and safe drink. Undesirable bacteria won't grow in this environment and therefore does not compete with the fermentation organisms. Some visitors who know the details of kumys might object to consuming it, but one should keep in mind that refusing to take this drink or any other offering of food can be taken as a great offense by the local people.

Among other drinks that may be difficult for Western visitors to accept is a tea called *Syr-tchai*, popular also among the Kazakhs and usually served after a meal. They boil the uncut tea leaves in salted milk topped with melted lamb fat and serve it in a large bowl. I was horrified the first time I drank it. I knew there was no way I could refuse it, so I closed my eyes and drank it as fast as possible. The host watched me and said, "I can see that you like our favorite drink. We do appreciate it." So he served me another bowl.

Most of the meals in Kyrgyzstan are like those served in the other republics of Central Asia. They consist of various pilaf recipes, shish-kebab (*shashlyk*), and noodle soups, most often with mutton. As in any Muslim country, pork is not served in public places, but horse meat (usually from a young mare) and sometimes camel meat are often consumed by Kyrgyz and Kazakhs.

At special celebrations the arrangement of food can be quite unusual. Such an occasion took place when I was part of an inspection team investigating the local tuberculosis control program. It was understandable that we were treated as VIPs. At one of the dinners, I was seated at the head of the table as the most important guest since Dr. Khomenko, the head of our group, was away in another village. My experience was somewhat similar to the dinner fantasized by Spielberg in the movie *Temple of Doom*. First, a plate with the head of a newborn lamb on it was placed in front of me. The local "consultant" on my left suggested that I cut the ears into tiny slices so that every guest at the table would be honored with a piece. Then he suggested that I remove the eyeballs, eat one of them, and give the other one to the second important guest on my right. Well, so far it was not too bad. Next, I had to open the skull and remove the brain, put it on another platter, then chop it and mix it in with the chopped liver. Everyone had to enjoy this delicacy as it was passed around the table. Finally the main course was served. The larger parts of the lamb's body had been boiled in salty water but no other spices. In fact, it was delicious! In this area Muslim customs did not allow the bones to be cut, so we had to hold the large pieces in our hands and eat the meat from the bones (like in scenes from films depicting Middle Age customs in Europe). After that a pilaf was served.

Visiting the republics of Central Asia during the dark years of the Brezhnev era was a valuable experience and an opportunity to escape the dismal Soviet reality.

6. In Caucasus Mountains and Other Places

Summer vacations provided another opportunity to escape from the tension of everyday life. I frequently went hiking in the Caucasus Mountains, where the focus was on reaching another peak or mountain pass, making camping arrangement in the wilderness, and just plain survival.

Mountain hiking is a good way to develop friendships and to test the human qualities of your companions, especially reliability. I was lucky enough to find a number of such friends. One of them, not really a hiker but a political leader of the whole area around Mt. Elbrus, was Noah Bezirov, a most controversial and interesting person to whom I dedicated a separate story in Chapter 7. Others were friends from Moscow whom I would invite to join me. Sometimes I hiked alone, or sometimes with my wife, Sima, or with my sons. One problem we always faced was the lack of geological maps.

They were a state secret, but, ironically, were available from foreign tourists! Once I was asked to help the local guide lead a group of German tourists and discovered that they had perfect maps of the area, probably copies of maps from the war where the battles took place.

Among the most interesting hikes were those with the family of Galiev, whom I met on one of the trips. They were Mars Galiev, his wife Galia, and their son Marat. One of the most memorable and dangerous hikes was when Mars and I accepted a plea from a group of physicists from Moscow who had lost their guide, to lead them through some high passes over the main Caucasus ridge.

We started our hike before sunrise and reached the pass, above 14,000 feet, around 11:00 AM. We discovered that the only way down the other side of the pass was an almost vertical descent to a glacier field below. We connected two thirty-meter long ropes and dropped them down, but it was still short by about eight meters. I went down first to secure the descent of the group from below, and Mars remained at the top. After Galia, Marat, and the five physicists safely reached the glacier, Mars dropped the rope and made a perilous descent by grasping the rocky wall and using the crampons on his boots. Somewhat amazed, I confronted Mars for not using the ropes to allow himself some safety; he insisted that we might need the ropes later on, and he was right. They were needed on two more hazardous sections.

The glacier field was covered with deep, fresh snow that could obscure dangerous crevasses. Mars and I went ahead to establish a secure trail while the group waited behind. Connected to Mars by a rope, I was out front with an ice axe, and he followed behind to hold me in case I plunged into a crevasse. This dangerous trek took about an hour; in the meantime, it started to snow. We commanded the rest of the group to start jumping up and down to stay warm, and they placed Marat, who was eight years old and small, into one of the large backpacks to prevent him from freezing. Finally, after negotiating another glacier, we went down safely and reached a green valley. It was almost the end of the day, and we barely had enough time to set the tents, have a bite, and go to sleep. We were up early in the morning enjoying the sunrise, the warm August weather, and the beautiful green landscape. After drying our clothes and supplies under the sun, we ate and continued our trek.

Very soon we were challenged again this time by a raging mountain river. We had no choice but to cross it using a sixty-foot tree trunk. With the rope ends securely fastened around my waist, I ventured onto the wet tree trunk while Mars and one of the physicists stretched the other ends of the ropes from the bank above and below the trunk. After I made the precarious crossing, Mars held the ends of the ropes; with those two guide ropes, we fashioned handrails for the group to hold onto as they crossed the raging river on this primitive bridge. Mars was the last to cross, and again he brought the ropes with him! These challenging and dangerous trips really lifted our spirits. I believe they also reinforced our mental and physical health to withstand the tribulations we would invariably face once we were back in Moscow.

Mars became my close friend, a term that probably had a deeper meaning in the Soviet Union than in the U.S. Generally, friendship meant deep interdependence and trust, and it was an important survival tool under an oppressive regime. Mars was the type of friend who exceeded even the highest level of friendship. I could easily put my life in his hands, both in the mountains and in everyday life in Moscow. He was an electrician at a tram station. He and Galia were not college educated, but their intelligence, general knowledge, sensitivity, and understanding of life was at a much higher level than most of my colleagues who had several professional and scientific degrees. Our families would frequently meet on weekends, sometimes joining other friends for a hike and a picnic, or just meeting at our homes. In addition to our love for the mountains and nature in general, we also shared concerns about the future of the country and the political changes.

Mars and Galia were Tartars, and because they belonged to an ethnic and Muslim minority, they often experienced discrimination from some of their xenophobic Russian neighbors. Being a minority was another element of our commonality, and I explained life as a Jew to their son, Marat, in order to overcome the prejudice he had absorbed from his friends. Altogether, having the Galievs as close friends was a highly meaningful part of my social life in

Moscow. I could never find other friends as devoted as they were, and I missed them tremendously after my emigration to the U.S.

Mars was physically very strong, tall, slim, and muscular. He never complained about any health problems, and he had very strong technical climbing skills. This combination enabled him to do amazing things in the mountains. Once, in the middle of nowhere in the wilderness, he developed a sore throat. I suggested some antibiotics, but he refused and found his way to fix the problem. Early the next morning while the rest of us slept, he climbed a nearby high peak. He felt better afterward, and we continued our trip. Mars hated to visit doctors so much that he neglected his health. He died in 2005 from a heart aneurysm rupture while driving in Moscow. His tragic death might have been prevented with surgery had it been diagnosed.

Another adventure to mention took place in a completely different part of Russia. Dr. Mikhail Alexandrovitch Karachunsky, a friend and a colleague at the TB Institute, suggested taking a canoe trip on the Kabozha River, located in a remote area north of Moscow. My son Herman joined us on this trip, and we traveled by train to a small stop. From there we walked, carrying the canoe and large packs to a river that was not much more than a large brook at that point. Mikhail insisted on carrying the canoe. This was remarkable because he was an amputee and walked with prosthetics! At the river he assembled the canoe, loaded it with our supplies, and we started our trip down the river. The trip lasted about two weeks, and most of the time we passed through areas with no sign of human habitation. It was reminiscent of landscape paintings by the famous Russian artist Kustodiev. In a number of places, we saw villages that had been abandoned except for a few bewildered chickens running around. Some villages had completely disappeared (perhaps burned), and only trees were reminders of where the village once stood. These depressing sites were remnants from the failure of the Soviet agricultural policies over the years. The young people would escape from the rural areas to the cities. The older generation died off.

A major part of our trip took us through the wilderness, and only at the end of our trip did we visit a few large villages that still existed. Many species of fish lived in the river. Fishing in the evening became a ritual, mostly for Herman and Mikhail, while I hid in the tent to escape the swarms of mosquitoes and emerged later to cook when the campfire would protect me from the annoying insects. Once we saw a bear on the opposite bank drinking water. The river separated us from the beast by only about twenty or thirty feet. Perhaps the bear had never seen humans before; when he realized that strange creatures were watching him, he stopped drinking, roared loudly, and ran away.

In 2004, while I was visiting Moscow at a scientific conference, Mikhail came to see me. He jokingly asked me, "Have you come back to Russia for another trip on the Kabozha River?" I answered him saying, "I would consider it if you could suggest a really effective way to combat the mosquitoes." Dr. Karachunsky was a delightful person to spend time with, not just in the wilderness, but professionally as well. He was one of the leading experts in treating tuberculosis patients and was one of only a few medical professionals in Russia who read the foreign scientific literature. He successfully treated my friend Bezirov, who had a difficult-to-treat form of tuberculosis called "tuberculoma" (chapter 7). During my 2004 visit to Moscow I also learned that Dr. Karachunsky had done an excellent translation of my chapter on tuberculosis bacteriology from the American Society of Microbiology publication, for the Russian version of that book. While writing this story I sent a letter to Mikhail to get permission to cite his name in case of publication. He did not respond, which was unusual. A few weeks later, in February of 2007, I was informed that Mikhail had died. Until his last days, Dr. Karachunsky was very active in research and clinical work. Knowing him during the time I worked at the TB Institute in Moscow which was one of the highlights of my life there, and another great loss now.

7. Family

The twenty-year period described above began with great hopes and expectations when my family moved from Arkhangelsk to Moscow in 1957. Back then, the only way to settle in Moscow after return from Arkhangelsk was to buy a house. Fortunately, I had saved almost enough money during my years in the North (plus an inevitable loan from some relatives) to buy half a log house in the suburb of Moscow in the area where my parents lived. I renovated the house, and the following year, my wife, Sima, arrived with our sons, Michael and Herman. We hired a young girl from a village to take care of three-year-old Michael and his one-year-old brother Herman. The girl's status in Moscow could not be settled, and we had to hide her from the police. Somehow we managed to do that until the boys were eligible to go to kindergarten.

Another problem was finding a professional job for Sima. It was a time of growing anti-Semitism and having her nationality classified as Jewish in the infamous paragraph number five of her internal passport was a serious obstacle in job seeking. Knowing how the system worked, I suggested a simple trick to overcome the problem. In order to obtain a job as a senior researcher at a medical institute, one had to submit an application-questionnaire. Then the Research Council would make selections by reviewing the applications and interviewing the applicants. The internal passport was not presented at that point in the hiring process. Since Sima's last name, Apsit, did not sound Jewish but was a typical Latvian name, and her appearance was not typically Jewish either, I suggested she should indicate "Latvian" in her application. Sima felt uncomfortable with this subterfuge, but I succeeded in convincing her. "After all, they did not say that you had to fill in that paragraph as it is in your passport," I said. "If they catch you on that, you could say that Latvian is how you felt when filling out the application and in memory of your father." The trick worked, and for many years Sima kept forgetting to bring her passport to the personnel department of the Institute for Heart Surgery where she worked as a senior researcher.

Although anti-Semitism became more and more apparent, the overall political climate in the early 1960s was still somewhat comfortable; it worsened in the early 1970s. Without any clearly defined goals, I decided that the children should start learning English during their pre-school years. We hired a private teacher for this purpose. Then, still lacking a clear goal, I pursued a way to enroll them in schools where English was intensive and some subjects were taught in English. These were quite privileged places, and enrollment was difficult. One had to know the system to find a loophole, and these schools were far from our home. It took an hour or more each way on Moscow's busy public transportation system. My sister accused me of torturing the children, and Sima was not happy when she had to pick them up on the way home. But I defended the need for the children to know English as an avenue to a better education and better professional opportunities, still keeping my secret hope the possibility that someday we could leave the country.

During the dark political years, my children graduated from high school when they were seventeen—Michael in 1972 and Herman in 1974. To become a university student immediately after graduation was important to avoid the compulsory three-year service in the Army. Military service would make emigration far more problematic. We invested substantially in private lessons for our sons to ensure high marks on their final exams at the school and the university entrance exams, but we knew that good marks alone were not enough.

Michael dreamed of becoming a biologist, but we knew that it was unrealistic for a Jew to be accepted to the Moscow University, which had the only quality biology department. There were no official policies against the Jews, and the authorities would deny such bias, but everyone knew that no Jew would pass an interview for acceptance to any of the prominent schools. I convinced Michael that education at the medical school could also be a pathway to becoming a biologist; however, even the medical schools in Moscow were becoming off-limits to Jews. So it was time to manage a circumvention of the system once more.

Sima and I went to the city of Arkhangelsk and approached the dean and other authorities of the medical school, who happened to be our former students. Jews, particularly from another city, were not very welcome to the Arkhangelsk Medical School either. To arrange an exception for Michael, the dean visited the "boss" (the Communist Party district secretary) and told him that the boy's parents had contributed greatly to the success of the school in the past and were currently helping with necessary upgraded training and consultations for the faculty members.

Michael was enrolled as a medical student at Archangelsk, but we needed him to be in Moscow. Transfer from one school to another appeared to be more feasible than initial enrollment in the Moscow Medical School if one could find a way to overcome some technical problems. The common avenue in the Soviet Union for resolving such problems was "favor for favor." The only favor I could offer was my capability of writing scientific papers and performing data analyses. I inquired through my numerous friends about people in power who may need such a service.

A scientific degree—Candidate of Science (Ph.D.)—and the highest degree—Doctor of Science (ScD)—afforded people a better position and a substantial salary increase. The degree had become desirable not only among the scientists but also for various administrators. It was not surprising that some people had significant problems preparing an adequate thesis and acceptable analyses of scientific data. These were not problems for me. Within eight or nine months, by working at home on the weekends, I wrote two dissertations, one for a Ph.D. in the field of organization and management of medical services, and the other for an ScD in epidemiology of the neurological disorders in the country. The latter was based on classified data. Carloads of classified documents were delivered to my apartment. Both dissertations were successfully defended, and the psychiatrist with his ScD had an opportunity to become a professor and chairman of the department in one of the medical schools outside of Moscow. (It also helped him on a personal level as well to finalize his divorce and escape the tenets of his wife.) Michael was accepted at two medical schools in Moscow, and after finishing the first year in Arkhangelsk, he was transferred to the First Medical School (now known as the Sechenov's Medical Academy), the best medical school in the country, from which he graduated in 1978. At the time of graduation, Michael was already married and had a son, Boris, born in 1977.

In 1974 Herman was admitted to the School of Railroad Engineering and took classes there, majoring in mathematics and computer science. That was one of the university-level schools known to admit Jews, and its curriculum fit Herman's interests, but he was unable to finish school there because of our emigration to the U.S. in 1978. He began his professional education again after our arrival in Denver in 1979.

My father had died in 1968 at age sixty-five from his chronic heart conditions, and his death caused me much grief, guilt, and self-examination. Observing daily Kaddish for a year helped me substantially in coping with the sadness of his premature death; however, for many years, unfinished conversations with him kept running through my mind, and my feelings of guilt mostly related to the lack of communication. We had both been guilty of this. My mother developed Parkinson's disease and lived with my sister and her husband. They emigrated from Moscow to Israel in 1972 and, subsequently, from Israel to Canada in 1975. My mother died in Canada in 1987.

In the mid-1970s it became quite apparent that my personal and professional success in the past and my ability to make favorable arrangements for my children was nearing an end. Along with my personal problems because of the conflict with Deputy Minister of Health Burgasov (Chapters 8 and 9), the growing anti-Semitism eliminated any hopes for a successful and secure life for my children in the Soviet Union. The feeling of being a second-class citizen was so humiliating that I saw emigration to Israel as the only solution to the problem. Set on Israel, Michael, Herman, and I (and, subsequently, Michael's wife Helen) started taking private lessons in Hebrew. When the teacher came to our apartment, we would close the curtains, place a pillow on the telephone (it was most likely bugged), and take the lessons in full secrecy. They were scheduled mostly when Sima, who did not approve of them, was out of the house. There was no need for secrecy when I took English lessons. Persecution was only a danger with Hebrew.

Although the option of emigrating to Israel, the U.S., or Canada was a welcome development in the Soviet Union, this new option also created disruption in many families and numerous personal tragedies. It was a view at that time that the émigrés would never again see those who were left behind. One pointed story was that of our Hebrew teacher, who was a successful professional in his early thirties. A common text to learn the language was the Torah, the five books of Moses. Just reading it in Hebrew and understanding the deep meaning of certain passages (many not fully translatable to other languages) converted some who were originally atheist toward a new direction and a new view of religion. That is how our teacher had become not only an expert in Hebrew, but also a religious Jew. His dream was to emigrate to Israel, but he had a problem. His father was a devoted old Communist who contemptuously resented any religious feeling, especially sympathy for Israel. Our teacher had to keep his conversion and his emigration dreams a secret from his parents. So he lived his dual life until after our emigration, and soon after that he ended up in a psychiatric institution.

Our own family was not exempt from a somewhat tragic situation. From my perspective, I felt that the overall situation in the country was becoming more and more depressing. Anti-Semitism was obvious in all facets of our lives. I did not see any good perspectives in my work, and I did not see any future for my children. I could no longer pretend to be happy or ignore the reality. In my desperation I started to become occasionally irrational and dangerous. I started to lose my usual patience with certain humiliations in the workplace and with life in general. I felt that I could not continue to live there anymore and, at times, thought of suicide in case our emigration was refused. Michael and Herman understood it well and made their decision to emigrate, not only because of my influence but also because of their own assessments of the situation. The problem was with Sima. On one hand, she clearly understood the situation with our sons and encouraged them to emigrate; on the other hand, she was concerned about the future of her daughter, Olga, who had graduated from the university and worked at the university as an instructor in the Department of Marxism-Leninism. She had already been married and divorced and had a little girl. Olga was listed on her internal passport as Russian and was a member of the Communist Party. She tried to hide the fact that her mother was Jewish. Under these circumstances, Sima felt an obligation to help her adult daughter (thirty-five at the end of 1977) settle her personal problems. Sima's decision at that time was not to emigrate. She signed the required letters permitting our sons, Michael and Herman, to emigrate, and then we had to get divorced. The choice she had to make was awful and dramatic. By allowing them to go with me she knew that she may never see her sons again. This was a brave move, but at the same time, her decision not to come with us seemed to me unwise.

In addition to this painful family problem, we had to pass a number of obstacles, both obvious and hidden, to finally emigrate from the country. Herman and I left at the end of October in 1978. Michael, his wife Helen, and their little son Boris, left in the summer of 1979. The success in overcoming both obstacles and real danger was not just luck but more a result of years of careful planning. The twenty-year period of our lives during the post-Stalin era was over. Ingrained in our minds were memories of bitterness at the overall unfairness from the authorities, combined with the sweet memories of our friends who helped us spiritually and physically to succeed in the harsh reality and to survive, literally and emotionally.

CHAPTER SIX

Russian "Shaman" in Africa

"The darkest thing about Africa has always been our ignorance of it."

George Kimble

1. In Moscow, 1960
2. To Congo, 1960
3. To Congo again, 1962
4. In the Ituri Forest
5. "Russian Medicine Man" in the Ituri Jungle
6. Pygmies
7. Farewell, Congo

Fig. 23. In Africa: pictures taken during the 1960 expedition (top to bottom):
- A typical village environment, Kivu area;
- Another village site;
- An old woman with *mpata*, a wooden plate inserted into her upper lip when she was young to make her unattractive to prevent her from being captured by the Arab invaders (Eastern Province); and
- A psychiatric patient.
-

Fig. 24. 1960 expedition (left to right, top to bottom):
- An African mother with a child (photo by Salmin);
- Andrey Arapov with the UN troops;
- Vaccination against plague; and
- Guramy Arabidze (on the right); with Dr. Shishkin, the Egyptian WHO expert, and the pilot.

Fig. 25. Expedition of 1962 (left to right, top to bottom):
- Our group at the Russian embassy in Cairo (I am on the left);
- David Bointuasu;
- With Domenique Nkwa, director of the hospital in Oshwe, and his wife; and
- With Paul Besoy.

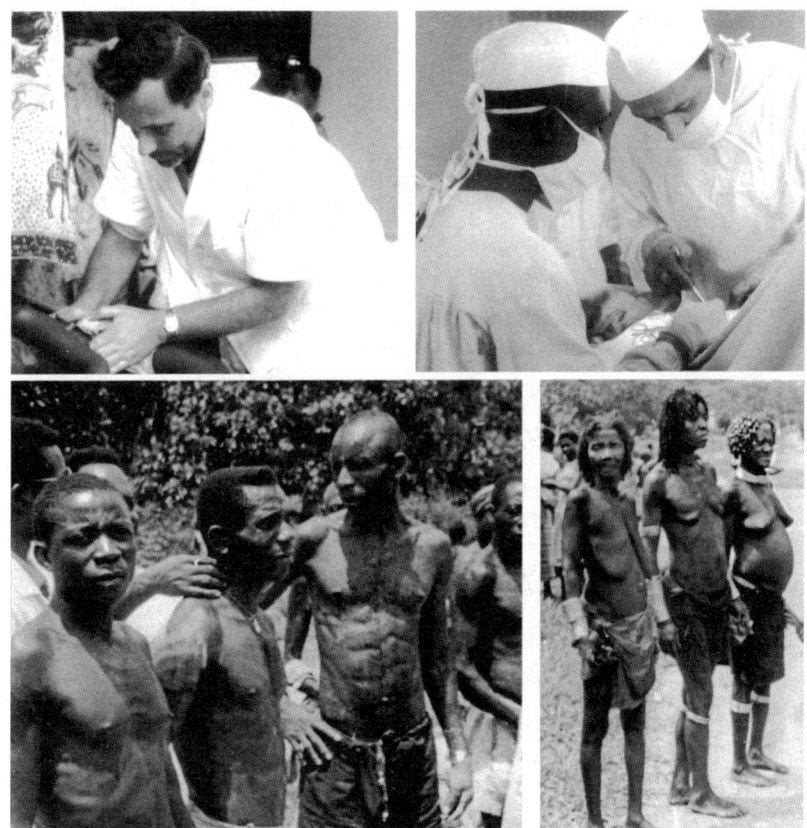

Fig. 26. Medical practices in Africa (1962):
- Examining a child with malaria;
- Surgery;
- Paul and David (behind the men) are examining the neck glands (for detection of sleeping sickness), this group of men had syphilis and labeled by Paul as *Equipe Syphilitiuque;* and
- The oldest women in the village in their forties.

Fig. 27. In the last village – Belonge (lef to right, top to bottom):
- Paul with his girls;
- Village chief;
- A happy family;
- Ludmila is watching the dances by the Batwa tribe pygmies; and
- Dancing children from the Batwa pygmies' village.

1. In Moscow, 1960

In July of 1960 the director of the Metchnikov Institute for Vaccines and Sera, Dr. A.P. Muzychenko, called me into his office and announced that "someone at the top" was organizing a Soviet Red Cross medical expedition to the Congo, an African country that had just gained its independence from Belgium. The official goal of this expedition, as he explained to me, was to prevent expected epidemics of infectious diseases resulting from political instability and chaos, as well as inadequate medical infrastructure after the departure of Belgian doctors. The true goal of the expedition was to provide a humanitarian cover for Soviet penetration into this country by seizing the opportunity to fill a suddenly emerging political vacuum. Muzychenko asked me, "Would you be interested in becoming a member of this expedition?" Without hesitation, I answered, "Yes!"

During that time, travel abroad was a rare opportunity for a Soviet citizen. Most importantly, such a trip would satisfy my appetite for adventure and danger. It was also a unique opportunity from a professional point of view, especially because of my interest in infectious diseases.

Dr. M.I. Khazanov, the head of the Department of Epidemiology (who was also my superior), and I sat in Muzychenko's office while he telephoned the person in charge of organizing the Soviet delegation to Congo—a high-ranking member of the KGB, as Muzychenko told us later. He said on the phone that he was recommending my inclusion in the delegation. He provided some details about me and emphasized that I had already published several scientific papers in first-class journals and that I was known abroad (particularly at the WHO) as a physician-scientist. During the conversation, and in response to some comment from the person on the phone, he said with some agitation in his voice, "So what that he is a Jew? I am telling you that I know him well, and I am giving you my personal guarantee of the loyalty and reliability of this young man. Is that not enough? Don't you trust me anymore?" Khazanov and I looked at each other with surprise at witnessing this conversation.

2. To Congo, 1960

A group of physicians (B. Shishkin, N. Plotnikov, L. Klassovsky, V. Tsibulsky, L. Heifets, L. Salmin, B. Godovanny, I. Shkhvatsabaya, A. Arapov, G. Arabidze, V. Frolov, A. Kuzmitchev, A. Tatchenko, and M. Gleser) from various specialties, along with several nurses (or so they were called) and an official representative of the Soviet Red Cross (a KGB man by the name Byelorusets); were assembled at the Ministry of Health. Our official assignment was to represent the Soviet Red Cross. Our mission was to travel to Africa to provide health care, as well as to help prevent epidemics of infectious diseases, because the Belgian medical professionals left Congo after the country received its independence on June 30, 1960. It was remarkable that all the physicians in this expedition came from various research institutes, and they all had Ph.D.s, in addition to their MD degree and several publications to show that the group was comprised of medical professionals rather than KGB agents. None of us knew French, which was the official language of Congo; however, the "nurses" and "medical assistants" from the Red Cross just happened to be our interpreters!

Our knowledge increased as we learned about the Congo, one of the largest countries in Africa, close in size to Europe. We were told that its population was approximately fourteen million (now sixty-two million) and consisted of approximately two hundred ethnic groups. The country had been a Belgian colony since 1908, and after its independence on June 30, 1960, Patrice Lumumba, a leader of a party called the Congolese National Movement (CNM), whose principles embraced the Soviet ideology, was elected as its first prime minister. Joseph Kasavubu, the leader of another leftist party (ABAKO), was elected as president. We were told that our delegation was organized at the personal request of Lumumba, who was fast becoming a friend of the Soviet Union.

In early August of 1960, after a few weeks of an expedited refresher course in tropical infectious diseases and basic French, we were on our way to Cairo in a special plane loaded with medications, blankets, and other supplies. Most of us had never been abroad before, and just spending the first night on our trip in such a unique place as Cairo was a shocking experience. Our next stop was at Khartum in Sudan, and then in Leopoldville (now Kinshasa), the capital of Congo.

When we arrived, the members of the temporary Soviet diplomatic mission in the Congo finally had an excuse to interact with the new government, to offer help and to discuss our work assignment. Other countries also used medical delegations as a shield to enter the political vacuum. For the Soviet Union, it was clearly an avenue to establish diplomatic relationships with this strategically important country.

From Leopoldville we traveled to Stanleyville (now Kisangani), the capital of the Eastern Province, a stronghold of Lumumba's Party. We spent approximately one week in a large hospital in Stanleyville, mostly getting acquainted with the local situation and working with another foreign medical delegation from Israel. We were divided into three groups: a small group remained in Stanleyville, and two other groups received assignments for two of the five provinces of the country. One group went to the Bunya in the Kivu Province, and the other group went to Buta in the Eastern Province. I was in the group sent to the Eastern Province.

In Stanleyville, I had the opportunity to visit the Institute of Hygiene, which was actually a large, modern clinical laboratory that provided services to the whole province. I went there with a representative from the World Health Organization, an epidemiologist from Egypt, and another epidemiologist from Israel. The services of the Institute included various tests with diagnostic specimen as well as research and development opportunities. It was much better equipped than any similar facility or research institute in Moscow. The director of each laboratory was a Belgian doctor (Ph.D.) whose desk was usually in the middle of the room, and the technicians, who were local young people, worked at the laboratory benches situated around the perimeter of the room. When I visited the place, the Belgians had left the country, but the laboratories were still functioning. I was told that similar institutes existed in each of the five provinces and were working in consultation with and under the direction of the Institute of Tropical Medicine in Antwerp, Belgium.

While in Stanleyville, we met Lumumba and had the honor of shaking his hand. After this momentous occasion, four of us—

Tolya (an interpreter), Guramy Arabidze (an internist), Andrey Arapov (a surgeon), and I—were sent to a small town called Buta.

The hospital in Buta was large (about two hundred beds), with a clinic for ambulatory patients, and it had only three medical professionals—three Belgian Catholic nuns. These elderly ladies spent the entire day, from sunrise at 6 AM to sunset at 6 PM, in addition to urgent calls at night, with their patients. The sisters' commitment to the well-being of the patients enlightened me as to what the work of a real nurse should be—nothing like I used to witness back at home. Because there were no doctors in the hospital, the nurses' duties included the whole range of medical care, except surgery. The hospital consisted of several barrack-type buildings; each served as a ward with twenty or more beds in it. Patients arriving from a large area near Buta were usually accompanied by their families. The families would camp in the large hospital yard. They cooked for themselves and took care of the hospitalized person, as well. At night, the families slept in the wards under the beds; they were elevated enough to provide space for several people. During the day, the hospital's yard was full of people. In addition to the families of the hospitalized patients, about twenty to forty new patients stood in line waiting to be seen in the clinic. We helped the nurses with this work. Each patient was examined. They usually did not require admission to the hospital but just needed to obtain the necessary medications. The patients' care, as well as all their medications, was free, which had been established by the Belgian colonial administration and sponsored by the Belgian government and the Catholic organizations. The supply of drugs and other material was enough for another year.

While Dr. Arabidze was spending most of the day at the clinic, as well as attending at the hospital, Dr. Arapov was quite busy with surgery. I assisted with surgeries almost every day. Most of the cases that required surgery were due to various injuries, and there were frequent cases of gangrene which required amputation of the limb. Some of the predominant reasons for patients coming to the clinic were malaria, skin lesions, enteric infections, and children with *quashiorkor* (an illness caused by malnutrition, the result of insufficient protein contents in the diet), evidenced by a large belly, thin extremities, and large red spots on the skin.

In addition to my involvement with patients, I also planned to organize some measures against the malaria epidemic and contacted the local Catholic mission that had experience in this type of work, such as spraying insecticides against the mosquitoes within the city limits. We decided to restart this work and developed a plan which included preventive treatment of malaria. When we returned to Moscow, I was told that it was inappropriate for a Soviet scientist to seek collaboration with a religious organization.

It was eye-opening for me when I discovered that the Catholic mission took care of a variety of needs in the local community, including health care, children's education (mostly addressing literacy in French), and other social activities. Most of the local people were Catholic, but in other surrounding areas there were Protestants. Interactions with the priests and other workers of the mission posed an interesting challenge. All of them were well-educated, cultural men, some of whom were multilingual. One of my most pleasant memories of visiting the mission was listening to classical music records. At that time, a perfect stereo system was already in place there, and it was then that I experienced surround-sound for the very first time. Dr. Borghese, a physician from Italy, was the person responsible for our visit to the mission. For some unknown reason, Dr. Borghese was not an employee of the hospital and mostly served as a private physician to a small white population of the city. We also socialized with a Portuguese couple. They owned a cotton plantation and had three children. One of the children, a boy about nine years old, was a mulatto, and his genetic origin was a mystery to us. We often ate dinners with this family at the hotel where we stayed.

We stayed at an *auberge*, which is the French/Belgian term for an inn or bed and breakfast, that happened to be the only available place in town. Each of us had our own very comfortable cabin with all necessary facilities. A separate building had a social hall, a restaurant, and a bar. We were the only guests, and there were several unoccupied cabins. A Greek man in his late twenties was the owner of the auberge. His mother served us breakfast and took orders for our lunch and dinner. In fact, it was quite an unusual, luxurious lifestyle for inexperienced Soviet citizens who had never been outside Russia. One day the owner decided to go the extra mile to please his only guests: He brought in four young ladies, all of whom were overdressed in colorful local fabrics. Their shining black faces smiled suggestively, but there was no language for maintaining a conversation, even in French with the help of Tolya, our interpreter. We drank beer served by the Greek man and silently smiled at each other. The girls left, and we were very proud of ourselves for following the strict instructions given us in Moscow, which forbade engaging in relationships with the local females. The owner of the auberge was disappointed and showed his obvious surprise and disbelief when we explained to him that we Russians did not have a need for women when we were occupied with an important mission. In fact, only two of us were really Russians—Arapov and Tolya. Arabidze was Georgian and I, a Jew, but how were we to explain that to the hotel owner?

Every day was routine and predictable. At seven or eight AM, a car with a driver assigned to us by the local administrator (another luxury of our life) would take us to the hospital; the car also brought us back to the auberge at noon. After lunch and a two-hour nap, we were served coffee and driven back to the hospital for four more hours of work. In the evening, after dinner, we had a few hours to socialize at the bar with Dr. Borghese and other locals (mostly whites), while hoisting a few excellent quality local beers. Tolya preferred much stronger beverages, and he began showing signs of becoming an alcoholic. After heavy drinking he suffered severe hangovers and became an embarrassment to us; he often could not properly perform his duties as an interpreter, which was sometimes necessary during surgery. In the old-fashioned Russian schoolboy tradition, we decided to teach him a lesson. We went to his cabin and waited there in the dark for his late return from the bar. When he finally arrived, we threw a blanket over his head and beat him sufficiently hard so he would feel the pain the next morning when he was sober. In Russian this is called *tyomnaya* (meaning "in dark"). This technique was used in Russian high schools on informers so they would not be able to identify the perpetrators. Tolya's behavior improved, and he never reported us to the authorities back in Moscow. Indeed, some traditions did work.

Andrey Arapov, Guramy Arabidze, and I became good friends, and we had an opportunity to see each other back in Moscow. In

Denver in 1994, I received a letter from Guramy, who became a chairman of the Moscow Society of Cardiology and served as department chairman and professor at the Cardiology Research Center. He informed me that Andrey, as well as another member of our delegation, Dr. Igor Shchvatsabaya, had died prematurely. That was the last time I heard from Guramy, and later I was told that soon after I received his letter he died also.

We worked in Buta really hard for almost a month, and we planned to take some time off later to see Africa. Unfortunately, this never happened. On the fifth of September, Kasavubu, president of the country, fired our friend Prime Minister Patrice Lumumba and placed him under arrest. One of the Russian military planes stationed at the Stanleyville airport suddenly arrived in Buta early that morning with the news that we had only fifteen minutes to collect our belongings and leave for Stanleyville; the other groups of our delegation were already there. Upon our landing in Stanleyville, the Congolese security police (*gendarmes*) surrounded our airplane. We were ordered to get under the airplane and were forced to sit on the ground at gunpoint and without water! Finally, an Ethiopian officer from the UN troops brought the commander of the Congolese gendarmes who allowed us to have some orange juice. We sat under the plane until sunset, at which time we were ordered back inside the airplane for the night. Early the next morning the confinement was lifted, and we were allowed to leave. We headed back to Moscow.

Later in Moscow we learned that Kasavubu had handed Lumumba over to his sworn enemy, Moise Tchombe, who was the president of the separatists in Katanga Province. Patrice Lumumba was killed in January or February of 1961, and soon thereafter, Kasavubu appointed Tchombe as prime minister of the country.

On the way home we stopped for a few days in Cairo. We went sightseeing and spent our foreign currency on gifts for our families; that was my first chance to see a large foreign city that was not decimated by war. The dominating impression was not of the pyramids and other attractions, but, rather, what we observed in the streets, a reflection of day-to-day life in general. Obviously, Cairo was not a part of the "free world." There were annoying beggars on every corner, abject poverty, the stench of garbage strewn in the streets mixed with the smell of cooked food, and large dense crowds of people everywhere. The most striking observation was the abundance of portraits of "the great leader" of the new Egypt, Gamal Abdel Nasser, a friend of the Soviet Union! Of course, we did not see the luxurious mansions and palaces located in different parts of the city other than the downtown, but even so, the reality of life there was quite clear.

Our families met us at a military airport near Moscow. The next day the Minister of Health, Dr. Kurashev, expressed his thanks on behalf of the Soviet government. He said that although our mission in the Congo happened to be shorter than planned, one important goal had been achieved. Thanks to our presence, the temporary Soviet diplomatic group had the opportunity to maintain contacts with the Congo government, with a goal of establishing a diplomatic relationship with the country. He also said that this work would continue, and that sometime in the future we may again be asked to become involved. A large group of Russian journalists assembled outside the Minister's office, and they immediately surrounded each member of our delegation for interviews and photographs. That is, everybody except me! I was puzzled but soon understood the reality of Soviet life. The purpose of any interview in the Soviet Union was pure propaganda that met the needs of the Party line. In this case, the goal was to show how the heroic Soviet (Russian) physicians had efficiently represented the Motherland by helping the Congolese who had suffered under Belgian colonialism. A Jew (easily identified by the name Heifets, as well as by my appearance in a photo) would not fit well into that scheme.

Our short trip to Congo was highly educational. We learned that, contrary to Soviet propaganda, during an eighty-year period, the Belgians built modern cities, roads, and a communication system; established basic state infrastructure; organized free medical care; and established basic education for children. Of course, all this was not at the European level yet and far from perfect, but it could have been used as a basis for further development. Unfortunately, within one or two weeks after receiving independence, the country became rife with civil unrest, intertribal conflicts, and power struggles among the leaders of political parties.

Contrary to Soviet media reports, this situation was not a revolt by the Congolese people against the remnants of the "Belgian imperialism, colonialism, and exploitation." In reality, two of the five provinces, Katanga and South Kasai, seceded from the new republic, and civil war broke out, which was later followed by an army coup staged by President Kasavubu. Beginning with Lumumba's death, political assassinations became the way to resolve political and ambitious differences between the new leaders of the country. An ongoing war that is responsible for a large number of civilian casualties continues today, as well as an extreme level of corruption among the country's leaders.

3. To Congo Again, 1962

The new prime minister of the country (renamed Zaire), Moise Tchombe, requested medical assistance from the Soviet government, specifically stating that he only wanted those physicians who had participated in the first mission. I was among the chosen. The new team consisted of five physicians and four "nurses" (interpreters from the Red Cross office). We departed at the end of December, 1961 on a large four-engine Aeroflot airplane assigned to take the nine of us, along with supplies of blankets, medications, and canned food, from Moscow to Leopoldville. It was a very cold winter in Moscow, and we left our warm clothes with our relatives when we boarded the airplane. A few hours later, as we flew over Yugoslavia, one of the engines failed, and we returned to Moscow. When we arrived, our relatives brought back our warm clothes, and we spent the night at the airport. We left the next day, and this time we successfully reached Cairo. It was December 31, and we were invited to celebrate the eve of 1962 at the Soviet Embassy, where an artificial pine tree had been placed in the yard. It was an unusual New Year's celebration; we just sat around the tree in hot and humid air knocking back our drinks.

The next segment of our trip, from Cairo to Khartum, was another adventure. As we approached Khartum, we were attacked by Sudanese military planes and received a signal to land. Fortunately, our plane was much faster than the Sudanese fighters, and we successfully escaped their bullets. When we landed at the

Khartum airport, we were politely taken into custody by the airport guards. The Soviet ambassador arrived in panic and explained to us that someone back in Moscow had not made the proper arrangements for us to fly over Sudan, thus, we had violated Sudanese air space. Although we were under arrest, I must say that it was a very pleasant experience. The nine of us boarded a large Nile riverboat occasionally used as a resort. Each of us had a cabin, and the stewards provided us with excellent colonial-style service. We were free to move around the city, and one member of the Soviet Consulate took us on a tour to Omdurman, a holy place forbidden to non-Muslims. The secret of our visit to Omdurman was that our tour guide happened to be a Kasakh, well-known to the locals as a Muslim, and had all the necessary local connections. Altogether, this arrest delay turned into a pleasant ten-day vacation at the expense of the Soviet government. Our vacation ended with an intervention by the U.N. Secretary-General, U Thant, in response to an appeal from the Soviet government.

After an overnight flight from Khartum, we arrived in Leopoldville in the morning and were met in the airport by a crowd of local officials—and Tchombe himself! We were well prepared for this honor. Lev Volodin, one of the Russian journalists, had informed us of this possibility. On the advice of Volodin, we brought with us a case of Russian champagne, Tchombe's favorite drink. We stored it in the cabin and brought it with us to a large room at the airport that had been prepared for our reception. At the table, I happened to be seated at the end of the table next to Tchombe and kept making toasts and shaking hands with this brutal man.

While waiting for our assignments, we stayed for about a week in a ten-story building that had been purchased by the Soviet Union for an embassy. One group (Drs. Alexander Kuzmitchev, Vasily Davydov, and I); was sent to a small town called Oshwe, it was located deep in the Ituri forest within the Leopoldville Province (now called Bandundu Province). The second group (Drs. Vadim Tsybulsky and Irat Ishmuhammedov) went to a town called Kahemba on the border of Angola. Our group also included two "nurses," Ludmila and Yelena.

To reach Oshwe was not a simple task. We had to travel by steamboat for several days on three rivers: the Congo, the Kasai, and the Lukenie. Our group was given a house on the bank of the Lukenie River. On the other side of the river, right across from our house, was a jungle from where sounds of wildlife were heard, especially at night. The house was a Belgian colonial residence, and it was large enough to accommodate each of us with an individual bedroom. There was no electricity in this town, but our house was comfortably equipped with two refrigerators that were run by kerosene lamps. To make sure that we would not starve, while in Stanleyville we purchased American Army food rations in boxes labeled "breakfast," "lunch," and "dinner." Later we discovered that most of the canned food, such as Spam, could not be eaten for too many days in a row. In addition, the flour purchased in the city turned out to be infested with tiny worms that we could not eliminate by sifting. At the end of our stay in Oshwe, we could no longer eat the U.S. rations or make bread or pancakes, and we started hating all varieties of bananas that were our predominant diet. At the end of our venture in the Congo we were starving.

Oshwe was populated (perhaps about two thousand people or less) with Kundu, a part of the predominant tribal conglomerate of Bantous in the Congo. (Bakundu, with the *Ba* prefix meaning "people of," is usually added to the name of any tribe.) Formally, the people of this town were Catholics, but I did not see any activities that indicated such an affiliation. There was no Catholic Mission in this area such as those I had seen in Buta during my previous trip. Although they all belonged to the same tribe, not all the residents were equal. There was a hierarchy, with individuals who were considered tribal chiefs and medicine men at the top. Some families had slaves or serfs who had been captured during past military conflicts or were descendants of those captives. In addition, there were members of secret societies, such as worshipers of leopards or crocodiles, both, previously persecuted by the Belgian colonial administration, as told to us by some of the locals. Some of these stories may have been the product of local folklore and fantasy and nothing to do with the truth. One person assigned to our group as a servant had his upper front teeth carved from both sides to resemble animal teeth. Someone had told Yelena that such teeth indicated that this man was not only a crocodile worshiper, but also a cannibal. It could have been a plot by someone who wanted his job, but Yelena took the story seriously and insisted that he be fired. I made fun of her for being scared by another African story. Dr. Kuzmitchev, the official head of our group, did not want to alienate her (perhaps considering Yelena's connections back in Moscow) and fired the man, which gave me the opportunity to make jokes (not much appreciated by others in our group) that Yelena might now become a real target for cannibalism.

During both expeditions, I noticed a very high level of xenophobia and racial prejudices among some of my Russian colleagues. Yelena was one of them. She was really afraid of "these wild black people." The locals perhaps felt it and tried to avoid any direct contact with her. Two episodes marked the feeling of some young people toward her. Once I went with Yelena to the open market, and we passed a bench where a local man, perhaps a hunter, was selling meat that happened to be parts of an ape's body. Yelena was horrified and, with an obvious tone of disapproval, asked the hunter, "Do you really eat this?" The young man, with a sense of humor typical for local people, responded with a quite sarcastic expression on his face: " O yes, madam, it is delicious, though may be not as tasty as human flesh." With her panic barely suppressed, Yelena insisted on leaving the market immediately.

Another episode occurred when Yelena and I were walking through the village. A group of young men were walking behind us laughing and intentionally speaking in French loud enough for us to hear. Suddenly, Yelena started walking very fast, almost running. When we got home, she told me they were talking about her body possibly being good for cannibalism. I said that I could hear only one French word: *jambon,* that could mean "thigh" or "hip," but also "ham." Nevertheless, even if they were referring to her body, they might not have been discussing eating her, but had a completely different purpose. After all, she was quite an attractive young blond woman with a well-developed body! She could neither appreciate the humor of the local young men nor any of my comments. To calm her down, I suggested that their conversation achieved exactly what they intended: to scare her. Otherwise why would they not speak among themselves in Swahili, but in French?

4. In the Ituri Forest

While Alexander and Vasily began working in the hospital similar to the one described during our first visit in 1960, I worked in the laboratory and started organizing an expedition across the area around Oshwe. This was requested as part of our assignment from the country's Ministry of Health, based on a recommendation from the Belgian Institute for Tropical Medicine in Antwerp. One of the major goals of the expedition was to assess the prevalence of sleeping sickness in the area. Another task was to estimate the spread of leprosy, because the leprosaria were closed when the country became independent in 1960, and the patients were free to go back to their villages. In reality, my mission became much broader. I was just a doctor in the eyes of people in the villages I visited, and many among them needed a wide range of medical attention.

The director of the local hospital, Dominique Nkwa, and the local administration were in charge of organizing our expedition. We were given a large truck equipped for navigating through the dirt roads that sometimes became swamps. The truck was loaded with a variety of medical supplies, antibiotics, microscope and other laboratory equipment, folded iron beds, mattresses, etc. The plan was to travel through the Ituri forest and visit about twenty villages in the most remote areas. In addition to myself, the team included a truck driver (who demanded to have his wife with him), two *feldshers* (similar in education and experience to physician assistants), one laboratory microscopist named Joseph, and Ludmila, one of the two interpreters. David Buintuasu, one of the medical assistants, was a family man in his thirties. He was a Protestant and was very calm and gentle in his relationship with others. Paul Besoy, the other medical assistant, was a young man in his early twenties who had just graduated from nursing school. He was Catholic, single, and very emotional—just the opposite of David. Ludmila was a petite, slim woman in her late thirties, never married, and confessed that she had never had a relationship with a man.

We traveled for about a month during February of 1962 and had no communications with Oshwe or any other place during that period. We did not come back to Oshwe as scheduled and, eventually, were thought to have been lost in the jungle. Reports that "the Soviet doctor Leonid Heifets and the nurse accompanying him were lost in the Ituri jungle" appeared in *Izvestia*, the leading Soviet newspaper. An expedition was set up to find us, and Domenique Nkwa, the director of the hospital in Oshwe, headed up the expedition himself. We were found almost two hundred and fifty miles from Oshwe on our way back. One can only imagine the reaction to these events in Moscow, especially my wife's reaction to the report that "Dr. Leonid Heifets and Ludmila were lost in the jungle." Later, back in Moscow, it took great effort to convince her that nothing happened between Ludmila and I. More precisely, as it is common to say today, I said, "I did not have sex with that woman, the KGB spinster." In fact, I invented this phrase long before Clinton, but it was in Russian. The other difference between Mr. Clinton and me is that, in my case, it was the truth!

Traveling through the jungle was a challenge. Ludmila and I sat in the cabin with the driver while the rest of the group and occasional passengers sat in the back. Sometimes I would join the group and take the opportunity to talk with David to learn about the places we passed. David knew a little bit of English, and my French was at the same level as his English. Our conversation was based on an unusual mixture of French, English, and Swahili. Ludmila would help me to understand some issues afterward or when we stopped, but she refused to give up her comfort in the cabin to join us during the trip. One thing David was reluctant to explain, even when we stopped, was about the remnants of abandoned villages. During these times, our team and the group of passengers, who were usually very noisy, would become silent. When I would question David, he would make a silent sign by placing a finger to his lips. Sometimes, he would mention something about war, Russia, and epidemics, but these comments never made any sense. I was not able to find out about the mystery of these abandoned villages, neither during the trip nor afterward.

Sometimes, the truck would become stuck in the mud, and everyone, except Ludmila and I would help push the vehicle back onto the road. That was really a very tough job, taking into account the constant hot and very humid air (only 30°C, but with relative humidity of 90% or higher). Once, something (maybe a spring) broke and needed to be replaced. The driver decided to replace it with a piece of wood from the "iron tree." (Perhaps not a very clear definition, but it was a very hard wood, indeed.) To cut wood from this tree was a challenge by itself, and the whole operation took at least three hours. We were close to a village, and some local residents came to help. Someone suggested that it would be better for Ludmila and I to walk to the village.

After about a two- or three-mile hike, exhausted and soaked with sweat, we were escorted to a large house that had been built by the Belgians. There were two beds with mattresses on them, and we immediately stretched out on those beds to recover from our hike. The door was open and the pleasant breeze was quite welcome. Suddenly I noticed an unwelcome visitor entering the open door. It was a very bright green snake with large eyes, about three to four feet long and probably half an inch thick. It started to rapidly circle the room. Without any hesitation or concern about preservation of a possibly rare species, I killed the invader by throwing a large rock I had picked up during our hike. Someone came in response to Ludmila's screaming and told us that the snake I killed was very poisonous and aggressive. Perhaps it was the Green Mamba, but I did not care about the correct species identification, and I did not even take a picture of it. A local man said that these snakes usually travel in pairs (male and female), and we should expect the "spouse" to come soon. He suggested we keep the door closed, and so we did, but it took awhile for Ludmila to recover from her panic.

The real danger to health and life in Africa comes from small creatures, some of which are difficult to avoid, particularly infections transmitted by mosquito bites. In Africa, about twenty-five million people are infected annually with malaria and two to three million die from this disease alone. During only three months there, and despite taking antimalaria medication to prevent it, I became infected with two types of malaria parasites: *Plasmodium falciparum* and *P. malaria*. Later, when I came back to Moscow, I provided my blood for the medical students to make smears. When I examined some of these smears, I saw that I was also infected with tiny filarial worms (*Wuchereia bancrofti*), also transmitted by a mosquito bite. This parasite causes elephantiasis, which is a massive, chronic swelling of the legs and genitals. It took me almost a year to recover from these illnesses. Millions in Africa suffer (and many die) from *schistosomiasis*, a severe illness affecting liver, kidney, and other systems and is caused by a worm called *Schistosoma*. *Schistosoma* can penetrate the human skin from water in most of the open reservoirs in Africa. Sleeping sickness, *tryponosomiasis*, is caused by a microscopic parasite *Trypanosoma*, which is transmitted by a bite from the tsetse fly. The prevalence of this illness is about 300,000 new cases annually in Africa. Quite often I experienced stings from the tsetse, which can even penetrate through fabric and feels like a needle stick. I took a collection of tsetse to Moscow for educational purposes.

Most often, we would stay two or three days in each village, but sometimes we visited more than one village in one day. The houses built by the Belgians for the administration visitors were diverse in size and comfort. Most often they had three or four bedrooms, sometimes equipped with refrigerators (powered by kerosene lamps), and had shower rooms where water tanks were warmed by natural heat on the roof, and, most importantly, there were replaceable filters to protect from *Schistosoma* parasites.

Although we were very busy in each village, I would not miss an opportunity to learn about the everyday life in this part of Africa, and David enthusiastically helped me. The landscape of these villages was not much different from that in Oshwe. There were narrow dirt (often red clay) roads, huts constructed from primitive forest materials, and the fetid odor from bananas and manioca baked and wrapped in banana leaves. Typical African traditions could be seen everywhere. There were women pounding with large wooden mallets in large wooden mortars. I learned that this was part of processing the manioca roots. Originally brought to Africa by the Portuguese from South America in the sixteenth century, manioca plants became an important food product. On the outskirts of every village were areas cleared from the jungle to be used for communal purposes, ie to plant manioca and banana plants. Women easily pulled up these approximately six-foot-high plants and stripped the roots that were one or two feet long. Later they would soak these roots in water for a long time, and then dry them in sun. Once the roots were dry the women crushed them with wooden mallets, producing manioca flour. The nutritional value of manioca is very poor, consisting mostly of cellulose and very little starch.

A typical household consisted of several huts, each having more than one opening for better air circulation that created cool conditions. The area around the huts was very clean and maintained by cutting the grass and bushes, which was necessary for spotting encroaching animals, particularly snakes. A separate hut was reserved for various food supplies. Each household had an outhouse cabin. A very small opening, always covered, was centered over a very deep hole down to water level. It looked very clean, without any odors. Women would get water from distant creeks and carry it on their heads in large calabashes—dry, hollow gourds similar in size and shape to a large bottle. The women carried everything on their heads, including large baskets of crops, or wood for a campfire. Each household had a small cabin where a special calabash was installed that provided a slow stream of water that served as a shower. Instead of soap people used leaves from a certain plant. The environment appeared to be very clean and healthy, in dramatic contrast to places located near the larger cities or smaller towns like Oshwe or Buta. Perhaps the slums on the outskirts of large cities, as we saw near Stanleyville, were the result of partial cultural development, which seemed lost between local traditions and not yet fully achieved "benefits" of the Western civilization. Nutrition of the local people in the villages of the Ituri forest was also much better than in any other part of the country. People looked much healthier, and I did not see a single case of *quashiorkor* among the children, as I had observed on our previous expedition in 1960. The reason was the availability of more protein in the diet, mostly from eating small antelopes.

Although they were usually Catholic, many men had two, three, and sometimes even four wives. Intimate relationships would cease when a wife became pregnant and resumed only when the child was two years old and no longer nursing. Each wife and her child had a separate little hut. David stressed also that it was easier to handle family life when there were more family members to share the work—for example, taking care of the children, preparing food, banana cultivation, planting and processing the manioca, and even in hunting. I would routinely rise at sunrise and have an opportunity to observe the family team consisting of wives, children, and dogs as they went hunting.

The hunter would set up a net deep in the jungle, while all members of the team encircled the large area where small antelopes were expected. Then they would make a lot of noise to herd the animals toward the net where the hunter waited to kill them with a spear. The exhausted family team would return to the village just before sundown. The catch would receive immediate care. The body of the animal was cut into large pieces, clearing only the internal organs, leaving the legs and skin untouched. All the pieces were placed in a large bowl of boiling water over a very slow-burning fire made from a special type of wood. At six AM the next morning, the pieces were removed from the boiling water, cleaned, skinned, and the meat cut in small portions. The water was then filtered through fabric; the bullion and meat were placed in a bowl along with a substantial portion of palm oil and *piri-piri* and cooked over a low fire until afternoon.

From time to time our expedition team had the opportunity to feast on the fresh meat prepared in the manner described above. The major impression that remains in my memory is that the meal was like a fire in my mouth, caused by the piri-piri, which is incomparable to any other spicy food in the world. After my first unsuccessful attempt to eat (the food fell uncontrollably out of my mouth), my mouth became so numb that subsequent bites no longer hurt. In addition to the very seductive flavor and good taste (after all), it was really a feast for the members of our expedition, who were hungry most of the time because our usual diet consisted mostly of bananas. We had a lot of Spam, but we could not eat it anymore, even when we were very hungry. I also developed an intolerance for all bananas, small or long, sweet or soft, and those with a wooden texture, which were smashed with oil and baked. I hated bananas for the rest of my life, and to this day I avoid anything that has bananas. Once we were served *fufu,* which is a product that looks like bread and is made of the manioca flour. Ludmila enjoyed this bread so much she could not stop eating it, despite my warnings that it was almost pure cellulose and might severely irritate her intestine. She paid the price for her imprudence with frequent trips to the bushes.

Once we met with the commissioner of the area, whose residence and headquarters was in one of the large villages. He was a handsome, physically strong Kundu man, well-educated and in his mid-twenties. He wore a full suit and smiled most of the time. He had two wives, and one of them had a six-month-old baby. David became a friend and confidant of this beautiful young mother, who often discussed her personal problems with him. She had met her husband when they were classmates, and after graduation they were married in the Catholic Church. Her husband had promised her that as a Christian and an educated person he would not take another wife. She complained to David that her husband had broken this promise as soon as she became pregnant, and that now he takes "this prostitute," as she called the second wife, on all his frequent inspection trips around the district. On the day she was repeating this story to me with David and Ludmila's help, her husband had already left the village on one of these trips. Tears streamed down her face as she told the story, and, at the end, she stressed that their life was not as happy as it may have looked at first glance.

5. "Russian Medicine Man" in the Ituri Jungle

David told me that people in some villages viewed me as a medicine man, which, according to him, imposed certain obligations in personal conduct, such as exhibiting absolute confidence in all situations. He mentioned that this impression of me as a medicine man was reinforced by my appearance, particularly my eyes, which were very similar to the eyes of some African people. He also said that, because of my eyes, African people categorized me differently from the other Russians. How could I explain to him that I was not really a Russian, but that my appearance was typical of another "tribe" called Jews?

With the exception of malaria, leprosy, and sleeping sickness, most of my efforts, as I traveled throughout the villages of the Ituri forest, were not related to rare illnesses, but rather to common health problems. Usually, I felt confident enough, but sometimes the challenge was greater, and I would rather the patient consult with someone else. Nevertheless, for the sake of the reputation of the expedition, and sometimes even for the sake of our physical safety, there were situations when I had no other choice than to behave with the confidence of a medicine man.

The routine in each village would start with all the residents assembled in a central part of the village. Most of the men wore shorts, and some of them also had T-shirts. Women did not cover their chests and wore skirts that were sometimes made of fabric derived from bark. All the women's underwear was fashioned like a hygienic belt. Most of them, especially elderly women, wore decorative brass wires, five to seven rounds around their necks, and ten to twenty rounds around their arms. Although the villagers wore scant clothing, they managed to keep valuables such as their documents, and even coins, in their clothing.

They would line up according to the order established by the Belgian administration in three rows: men, women, and children. Paul would collect their medical certificates (to later stamp certifying that the person passed inspection), while David and I would go behind each row and examine the necks and underarms for enlarged lymph nodes, a possible early sign of sleeping sickness infection, and also observe the skin for detection of leprosy. In cases of suspiciously enlarged lymph nodes, I would puncture the lymph node to collect a sample for smear examination. The laboratory technician would stain the smear for microscopic examination and look for protozoans of the genus *Trypanosoma*. If the smear revealed *trypanosomes* the technician would alert me.

There was an interesting detail about how the Belgian administration made it possible for all these illiterate people to preserve their health certificates. A penalty of five franks (*mpata*, or a disc, as they called it, of very small value but still a treasure in this remote area) was imposed on those who lost their certificates.

The major problem was the quality of smear examination. A positive smear was very rare, and the microscopist who did not anticipate finding the parasite was quite negligent in his work, often not spending enough time examining each smear but engaged in social interactions with people who were waiting. Microscopic smear examination for any purpose is boring, monotonous, and tiresome work that requires certain discipline and concentration. It is very difficult to find suitable individuals among people who are not professional lab technicians and are poorly compensated for their work.

After completion of the mandatory inspection and after a break (and sometimes the next morning), I had to meet the expectant villagers regarding their medical concerns. Sometimes the priority was an epidemic of whooping cough, often complicated with pneumonia, and I had to give the children the penicillin injections and then stay in the village an extra day to continue the treatment. Often there were children with severe manifestation of malaria who required immediate treatment and distribution of the anti-malaria drugs for subsequent treatment. There was a high prevalence of venereal diseases, even several cases of fresh syphilitic ulcers. It was of great concern, but the only thing we could do was register the case, make a note on the person's health certificate, and include it in our report to the local administration. Paul was fascinated by the high prevalence of syphilis and from time to time asked me to take a picture of groups of such patients, groups that he called *Equipe Syphilitique*.

Working conditions were extremely tiresome. The air was so humid that the condensed water on the tree leaves dripped, creating a constant shower in the forest. We could never see blue sky because of the high humidity. In addition to the hot and humid air, tiny insects and mosquitoes were a constant presence. It was too hot to wear long pants, so I wore shorts. To protect us from bites, David would prepare a basin with liquid soap. We would cover all open areas of our bodies with it, which formed an unpleasant film on the skin but was much more preferable than the annoying bites. Liquid soap was also a useful tool for self-protection against diseases because we did not have enough gloves to last through the length of our journey. After examining each patient, I would wash my hands in a basin with water and then cover them again with soap. Sometimes, I would cover my hands with iodine solution, particularly when performing a gynecological examination. I recall a pregnant woman who came to see me. Her skin was completely covered with a bright red substance. I learned that the red substance was a powder made from the bark of a specific tree and was mixed with palm oil; this protected her from insect bites. I was told that only pregnant women were allowed to use this protection.

Perhaps this restriction was introduced for the protection of the rare trees that had this power.

The prevalence of leprosy was quite significant in this area, and we identified many cases, even in children. There was clear evidence that it had recently spread after the patients with leprosy had been dismissed from the leprosaria less than two years before. They were left unattended in the war-torn country with no option of re-establishing the leprosariums. Most of the cases were a tuberculoid type of leprosy, which is relatively moderate in severity and is now easily treated with antimicrobials. During the entire period I spent in the Congo, I saw only one case of lepromatous manifestation with the classical "lion face" appearance. Another severe case was a young woman with a neurological manifestation affecting her arms. We were passing through one of the villages, and the local people stopped the truck and insisted we see a sick person. The woman was sitting at the threshold of her house with her arms lifted up, and she was constantly screaming and crying. She suffered from extreme pain in her forearms and could not tolerate any touch to her skin. I gave her intermediate strength painkillers from our supplies.

I saw several patients, mostly men, with skin ulcers on their legs and sometimes with missing toes and deformed feet. I made smears from these lesions, stained them, and examined them microscopically. In almost all the cases, I saw clumps of red-colored bacteria (called Acid-Fast Bacilli, or AFB, when the smear is stained by a method specific for this purpose) typical of the leprosy bacteria, *Mycobacterium leprae*. I thought these patients had leprosy. Retrospectively, I learned that perhaps I was wrong in my diagnosis in some cases. At that time, I did not know about another disease that is caused by related bacteria, *Mycobacterium ulcerans*, which causes the Buruli ulcer that is typical in some tropical countries. If I had had a more investigative mind and more time, I could have become one of the scientists who pioneered the description of this illness.

A common medical complaint of women in most villages was the inability to become pregnant. According to the custom, the husband had the right to send his wife back to her parents if she did not conceive within a couple of years. In addition to having more than one wife in the family, the men were quite promiscuous, which explained the very high prevalence of venereal diseases among them. Usually, infertility was caused by gonorrhea, and the only help I could provide during my short stay was the penicillin injections.

Some of the very large villages had a medical station. In one of them I met a young medical person, *feldsher*, a graduate from the nursing school in Leopoldville, who kept his job despite the disastrous situation in the country and irregularly paid wages. He was quite intelligent and knowledgeable in medicine, perhaps more so than David and Paul. He was proud of his assignment to help with the medical needs of his native village people. After finishing our two days of work, he approached me confidentially and asked for advice. He had been married already two years, but his wife still was not pregnant. Once, while visiting the city, he underwent an examination and was told that he had no fertility problem, causing him to assume that the problem was with his wife. So he asked me to examine his wife. My knowledge of gynecology was one of my lowest achievements in medical school in spite of the A grade I had received in all subjects. Nevertheless, a refusal to examine his wife would have been perceived as an insult and therefore was out of the question. Fortunately, during the examination (that was something I knew well how to properly perform, as an A student) I found something that could have explained the woman's unsuccessful attempts to conceive. Her uterus had a very significant retroflex, perhaps under an angle of 90%, which could block, according to my primitive thinking, the entry of sperm into the uterus. I shared this possibility with the husband who said that he, too, had noticed the same thing upon his own examination of his wife. What advice could I offer? First, I suggested that at the next opportunity he should take his wife to the city for a proper examination by a gynecologist. This was not a realistic proposition at that time because of ongoing military conflict and unlikely availability of specialized medical services, even in Leopoldville. In the meantime, what else could I recommend? He was so open that I entered into more intimate discussion about his sexual habits. He told me that the Africans, at least people of his tribe, have sex where men enter the woman from behind, or, as he said in French, *a la vache*, but he believed that this position was too animal-like, and as a cultured man he had sex only in the European missionary style.

I had to suggest something, so I proposed to this gentle young man, "Why don't you try the African style? Maybe in this position the uterus would come forward and your sperm would have a better chance to enter." I did not know whether my advice was sound, but I escaped a difficult situation, and I acted, perhaps, according to the standards of any other medicine man. The peculiar part of this episode was that, with my poor French, I had to ask Ludmila to help explain some of the sexual details. I have to admit that, along with some discomfort in this situation, I did have some fun observing the embarrassment of this aging, hypocritical virgin for whom any conversation about sex, even much more moderate than we had, was a taboo. After all, we had to comply with our medical duties, and I tried to maintain a most serious and concerned expression on my face! A year later, back in Moscow, I received a letter from David telling me that the couple had a newborn girl whom they named Leonida! Was it my contribution to an increase of the African population?

A much more dramatic situation occurred in another village when I was faced with work as an obstetrician. I had relatively good training in this field of medicine because I spent a whole month one summer after the fourth year of medical school in a large maternity hospital in Lubertsy, a city near Moscow. I was actually assigned to live in this hospital (along with two other students) because most births and associated events had taken place at night or early in the morning.

While staying in one of the large villages, in the middle of the night David woke me and requested that I go to a house where a woman was having difficulty giving birth. We entered the house (rather, a hut) filled with people. Some were sitting around talking and a group of children were observing the event from the upper level. It seemed that giving birth was a social event for the village. The woman was in a semi-sitting position, and two elderly women (perhaps local midwives) supported her. She looked exhausted. Not only the woman, but everybody else was sweating in the stuffy atmosphere in the house. I was told that the contractions had started about eight hours earlier. Upon examining the woman I could not detect the baby's heartbeat, and after some questioning, I learned that the mother's water had broken about two hours earlier. Alarmed, I asked David to explain to the people that the baby was already dead, and, therefore, it was too late for the doctor to do anything. The problem was, perhaps, that this woman had a very narrow pelvis, which was unusual for an African woman, and it was her first pregnancy. A half an hour later the baby emerged. I tied up and cut the umbilical cord and tried to revive the baby by alternately dipping it into cold and hot water, slapping, rubbing, and moving. Nothing helped! After a while there was a dead silence in the hut, and I could feel the angry looks. Clearly, it was felt that I was the one to blame for the misfortune. David stood in the center and started delivering a long speech, accompanied by many gestures, at times pointing at the woman, at the midwives, and at me. When we finally got home, David told me that the situation was very dramatic and dangerous. He had spoken to calm the people down and to remind them that I had already told them the baby was dead, and that such things happen when labor is so long and her water had broken before I came. Perhaps it was not so much his arguments, but the very long speech he made to these tired people that calmed their emotions.

There were many other less dramatic episodes of my medical practice in the jungle, one of which I remember very clearly. One day, in the late afternoon, a couple brought their seven- or eight-month-old child who had diarrhea and was dehydrated. They came from more than fifteen miles away, but there was no medical facility or any other place to accommodate them overnight in the small village where I stayed. Accommodations were made for them under a large tree. Paul brought some mattresses and blankets and some food for the parents. With his help, I arranged an intravenous infusion of an electrolyte solution that I had previously spotted in the supplies in one of the trunks we had inherited from the previous expeditions by the Belgians. I was amazed at having this solution in the middle of the jungle, while back in the Soviet Union they did not have standard IV fluids. In addition, there was quite a large supply of sterile IV-tubing systems to connect an inverted bottle to the vein. The system had a drip vial and a clamp to regulate the flow of the liquid. Some of the bottles were clearly labeled for treating dehydration caused by diarrhea in small children. How smart! Paul helped me to fix the needle at the baby's temple, and all I had to do was adjust the flow of the fluid. I started cautiously with a very slow drip, as it was suggested in the instruction on the bottle's label, and increased the rate subsequently. Starting at six PM I frequently looked in (every hour or so), using a flashlight to check the baby's status and the performance and safety of the IV system. I fell asleep around three AM, and during the night no one came to wake me up, as I had requested. When I woke up at six AM, I rushed to the tree to check on the family. They were gone, and the IV system was hanging on the tree branch. Paul told me that the baby was "fully recovered" and the family had left for home since they had to travel a long distance. So, I saved the life of a child using a Belgian-made apparatus for rehydration. It gave me certain satisfaction, but I was somewhat upset that the parents did not allow me a chance to check the child before they left.

6. Pygmies

The village of Belonge was at the end of the road from Oshwe, and we were to turn onto another road to visit more villages on the way back. On February 17 we were finishing our work in Belonge when suddenly it started to rain. In fact, it was pouring, a typical tropical rain. Immediately the veranda of our house was crowded with people who were coughing and sneezing. This was not a very pleasant situation, taking into account that, particularly in this village, many of our guests had leprosy, which is usually transmitted in this manner. Suddenly, through the noise of the rain, we heard the sounds of drums, and a row of about thirty children and five adults entered the village singing (*Singing in the Rain*, African style?) and carrying two flags. The group was a delegation from the Batwa tribe coming from villages beyond Belonge where no road was available. The new arrivals, wet and cold, joined the crowd on our veranda. The hostile reaction of the local people from the Kundu tribe was immediate. They backed off, leaving an empty space between themselves and the newcomers. The situation was tense. I approached the five adults and shook hands with them, ignoring the negative looks by the locals. Afterward, one of the adults who was wearing a full, dark suit, white shirt, and a black bowtie introduced himself in perfect French (obviously much better than mine) as a teacher of the school in the Batwa village. He also asked for a glass of water, and I directed our driver's wife to bring him a glass of water. She did so, but she handed the glass to me, and I gave it to the teacher, which was another gesture of acceptance of which the locals did not approve. Later on, the driver's wife insisted on breaking the glass because it had been defiled by the Batwa touch. Paul objected, saying that he would drink from the glass, as well as the doctor (me), and the mademoiselle (Ludmila). The aim of the visit by the Batwa was to invite us to their three villages and enlist our help with a large number of ill people. The teacher explained that his people could not come to Belonge because the hostile Kundu people would not allow them to stay overnight. I winked at Paul, who correctly understood my signal, and said, "Yes, we will come, but send strong men to carry our luggage." Paul also added that he considered Batwa equal to Kundu in all aspects, which was a final signal to both sides, making the visitors positively excited. The delegation left, walking in the rain while singing and dancing.

Batwa (*twa* with a prefix of *ba* means "people of") is one of the Pygmy tribes of Africa. Other groups of Pygmies are better known from popular literature. The three or four Bambuti (*Mbuti*) tribes (*Sua, Aka, efe*) of the Ituri forest are the shortest group of Pygmies, usually under 137 cm. (four feet, six inches) in height. Because of their dependence on natural resources and their hunting skills, they were called "the Forest People" by some authors. The Batwa, also short in stature but usually taller than the Bambuti, are called "Pygmoids" by some anthropologists, though they are genetically related to other Pygmies. For example, a guide who accompanied me while visiting the Batwa villages was even taller than I was. Most of the Batwa people live in Rwanda and Burundi, but some live in different parts of the Ituri forest. Only three villages were in the area bordering Belonge where I met them. All the pygmies, Bambuti and Batwa, are considered the ancient inhabitants of the continent, having lived there even before the last ice age and known to the ancient Egyptians around 2500 BCE. Throughout the centuries they were subjugated by Bantu tribes and pushed to the most remote areas of the forest, to places the Bantu people considered frightful and to be avoided.

We began preparations for our trip to the Batwa villages, which were not listed as mandatory by the health authorities on the list of villages assigned to our expedition. I was excited at this unusual opportunity, but immediately met with negative reactions from the local Kundu people regarding our intentions. While Paul and David were also enthusiastic, our driver (who had some administrative functions as well) and, particularly, his wife got into heated arguments with Paul and David.

It was a great honor to have the chief of the Belonge village to come to see me; and we had a lengthy conversation, albeit through two interpreters, Paul and Ludmila. He tried to convince me that it was wrong and very dangerous to visit the Batwa. He told me that no one ever went there from his village; he also said that the Batwa people were very wild, vicious, and dirty. Furthermore, he said they ate uncooked meat, and therefore smelled awful. There were even vague threats that our visit to the Batwa may cause some mysterious spell of misfortune to befall his people. I assured him that none of his people would go with us, and Ludmila was not going either, and that I was counting on his kindness to take care of her safety while we were gone.

Ludmila and I also learned that complete separation from the Batwa was very stringently observed, and close contact with them (for example, sexual interaction) usually led to the expulsion of the violator from the village and even from the tribe. Batwa people were not allowed to take water from wells used by Kundu or even approach such wells, and they had to avoid any physical contact. Batwa would yield to a Kundu person should they happen to meet on the forest trail.

In the afternoon the driver came to me and threatened to leave because our expedition was already extended; he would return to Oshwe, he said. I invited him to dinner, and with David's help I finally convinced him to stay a few more days. That was a day full of political maneuvering in the middle of the jungle.

The next morning, another Batwa man came to visit us. He was a pastor, a spiritual leader of the local Batwa people, and an old acquaintance of David, who introduced him as his good friend. He was a short man, perhaps five feet tall in full regalia. He explained the difficulties the isolated Batwa villages were facing, and that our visit would not only help with health care, but also may lead to a breakthrough in alleviating their isolation. I promised him that we would do our best. We continued our routine work. It was a difficult day. People from other places near Belonge brought their children with whooping cough complicated with pneumonia, and we were quite busy examining them and administering penicillin injections.

Again, a row of Batwa children entered the village in the same manner as the previous day. This time the weather was bright and warm. The Batwa children entered the square in front of our residence. They formed a circle around four children: a conductor, who was a ten- or eleven-year-old boy; two boys with drums; and one with a very unusual trumpet. I had an opportunity to witness this most interesting performance, which was later repeated in a different style in the Batwa village.

This performance in the middle of a Kundu village had a clear political purpose: to demonstrate that the Batwa people, even their children, were intelligent enough to stage a whole show. The show was about the need for unity among the people of the newly independent country and contained some cautious critique of traditional tribalism. Children who played various roles, such as a white Belgian man (in a tropical helmet) and representatives of various local tribes, demonstrated their obvious performing talents. The most impressive were the dances and songs. The songs were unique and very different from what I had heard before in other villages. Previously I had an opportunity to attend some of the evening meetings of the villagers when they discussed their communal problems. At the meetings, usually held in the evening, people would sit in a circle, sometimes around a campfire, and most of the "discussions" were presented in songs, with a "speaker" who would enter the center of the circle and make a point through dance, gestures, and songs. What the Batwa children presented was quite unique in the quality, harmony, emotional expression, and overall performance. I was left with the impression that Batwa children definitely had musical talent.

The teacher told me that the trumpet used by an older boy (fifteen- or sixteen-years-old) was a unique tribal instrument made of special wood and was only used for sacred mystical purposes. During my conversation with the teacher I learned that twelve or fifteen years ago a Swedish missionary had taken him and the pastor to Sweden as children, where they received their education. They were then brought back to this area as adults.

Early in the morning, before sunrise, a group of fourteen Batwa men came to carry our luggage and to take us to their villages. They took all our seven, large, heavy, iron-reinforced trunks on sturdy wooden rails that they brought with them. They also offered to carry me in a chair placed on wooden rails, but, naturally, I refused. I was very impressed with the physical strength of these relatively short men, especially when they took the trunks and *started running*. Paul, David, two Batwa guides, and I could not keep up with them and walked at our own pace. The total hike to the first Batwa village took more than three hours. After we entered the jungle, the narrow road became a trail, often overgrown with vegetation and sometimes swampy. The forest was full of monkeys jumping noisily through the trees. Birds also made noise, but the loudest noise came from the frogs in the swamps. The fresh elephant and antelope dung on the trail was always covered with many large, colorful butterflies that were not scared away by our approach. The air was extremely humid and condensation dripped from the trees. We were sweating profusely, and after the first hour of brisk walking, our clothes were drenched with perspiration. We had to keep moving because if we stopped, it would increase the probability of being bitten by insects.

At the end of our walk, as we neared the villages, we saw fields of manioca and banana plants; some individuals appeared out of nowhere once we entered the Batwa land. One hunter laid down his bow, arrows, and a few heavy timbers he was carrying when saw us approaching. He stepped to the side of the trail and greeted us by saying *"Mbote,"* or "Hello" in the Kundu language. We also saw a few women carrying heavy baskets with manioca and bananas on their heads. They not only stepped off the trail, but also tried to merge completely into the forest. The facial features of the people we met were quite different from the Kundu; the main difference was in the shape of their noses, which were straight, sometimes even aquiline, instead of flat. This difference was most noticeable in the females. It was obvious that we were being watched. From time to time the sound of drums could be heard from somewhere in the jungle—most likely an African telegraph sending messages about our arrival.

Contrary to what we experienced on the trail, there were no signs of shyness when we met the people of the first village. A large crowd of almost-naked people came running from their huts to see the unusual sight of a white man and two Kundu people. For some of them, the appearance of Kundu in their village was perhaps more surprising than the sight of a white person. Many small children who had never seen a white man became frightened as I approached and ran crying to their mothers. We were escorted to a newly built (for us) hut. Inside, to our great surprise, was a round table loaded with a variety of fruits and four modern soft chairs! The hut had two entrances, which provided a pleasant cross breeze. After a short rest and recovery from our hike, the sound of music lured us outside. The group of children we had already met appeared in front of our hut. This time it was not a politically motivated show, as it had been in Belonge, but a show designed to entertain us!

This time the dances and the music were even more impressive. The performers put on a dramatized show, a pantomime, about human life, a comedy depicting a relationship between a crooked man and a naïve man. Again, the music was mysterious, and I wonder whether it was ever properly recorded. The sounds from the drums were different from those brought to Belonge. Long hollow tree trunks were the traditional Congo drums used for producing both music and sending messages. We could have watched this show forever, but our time was limited. It was already afternoon, and we had work to do. The ambulatory work was arranged in the school, a large hut with a roof made of banana leaves, with two real blackboards and wood planks that served as benches. During the remaining two hours of the day, Paul and I examined more than twenty patients affected with leprosy, tuberculosis, malaria, and all types of skin ulcers. Severe cases of TB were obvious even with a cursory physical examination, and a few patients were in very bad condition. Paul said that there was no way we could send them to Oshwe for further treatment. We did not see a single case of syphilis or gonorrhea among the patients we examined, perhaps a benefit of their enforced isolation from other African tribes.

In the evening I walked around the village to explore the Batwa lifestyle, as requested by the Belgian Institute for Tropical Diseases. The setting of households and the design of the houses were not different from those in the Kundu villages, though they appeared much cleaner and better organized. The Batwa were known as skillful hunters who used bow and arrows but no firearms, and their houses had special places to preserve meat. Most houses had a supply of honey that was collected from the forest. Every man had two or three wives, and the family structure was not different from what I had previously observed. Women were in charge of harvesting banana and manioca plants, food preparation, caring for the children, and helping their husbands in the hunts.

Contrary to the rumors spread about the Batwa by the Kundu, they did not eat raw meat, and the hygiene of their facilities was superior to the Kundu villages. With the help of my guide, a man who was approximately my height or perhaps somewhat taller (a giant among the pygmies), I went to investigate the sources of water. A group of children accompanied us, carrying and placing boards and logs on the trail to help pass through the swamps. The water wells were not open streams or brooks but small springs producing clean, cold water. I could not find any snails, which are the natural hosts of *schistosomes*, parasites belonging to the genus *Schistosoma*. It seemed likely that the water used by the Batwa was not infested with these parasites.

The next day we continued our work with the patients, and then the pastor came from his home in the second village. He told us that many patients needed medical attention in his village, and that some people from the nearby third village were also at his place in anticipation of our visit. Paul and I took a short ride on bicycles on a solid trail to the pastor's village and spent most of the day there, while David continued working in the first village. In the afternoon my work was finished, and I decided to go back to

Belonge. Paul and David had to stay in the Batwa village for two more days to administer treatments that I prescribed to several patients. Two Batwa guides accompanied me on the three-hour walk through the jungle to Belonge—one in front of me (the tall man) and another behind me. We arrived after dark, and my guides immediately turned around and went back. Walking through the jungle at dusk and in the dark is not a very pleasant experience. Although it was a cooler day than during the previous hike, there were more mosquito attacks, so I constantly had to apply the repellent ointment (which was possible thanks to less sweating). The forest fell silent at dusk, but then became alive in the dark with a full range of new sounds. Sometimes, the guides would stop and listen to the voices of the jungle. Distant lightning and sounds of thunder enhanced the mystery of the jungle at night.

Back in Belonge, I had to again calm the driver down and convince him to wait for David and Paul's return by inviting him to share meals with Ludmila and I. I learned that inviting him for a meal or a drink was a useful way to avert a confrontation. It works not only in Africa but in industrialized countries as well. Perhaps it is useful even today in the U.S. when one has to address his bosses.

Finally, we started our drive back to Oshwe. On the way we visited a few more villages and met the rescue expedition by Domenique Nkwa, with whom we returned to Oshwe. My work was over, and the leader of our group, Dr. Kuzmitchev, decided that Yelena and I could go back to Moscow, while the other three would stay behind until they heard from the Soviet authorities. In about a week, we had a farewell party with some drinks using our ethanol supply to make some vodka, which David hardly tolerated.

7. Farewell, Congo

A week after my return from the jungle, Yelena and I boarded a steamboat. Paul joined us for the trip to Leopoldville. It took three or four days to travel through three rivers, and there were no noteworthy events during this trip. In Leopoldville, Yelena and I stayed in the same building, which now hosted the Soviet Embassy with a red flag posted outside. Our mission was accomplished! With Yelena's help, I prepared a report about the expedition to the Ituri forest to be submitted by the Soviet Embassy to the government of Congo. The contrast between the living conditions in this modern city and the environment we experienced when traveling through the Itury forest was dramatic. My general impression was that the conditions of life, the cultural setting, and the social structure in areas we visited were not much different from those experienced by Livingston and Stanley more than hundred years before us. I even had a temptation to entitle my report "In Livingstone's and Stanley's Steps," imitating the title of the famous Stanley report about Livingstone.

After our arrival in Leopoldville, Paul disappeared. He did not come to visit us at the Embassy as promised, and we never heard from him again. On the other hand, back in Moscow I received a letter from David thanking me for my friendship and for the Russian watch I had given him as a farewell gift. He also mentioned in his letter about a baby girl named Leonida, in my honor, born in a distant village, and gratitude for my advice expressed by the parents.

From Leopoldville, Yelena and I flew on the Belgian airline, Sabena, to Brussels, where we had to wait for two days for the Soviet airline's Aeroflot flight to Moscow. To make this unscheduled stop in Brussels and to enter the city, we needed to obtain police visas. Yelena was very uncomfortable about that because she said she had previously visited Belgium under a different name... We could not stay in the airport as she suggested, and finally we were escorted to the police office in charge of such arrangements. There we faced a high-ranking officer in a uniform, a very tall man with red hair and a large mustache. Looking at our passports, he became very sarcastic and asked Yelena, "Well, you are coming from *our* Congo and you state that you are a nurse assisting this doctor, but why does he have a regular ("red") civilian passport, and you, his assistant, have a diplomatic ("green") passport? Do you need more protection than he does?" He definitely realized that Yelena was not just a nurse; he said that he was giving us a forty-eight-hour visa but suggested that Yelena not become involved in any business activities in Brussels.

The stop in Brussels gave us an opportunity to see the city (for me it was the first time in a Western city), to obtain our currency from the bank as payment for our work, and to spend this money on various goods. Those two days were very nicely spent and became the source of many stories I told my friends back in Moscow. In turn, this caused them to tease me sometimes, particularly in response to any of my criticism, with phrases like, "Of course, it is not like in Brussels."

Finally, we were back at home, and I had to undergo a long treatment for malaria and filariosis infections that I contracted in Africa. Overall, visiting Congo was a once in a lifetime opportunity to learn about another world and to better understand our own world and our own country, the Soviet Union.

CHAPTER SEVEN

Homo Sovieticus

"A real friend is one who walks in when the rest of the world walks out."

Walter Winchell

1. A party
2. Friendship Developed
3. Kabardino-Balkaria
4. Who was Bezirov?
5. People of Kabardino-Balkaria

Fig. 28. A party: Soviet elite group gathering in mountains. *Drawing by Edward Tabachnik.*

Fig. 29. In the Mt. Elbrus region (left to right, top to bottom):
- Hotel Itkol;
- With Bezirov (on the right) and director of the hotel (on the left) in front of the Itkol hotel;
- Herman (on the left) with Bezirov at Elbrus, with a local man (between Herman and Bezirov) and a local woman; and
- With Herman on the last trip to Elbrus.

Fig. 30. Balkarian experience (left to right):
- **Balkars' village;**
- **Balkarian children;**
- **Michael with the Balkarian peasants (1970); and**
- **Michael (in center) with Mars and Dr. Dmitry Kushnaryov, a friend from the Metchnikov Institute with whom we planned our emigration to the US, 1974.**

Fig. 31. In the Caucasus Mountains (left to roght):
- **At the Cheget mountain;**
- **At the main Caucasus range;**
- **With Herman in the high country; and**
- **Helping the local peasants (in the background is Michael and his future wife Helen).**

1. A Party

Guards wearing special security forces uniforms inspected each vehicle thoroughly as they approached the canyon entrance of this remote place. Approximately three miles down the road, beautifully placed amid tall, stately evergreen trees rising from the canyon floor stands a three-story hotel building on the slope of a mountain at the end of the canyon. It is a quiet and remote area with snowy peaks and glaciers surrounding the little valley, the sort of place meant for relaxation and self-indulgence.

The men begin to arrive early in anticipation of another memorable weekend. As each one enters the lobby of the hotel, the concierge (who is also a security officer) greets them personally. He knows why they are all here. For his careful consideration and discretion, the concierge and two of his assistants will be amply rewarded at the end of the event. Each guest is escorted to a luxury suite and then to the designated general meeting room. The meeting room is large and filled with opulent furnishings, which includes several plush velvet sofas and chairs arranged for intimate conversations. Elegant Persian and famous locally handmade rugs grace wooden floors. The imported crystal chandeliers cast a mellow glow in the mahogany-paneled room. Strains from soft music permeate the atmosphere, adding to the richness of the surroundings. The hotel has many beautiful rooms, but this particular room is the grandest of them all, and it is where a particular group of powerful men meet from time to time. The grandeur of the room is overshadowed only by its history of mystery and intrigue.

The group of men is quite ethnically diverse and is comprised of Russians and representatives of two local ethnic groups, the Kabardin and the Balkars. Each man is impeccably groomed. His suit is hand tailored from the highest quality of fabric and his shoes are of best leather. His jewelry is understated, consisting only of a gold watch, gold cuff links, and the flag pin on the lapels of those who are members of the government's Supreme Council. They congregate in small groups; some are playing billiards, some are playing cards, while others are seated around small tables talking. Regardless of their cultural differences, the men partake of the food and liquor before them. Large crystal bowls are filled with black caviar just delivered from the nearby Caspian Sea. They drink vodka, beer, wine, champagne, and cognac from fine crystal glasses. The gourmet food is eaten with gleaming sterling utensils.

Soon a special bus from the city arrives with a group of elegantly dressed, diamond-bedecked women. The unmistakable fragrance of expensive perfume wafts through the room. The women have been carefully selected for this occasion. The weekend is now underway. The women begin to move around the room smiling and making conversation with the men. After a little small talk and more food and liquor, couples discreetly disappear to the private suites. Each private room is luxuriously decorated and there is a refrigerator stocked with champagne, black caviar, and other unusual items. The bathrooms have private little saunas and round Jacuzzi-type bathtubs.

This is not a fictional story. Despite some similarities, it is not taken from any modern movies about the Mafia or Japanese corporations in the United States. In fact, it is my recollection of a party that took place in the former Soviet Union in 1978. The setting is in Kabardino-Balkaria, which, at that time, was one of the autonomous Soviet republics. (It has been one of the constituent republics of The Russian Federation since 1992.) The "hotel" was a special resort in a well-guarded area near the famous twin-headed Mt. Elbrus, which sometimes served as a retreat for high-ranking local and coming-from-Moscow Soviet officials.

2. Friendship Developed

My attendance at the above-described event happened under very peculiar circumstances. In 1978, I applied for immigration from the Soviet Union. This move placed me in the vulnerable position of a *persona non-grata*. To avoid potential danger and harassment from the KGB in Moscow, my son Herman and I spent a lot of time in the Caucasus Mountains and stayed at the Itkol, a resort hotel. We were invited to stay there by my good old friend Nukh (Noah) Bezirov, who was in charge of the whole area around Mt. Elbrus.

This story is actually about Noah. It is a story about a good and decent person who had to adjust to the Soviet system to survive and to be successful. There are many statements in the literature about the mystery of Russia and Russian character. I submit that since 1917 there have been no Russian characters anymore; they were replaced with Soviet characters. Also, I believe that there is no mystery about either Russian or Soviet character if one makes efforts to understand the nature of the past system and how it changed the nature of people, either of Russian origin or of any other ethnic group in the Soviet Empire. People were melted into a very specific brand of species, *Homo Sovieticus*, labeled as such by those who secretly opposed the system. The main feature of *Homo Sovieticus* was complete separation of deeds, words, and thoughts. My friend Noah unwillingly became one of these characters and description of my interaction with him may shed some light on the mystery of the Soviet character.

I met Bezirov more than ten years before the above-described elaborate party. I met him during one of my summer hiking trips to the Caucasus Mountains. One of the local people at the hotel approached me in the lobby and asked, "Doctor, can I talk to you privately?" Although we went to another room at a suitable distance from any unwanted ears, he still continued to whisper, " I am talking to you on behalf of my boss, Noah Bezirov, whom you met last year." I said, "Yes, I remember him—he was kind enough to accommodate me when I arrived without a reservation. We even became friends after he learned about my interest in this country and his people." The man continued, "Bezirov is very ill now and asks that you visit him as soon as possible at his home in Nalchik." After I accepted the invitation, he informed me that Bezirov had already sent his car to take me to city of Nalchik.

After a two-hour drive on mountainous roads and the chauffeur's attempts to entertain me with stories about the places we passed, we reached the capital of Kabardino-Balkaria. I was taken to Bezirov's apartment, where Bezirov, his pleasant Armenian wife, and their teenage son greeted me. Immediately, the reason for my visit was apparent. Bezirov was frightened as he told me that he had contracted tuberculosis.

There is a prejudice among many Muslim people that tuberculosis is not only a deadly disease but also a shameful illness. Bezirov, who was Kabardin, a member of a large Muslim ethnic group, was not free of this prejudice despite his erudition. He was overwhelmed by two fears: one was that he would soon die, and the other was that his friends and relatives might learn that he had this shameful illness. It was the latter that prompted the secrecy by which I was summoned to his home. When I examined his x-rays and other medical data I realized that he had *tuberculoma*, a form of tuberculosis that is quite difficult to treat.

Fortunately, I was able to find a perfect solution to the problem. He would travel to Moscow with me, and I would arrange for him to be hospitalized where I worked at the Central Institute for Tuberculosis. Bezirov was hospitalized for a whole year. Thanks to the outstanding efforts of his attending physician, my good friend Dr. Karachunsky, he was cured of his "shameful" disease. During his hospitalization I would find Nukh waiting for me at the main entrance of the building each day at 5:00 PM when I finished work. The institute was located in a large forest park in Jauza, a suburb of Moscow. We walked the trails of this forest, and each time the primary topic of our conversation was his condition.

Nukh was a short, stocky man with a round face, which showed a few features of the local tribes. When I see James Gandolfini as Tony Soprano, I am reminded of Bezirov, and sometimes for reasons beyond mere physical resemblance. Bezirov was not athletic at all and had a large belly, which contracted during his illness. After his recovery he regained his girth, and his chauffeur, who saw this progress when he visited him from time to time in Moscow, exclaimed, "I am so happy—indeed you now look like a boss again!"

Before the recovery and almost every day during our walks through the forest, I had to continually reassure him that he was not going to die. Each time I had to tell him that the treatment was progressing successfully, and he might not need surgery (often required for this form of tuberculosis). After calming his fears, the topics of our discussions ranged broadly from his personal life and interests to the criticism of Russian domination in his people's region. I had the opportunity to learn about the history and problems of the Northern Caucasus and the tribes living there. Before he became a high-ranking official, Bezirov had been a history teacher. He was extremely knowledgeable on issues and events, including those outside the bounds of Soviet censorship. These conversations could only occur in an atmosphere of strong mutual trust.

3. Kabardino-Balkaria

One of the frequent topics of our conversation was the history of Bezirov's native region. Ethnic groups and tribes of diverse origin with more than fifty languages (and, by some accounts, possibly exceeding one hundred) populated the large area between the Caspian Sea on the east and the Caucasus Mountains and the Black Sea on the west. They represent remnants of the movement of people for centuries from Siberia and Central Asia, including conquests by the Alans, Huns, Khazars, Arabs, Mongols, Persians, Ottoman Turks, and Russians. Most of the local population became Sunni Muslims. Again, the variability of ethnic groups is very broad, including the Mountain Jews, or Tats, in Dagestan, who are believed to be descendants of the Jewish Khazars. The area was under Russian control beginning in the mid-sixteenth century and experienced a significant influx of Russian people, especially after the bloody suppression of the twenty-year rebellion led in the mid-nineteenth century by Imam Shamil, the Dagestani religious militant leader. Ethnic Russians (mostly Cossacks) constitute 30–60% of the population, predominantly in the urban settings.

Shamil was a hero to Bezirov even though he was an Imam and an ethnic Avar; Bezirov was Kabardin and not particularly religious. During the 1970s many local people secretly viewed Shamil as a legend, simply because of his stand against Russian dominance. Bezirov was not exempt from these nationalistic sentiments, and he proudly talked about the great nation of Adyghe (the original name of the Kabardin) and more so about the possibility of the restoration of "Great Adygea." He spoke of incorporating Kabardian with other related groups existing under various names in other republics. Remarkably, at the same time, he also viewed the Shamil's war for independence from the Russians simply as an historic fact and considered the coexistence and collaboration with Russians as a positive aspect for his people and the region. I imagine that if Bezirov were alive today, he would surely condemn the terrorist activities of the Chechen leaders, as do most of the current leaders in Kabardino-Balkaria and other neighboring republics.

4. Who Was Bezirov?

The Soviet authorities skillfully used people like Bezirov, people with nationalistic feelings who were also loyal to the system of Russian dominance. Once they sent Bezirov as head of a delegation to Jordan and Syria, along with other prominent individuals of his republic, to establish cultural ties with a significant population of the Kabardian (often under the name of "Cherkess") in these and other Arab countries. In the past, Shamil himself was allowed by the Russian government to immigrate to Medina in Saudi Arabia. With pride, Bezirov told me how millions of his people (according to him) were respected and were successful in Arab countries and in Iran. It is quite possible that some members of his delegation were in charge of recruiting Soviet agents among the groups with whom they visited. Nevertheless, whether it is true or not, Bezirov's mission was considered a success by the authorities.

During the entire year of his hospitalization, it was said in his hometown that he was attending special continuing education classes in the field of tourism in Moscow. Therefore, the big secret of his illness was not revealed, and he returned home cured and with no record of having a shameful disease. The gratitude of this man was beyond limits. From then on, I was no longer just an ordinary tourist visiting my favorite area in the Caucasus Mountains. To the local people I was known as Bezirov's doctor." Each time I arrived at Itkol, the hotel's staff greeted me and my group as VIPs and provided us with free accommodations in this luxurious hotel.

Once I experienced Nukh's anger and learned that this well-educated and balanced man could have a surge of strong emotion. He came to me and said, "I have learned that you have bought the food coupons and are dining in the cafeteria. Why are you turning down my hospitality? I have arranged that you and members of your group dine in a special room for the management of this place. Please don't buy any coupons; it is insulting to me. By the way, the food in this room is not only free and available any time you choose, but it is also of the highest quality and is prepared by an expert chef." I apologized profusely, and afterward, with some embarrassment, began dining for free in a special place reserved for administration of the hotel.

From time to time, Bezirov would call me in Moscow and suggest that if I could not come to visit myself, then I should send some of my friends who were also accommodated at a place not usually available to most Soviet citizens. All the hotels in this area were under the supervision of the famous KGB-controlled "Intourist," the Soviet agency for foreign visitors. Every summer I would go with my friends to start hiking from Itkol. For a week or two, we would go through the wilderness over a number of mountain passes and visit places where no regular Soviet tourist would go. Some Russian tourists, hikers, and mountain climbers kept asking how we dared go to these dangerous places where the locals were known to kill and rob Russian visitors. They didn't know our secret: at any place in the wilderness, any shepherd or any other representative of the local tribes knew that I was a friend of Bezirov. Often in the wilderness some of them would greet us and invite us to the huts or tents and offer us bread, goat cheese, and the delicious milk-derived drink called *airan*. We were safe. We belonged there!

Bezirov's title was Chairman of the Elbrus Tourist Region. As such, he reported directly to the Central Office of Intourist in Moscow, which actually was under control of the KGB. At the same time, he maintained proper relationships with local authorities and local Communist bosses. According to the unwritten rules, every local business in this area serving the needs of tourists— such as restaurants, kiosks, shishkabob stands, etc.—had to be registered and meet Bezirov's personal approval. Though no private enterprise in the Soviet Union officially existed, in reality, all these businesses were run as private enterprises. That meant each business had to pay Bezirov in cash ("envelopes") for their continued existence, and the profit was not reported to the government. The wealth and the amount of money of this system probably exceeded any profit produced by racketeering in America or any other Western country. It was a network entrenched in bribery and corruption that had attained a status close to official sanction. Bezirov also had to give a significant portion of his profits to the local authorities and probably to some bosses in Moscow as well. All these activities created a system much more powerful and entrenched than any known Mafia family in the U.S. People in this system, high-ranking officials as well as lower-level managers, were tightly interconnected and interdependent. It was a true Soviet-style Mafia, but at the same time, it also meshed well with the feudal traditions of the region. Bezirov had a reputation with the local people as a fair and often charitable man. He was frequently noted for quietly helping families through troubled times, and he was available to those in need, either economically or politically. It was known among both Kabardin and Balkars alike that he never harmed anyone, and, at any given time, he was asked by many to facilitate conflict resolution, particularly in regard to "business activities."

It is interesting to note that there were almost no national uprisings, underground movements, or anything resembling today's Chechen terrorism. As Bezirov explained to me, peace was established through balanced appointments of representatives from the three major ethnic groups to various positions in the local government, the Communist party, management, manufacturing, education, etc., each reflective of their proportion in the population (Kabardian—50%, Russians—35%, and Balkar—15%). Even within the local KGB, positions were clearly determined on the basis of ethnic origin. If anyone was dismissed or died, then someone of the same ethnic group filled his position. Remarkably there were no conflicts between the Kabardian and Balkars, despite the fact that in 1943 Stalin deported the whole nation of Balkars (about 60,000 people) to Central Asia, along with a few other ethnic groups, accusing them of collaboration with the Nazis during the German occupation of this area. In 1956 the Balkars returned to their destroyed villages and restarted their lives. No negative feelings by Balkars toward the Kabardian (more favored by Stalin) have ever been noted. Most recently, some villages have been found to have a mixed population of both people.

As Bezirov told me, at that time, at each level of the governmental structure (particularly with the KGB) there were Russian individuals who had an unwritten duty to report local events to an office in Moscow. The only concerns the Moscow government had were political stability and loyalty; private entrepreneurial activity, economic corruption, and the bribery system were overlooked as long as there were no apparent scandals and everybody knew his place. It was a near-perfect combination of Soviet colonialism with a special style of Mafia-type activities and local feudal traditions. My friend Bezirov was a part of this system, and I must admit that by accepting his favors, such as guarantees of safety during the mountain hikes and free hotel accommodations, I also became a part of it.

Through the eyes of current standards and ethics this situation was far from kosher, but at that particular time and in the reality of existence in the Soviet Union, things did not look so bad. After all, people lived peacefully and the people of this area were much better off economically than in other parts of Russia. Regardless of his personal feelings, Bezirov had no choice in being a part of this system. Based on the trust that developed between us, I had the unique opportunity to learn the most interesting personal and social issues that had never become common knowledge.

Some recent changes in this republic with a generally peaceful history have surprised some observers. In October of 2005 I visited Moscow and learned from the local newspapers that a group of about two hundred young people, mostly Kabardian, recruited by Islamic fundamentalists, Chechens, and maybe some foreigners (Arabs), attacked the police stations and other places in Nalchik City. Most of these militarily inexperienced young people were killed by the police. The leaders escaped. In accordance with Russian law, the bodies of those who were identified as terrorists were not given to the families. Denying a proper funeral can cause the Muslim families more grief than the death itself. It caused near rebellion by the local people and wide coverage in the Russian newspapers; however, it appears that the Russians may have discovered a tool to intimidate potential suicide-bombing fanatics who were penetrating this and other Muslim regions.

5. Visiting with People of Kabardino-Balkaria

I started visiting the Elbrus region along with some of my family members and my friends quite often, usually every summer and sometimes during the winter. Bezirov frequently visited us in Moscow. Several events that occurred during this approximate ten-year period of our lives are useful in understanding Bezirov as a typical representative, not only of prominent members of the Soviet hierarchy in general, but also as a member of a particular group of people in that historic period.

During some of my trips to the Elbrus region, Bezirov would broaden my education with visits to the local Kabardin or Balkar families, who were mostly engaged in agriculture. There were usually large family gatherings to discuss their planning and sales. Most typical occupations of the Kabardin, who resided mainly in the plains, were corn harvesting and horse breeding; the predominant occupation of the Balkar who lived in the mountains was the care of their sheep and Angora goats, as well the processing of wool and knitwear. Balkar villages, with houses constructed from rocks, were often located on high cliffs, accessible only by hazardous dirt roads.

A typical gathering consisted of men sitting in a large circle on the floor being served tea and food. Sometimes a teapot contained vodka colored with tea, and only a few of the participants consumed this product. Muslims are not supposed to drink alcohol, but this law was not strongly observed by the majority of the middle-aged men. Others tolerated this violation, but the bottle of vodka was not exposed on the table for fear that it might offend some of the men. One element of these gatherings that most impressed me was the respect for age. With each arriving person, some would stand to welcome the new guest while others greeted the new arrival from a seated position. It was explained to me that only those younger than the new guest were obliged to stand. The eldest member of the family was seated at the head of the circle, and at the end of each discussion, the group would seek his final approval. Of course, it was a formal gesture, and often the man was too old to grasp the points of the discussion. Nonetheless, it was a strongly observed and beautiful ritual that imparted a tradition of cultural grace to the younger generation.

After his illness and successful recovery, Bezirov became obsessed with the power of antibiotics and started using them loosely for any illness or disorder. He would listen to me while visiting Moscow and stop this abuse for a while, but then back at home he would ignore warnings about the potential side effects of these drugs. One of these side effects was a severe complication of the digestive system, which eventually led to his death several years after I emigrated from the country. In the meantime, he developed a fear that he may have a severe undiagnosed illness, and during each trip to Moscow he asked me to continue testing him for various diseases. Once he became suspicious that he had syphilis and perhaps had already infected his wife, who recently had started feeling ill. I knew well that he was very loyal to his wife, but he argued that he might have gotten infected before his marriage. About three or four times during his visits to Moscow, I took his blood sample for informal submission under my name (quite an embarrassing situation) to my colleagues in a VD laboratory. Each time the results were negative, and that finally convinced him, but he did not stop the abuse of antibiotics.

Then came the final period of our most interesting and controversial relationship. I applied for emigration from the Soviet Union to Israel with my son Herman and felt obligated to cease all interactions with my friends to avoid potentially dangerous exposure for being associated with me. Nukh started calling, worrying that the season had started and that I was not coming to hike. I could not provide a proper explanation over the telephone, which, at that time, was most likely tapped. I told him the truth later when he came to Moscow in person. He was outraged! It wasn't the fact that I was emigrating, which was then considered by many as a betrayal of the country. He was outraged that I could think about him in that manner and that I would consider disassociating myself from him. This was not the case! He said, "Leonid, how could you think of me, your loyal friend, that I would not understand your reasons? I know that as a Jew, the Russian authorities have humiliated you. They are not capable of understanding that your emigration would be a significant loss for the country." He firmly stated that the most important thing was that we were friends—this overrides everything else. He was sorry I did not share my plans with him in advance. He suggested that he would find a better solution for me than emigration, perhaps moving from Moscow to the city of Nalchik, where he would arrange a position for me as the chairman of the Department of Microbiology at the local medical school. Fortunately or unfortunately, it was too late, and he insisted that Herman and I should now come to Itkol to rest before our journey. When I mentioned my concern about the mandatory registration at the hotel controlled by the KGB and full of foreigners, he simply said that we were not going to be registered and would stay there in his personal suite. This generous offer was extremely welcome since I had to hide Herman from the potential army draft, which was a trick often used by Soviet authorities to punish young people and prevent their emigration.

We had a wonderful time in Itkol. We visited Mt. Elbrus (5642 m) for the last time as well as other beautiful places and just relaxed. One day Bezirov told me that he wanted to take me to an interesting party, but this time without Herman. Nukh learned that I had no formal clothing with me, so he borrowed some. I was puzzled. This was quite an unusual requirement. It wasn't until we were in the car driving to this party that he told me about the nature of this gathering. The "big shots" from Moscow had come to inspect the local tourist activities and members of the local government, and, of course, the local KGB were coming to entertain their bosses because it was expected. I expressed my concern that maybe he should not take me to such a party. "What if they learn that I am going to immigrate to Israel?" I asked him. His reply was, "Don't worry. I know what I am doing."

We arrived at the hotel described at the beginning of this story, and it was clear that Bezirov was the host of this place, exhibiting his extreme hospitality to all his important guests. Immediately he took me around the room and introduced me to his guests as "this great physician from Moscow who saved my life." Among the individuals he introduced me to were the head of the Communist Party of the Kabardino-Balkarian Republic, the chairman of the local government, and… the head of the KGB! I took a moment at a break and inquired of him, "Nukh, are you crazy introducing me to the KGB man as your friend?" He started laughing and said, "Listen, Leonid, I am also a KGB man, but we are friends, and, as I told you many times, that is what is important! Besides, we all are here to have a good time, and we don't do any business at this place. Join the party and have fun." When I recovered from the shock, I managed to join the party crowd.

Attending the party was the last time I saw Nukh Bezirov, but after almost thirty years, my memory of this unusual man is still alive. He was a member of the KGB, but personal relationships were more important to him than his duties. He was a member of the Communist Party, but he never believed in its ideology. He was a Muslim, but he was not religious. He had definite nationalistic feelings as a Kabard, but he believed in joint arrangements and benefits for his people under Russian dominance. To this man, I owe the valuable experience of being immersed into a most unusual environment, learning about the Kabardin people, and most importantly, experiencing true friendship. I tell this story to honor the memory of and to pay tribute to the most extraordinary character I ever knew, a good and kind man, although a typical *Homo Sovieticus*—to my great friend Nukh (Noah) Bezirov!

CHAPTER EIGHT

Dangerous Assignment

"In a time of universal deceit, telling the truth becomes a revolutionary act."

George Orwell

"The truth will set you free. But first, it will piss you off."

Gloria Steinem

1. A Report from Behind the Iron Curtain
2. General Facts about the Efficacy of Vaccines
3. Vaccine for Bacteriological Warfare
4. In Tajikistan
5. In Dushanbe, Capital of Tajikistan
6. Clinical (Field) Trial with a Typhoid Aerosolized Vaccine
7. Back in Moscow
8. Outcome

1. A Report from Behind the Iron Curtain

The Isle of Man, which is located off the west shore of England, is not one of the most important places on earth. One distinctive feature of this remote area is that it is where the unique tail-less cats live. There are several legends about the origin of these peculiar animals. I have never visited the Isle of Man, but some events that occurred there have played an important role in my life.

Even less noticeable than the isle itself was the fourteenth Congress of the International Association of Biological Standardization, which took place there in 1975. A scientist from Hungary, Dr. Ishtwan Joo, gave a presentation on behalf of a group of Russian scientists (my group) reporting the results of a double-blind, placebo-controlled field trial using inhaled administration of a typhoid vaccine. Had anyone paid attention, they would have questioned some of the strange circumstances of this presentation. One question would have been why was a Hungarian scientist presenting these findings rather than the Russian authors? It should have been alarming that the double-blind trial methodology, appearing in the West in the 1960s, had already been done in Russia during the clinical (field) trial in 1963.

But the most extraordinary matter was that the typhoid vaccine had been developed for inhaled (aerosol) administration to prevent an orally transmitted infection and not through the air! A legitimate suspicion might have arisen that the Russians were developing typhoid as a bacteriological weapon and the aerosol vaccine was intended for protection against infection spread artificially through the air.

I published this presentation a year later in the Proceedings of the Conference (Hejfec et al., Dev. Biol. Stand. 1976; 33,93-97), but again no one was taken by surprise. Perhaps it was because this was considered a mere scientific report and not inside information implicating Russian work on bacteriological warfare. Perhaps it was because comfortable, cultured Western scientists were rather uncomfortable asking unmannerly, politically motivated questions. It was only three years later (1979) that the West was shocked by the news of an epidemic of anthrax in the city of Sverdlovsk, which resulted from an accident in a military facility manufacturing bacteriological weapons. The Russians continued to deny this occurrence until 1992, but even then only a portion of the truth was revealed to the world.

2. General Facts about the Efficacy of Vaccines

Not without controversy and drama, the history of vaccination for the prevention of infectious diseases started in 1798 with Edward Jenner and the first vaccine against smallpox. Throughout history, there have been concerns as to whether any of the vaccines invented could really prevent a vaccinated (immunized) person from contracting the disease, and what percent of them could be protected with less-than-full protection? This question is part of a greater issue in modern medicine, an unavoidable question of the efficacy of any new drug or method of therapy. In the 1950s and 1960s, it became evident that routine application of new drugs or treatments did not provide indisputable evidence of their efficacy. In the field of vaccination, where vaccines are generally less than 100% effective, attempts were made to establish objective criteria for efficacy based on the comparison between vaccinated and nonvaccinated groups of people. The problem, however, was in proving that the difference in morbidity between these groups was the result of vaccination. One could not guarantee that the vaccinated or nonvaccinated groups were equal in this regard, even if they were selected in the same place, at the same time, simply because the vaccination procedure could have biased the selection.

Historically, these problems led to the use of placebo for the control group. To ensure that groups were truly equal by any criteria, the participants were randomly assigned into groups (arms) of the study. In addition, to ensure full objectivity and equal probability, both the vaccine and the placebo vials were labeled with a code rather than the names of the contents. This type of study is called a randomized placebo-controlled double-blind trial. Double-blind means that neither the personnel who performed the vaccination, nor the personnel who assessed patients during the follow-up period were able to identify which individuals received the vaccine or the placebo until the completion of the trial. This methodology for testing vaccines and other preventive agents was summarized by the World Health Organization (WHO) in a special monograph published in 1968.

In 1958 I initiated a program of controlled trials in the Soviet Union, and this work became known to the international group working on the WHO monograph (under T. M. Pollock) from my publications. I was invited to participate in the preparation of this monograph, and was quite proud of having my name (spelled as Hejfec) listed in the subtitle of the book as a collaborator, along with Thomas Francis, Pierre Lépine, and other prominent international scientists. Subsequently, many scientists around the world introduced many details regarding trials of this type, and not only for the methodology of the controlled trials, but also to safeguard the health of individuals enrolled in such observations.

By 1963, the medical community of the Soviet Union was not yet ready to accept the concept of double-blind, placebo-controlled trials; however, the Soviet Ministry of Health at that time should be credited with having the insight to grasp this new concept and approve it. There were also some Russian scientists who opposed this concept, especially those who were not interested in the serious objective assessment of vaccines they had developed. This story is about one such group of Russian scientists, whose character defines their motivation and behavior.

3. Vaccine for Bacteriological Warfare

Several dramatic events could have happened following what appeared to be an insignificant meeting on the Isle of Man. It could have been perceived as a signal from behind the Iron Curtain warning the international medical community about the unusual scientific activity in the Soviet Union and raising the possibility of the development of bacteriological warfare. To the best of my knowledge, this message went unnoticed, even among the intelligence services of the West. (Are they really intelligent?) Also, it could have affected my life, but it did not.

The above-mentioned 1976 publication about the field trial was a reflection of my struggle for many years to reveal scientific truth in the field of vaccination and the efficacy of various vaccines, but the situation was much more complex than just another publication.

At that time I was near the end of my ten-year period of preparation (technically and emotionally) for emigration from the Soviet Union. That is how long it took for my previous security clearance as an epidemiologist to expire. To remove from my personal records any connections with state secrets, I had worked during this time not as an epidemiologist, but as a microbiologist at the Central Institute for Tuberculosis. Nevertheless, I was worried that my past involvement with the aerosolized typhoid vaccine might surface and be used by the emigration authorities as reason to deny me an exit visa because of my knowledge of state secrets. In fact, it was in a gray zone, since no official secrecy had been assigned to the field study conducted in 1963–64, but the aerosol development was covert. I decided to solve the problem by publishing the data from this trial submitted in my 1964 report to the Ministry of Health. I incorporated this data into a paper for the International Conference and submitted it for censorship clearance; after that, the paper was sent abroad by the Ministry of Health. Hejfec or, sometimes, Kheifets, was, at that time, the official international transliteration of my name from Russian in English-language publications.

Long before that, during 1958–69, I developed a system to conduct the first double-blind, placebo-controlled clinical (field) trials in Russia. I organized a department (laboratory) at the Moscow Metchnikov Institute for Vaccines and Sera; and every year, between 1958 and 1964, a new field trial was initiated in areas endemic to the infection in question, predominantly in Central Asia.

The trial with the aerosolized typhoid vaccine was organized in 1963. The vaccine was developed in one of the secret institutions of the Ministry of Defense, located mainly at the institute in Zagorsk, a small town near Moscow. In charge of this work was the supersecretive Main Directorate No. 7 of the Ministry of Defense. The deputy commander of the Main Directorate No. 7 was P.N. Burgasov, a three-star general of the medical corps. It is now known that during 1950–53 he was one of the leading individuals in the bacteriological warfare program. He worked under L. P. Beria, one of the most notorious heads of the State Security System. The typhoid vaccine was only one of several aerosolized vaccines being developed by the military establishment, along with broader research on aerosolized materials in general.

The Ministry of Defense had requested an evaluation (actually they expected a stamp of approval) of the new typhoid vaccine from the Ministry of Health. In turn, the Deputy Minister of Health, Dr. T. A. Nikolaeva, an enthusiastic supporter of my program, forwarded the request to me. I prepared a protocol for a double-blind, placebo-controlled field trial and contacted my colleagues in the Republics of Central Asia, where typhoid had reached epidemic levels. Eventually, I selected the Republic of Tajikistan as a trial site, where the school children in Dushanbe, the capital of Tajikistan, were most affected by the typhoid fever epidemic. At that time, there was no such thing as the Internal Review Board, or any other formal ethical standards for such a trial, particularly in the Soviet Union. All decisions were made administratively. The primary justification for the trial was high typhoid morbidity among children in selected areas, as well as the military manufacturer's preliminary reports with the proposed vaccine on the lack of any side effects in humans.

The trial was approved by the Ministry of Health of the Soviet Union and officially forwarded to the Ministry of Health of Tajikistan. The Ministry of Defense did not state any objections, although, as we learned later, they simply did not understand the terms "double-blind" and "placebo-controlled," and their high rank prevented them from asking questions that might constitute an admission of a lack of knowledge. Later, their lower-ranking representatives were confused and expressed concern when I explained to them what they needed to prepare a placebo powder that did not contain the active vaccine for the control group. They did not dare report this discovery to their superiors, and thus, they prepared the necessary materials. In the spring of 1963, two teams went to Dushanbe. My team was responsible for organization of the trial. The second team consisted of representatives of the Ministry of Defense who were responsible for actual application of the vaccine.

4. In Tajikistan

Tajikistan is a country in Central Asia comparable in size to Wisconsin, with a population of approximately seven million, mostly Tajiks who speak the Pharsi (Iranian) language and are Sunni Muslims. The republic borders Uzbekistan and Kyrgizstan (two other former Soviet Republics), as well as China and Afghanistan. Tajikistan gained independence from the Soviet Union in 1991. A large part of the country is mountainous (The Pamirs, with the highest peak being 7,495 m); only about 6% of the land is used, mostly for the production of cotton, and is totally dependent on an irrigation system for its water supply.

In the early 1960s, on assignment from the Ministry of Health of the Soviet Union, I investigated the epidemiology of typhoid fever in the Republics of Central Asia, primarily in Uzbekistan. I concluded that the reason for the high prevalence of this infection, which was mostly in the larger cities, was transmission through water from the irrigation system. The limited sewer systems covered only the central parts of the cities, while outhouses everywhere served the majority of the population and accounted for water contamination. The irrigation system ran not only in the fields but also into the cities. For the majority of the population this represented the only source of water. The narrowing of the canals resulted in an increased concentration of contaminants at their ends. Morbidity and mortality from typhoid among children was particularly high in the cities because they spent a lot of time playing in these canals, especially during the summer.

To draw attention to this alarming discovery I published my findings indicating that the main cause of epidemics of enteric infections in Central Asia was the unsatisfactory water supply. The Ministry of Health of Uzbekistan presented me with an award for this discovery and for my help in implementing the control measures. The data on typhoid, as well as data on other infectious diseases in the Soviet Union, constituted a state secret. To observe the standards of secrecy, I was unable to reveal in a publication the actual number of cases and the name of the city where most of the observation was conducted. The city was Tashkent in Uzbekistan; however, the situation was similar in other cities, including the city of Dushanbe. Development of proper sewage and water supply systems was out of reach at that time. Therefore, the main emphasis of the Soviet health authorities was on vaccination against typhoid fever, and the medical authorities of Tajikistan willingly accepted the recommendation (more so, an order) from the Ministry of Health of the Soviet Union to try an aerosolized vaccine.

5. In Dushanbe, Capital of Tajikistan

The two teams arrived in Dushanbe. I was immediately surprised to find that the military representatives contacted the local Ministry of Health to alter the original plan of the trial. They informed me of their intention to vaccinate the entire population of school children with no control group. Their argument was that it was unethical to vaccinate only a small group, leaving the majority of the population unprotected. The real reason was their fear that under the strict conditions of the double-blind, placebo-controlled trial the vaccine might not show the desired efficacy. They prepared the vaccine to be used in small doses to avoid or minimize side effects of the vaccine, and they feared that the small doses might be not effective. One of their goals was to exercise mass vaccination within a short period of time, for future implementation in the time of war.

It was quite interesting to listen to the "ethical arguments" put forward by this group of "Ten Colonels," as I called them, although one was a civilian—Dr. N.B. E., a female microbiologist. They were preparing for bacteriological warfare, and not all of them were medical professionals. One of them once told me in horrible details how he observed the executions of deserters when he served as the commander of a firing squad. Others were not much better, and all barely disguised their hypocritical statements concerning the health of the local population. They had their goals!

The "colonels" arrived in Dushanbe dressed in plain clothes, but they did not let the opportunity pass to flash their military credentials to impress the local authorities. I sensed trouble and contacted the Ministry of Health in Moscow. The official response (a government telegram!) was very clear that the study was to be organized according to the approved plan as a double-blind, placebo-controlled trial (not a mass vaccination) involving no more than 25,000 schoolchildren. Nevertheless, the final decision was up to the local Ministry of Health, and the colonels could have prevailed.

As often happened in the Soviet Union (perhaps not only there, and not only then…), I found a solution to the problem through a personal contact from my past. There was a very close friend, Hamid Mansurov, with whom I had attended the first three years of medical school in Samarkand in Uzbekistan from 1942–45, during the war, when we studied and shared hungry times together. I knew from past experience that Hamid was no stranger to secrecy and politics, and he was a trusted friend.

In 1963, Hamid, who was a member of the local elite, had become the most prominent person in Tajikistan as the director of the Institute for Gastroenterology, an academician, and a member of every council and entity in the republic. We spent a pleasant evening at his home discussing our past. His wife joked about my unsuccessful attempts to date her when we were students. After dinner I explained my problem to Hamid, and he said, "Don't worry, Leonid. I will talk to the Minister of Health, who is my good friend." He immediately called the Minister of Health at his home. After a long phone conversation in Farsi with the Minister of Health, Hamid told me that the Minister suggested we first visit the "boss," the Secretary of the Communist Party of Tajikistan, to cut off any potential pressure from the Ministry of Defense in Moscow. The next day, Hamid took me to the local bosses of the Communist Party and the Ministry of Health, who were at a much higher level than the colonels could ever dream of approaching. Both said they clearly understood that some people from Moscow were again trying to use Tajik children as guinea pigs for their own personal and even military gain. The Minister of Health stated, "We will address the issue in a democratic way, by vote of the Research Council at our Ministry of Health!"

The council met the next day. The group consisted of chairmen of various departments at the medical school, some other prominent local medical scientists, and leaders of the Ministry of Health. Both of our teams were invited, and we stated our positions. The colonels again appealed to the ethical issue and declared their desire to protect as many children as possible from typhoid fever.

My point was that we needed to be cautious and to find out first whether the vaccine was really effective. Almost all members of the council were Tajiks, but the discussion was conducted in Russian. Each member of the council spoke in the extremely polite Asian manner, complimenting the great scientists from the Ministry of Defense. A typical speech emphasized gratitude to the scientists from the Ministry of Defense who dedicated their efforts to benefit the children of this republic; however, after weighing all "pros and contras" they would rather wait until the next year to move forward with mass vaccination. They expressed confidence that the initial attempt in a limited population would show positive results.

The council's decision was prearranged; but the colonels did not know my secret, and they were quite puzzled. And so "democracy" prevailed over the declaration of "ethical concerns."

6. Clinical (Field) Trial with a Typhoid Aerosolized Vaccine

At each school chosen for inclusion in the trial, two rooms of approximately the same size were selected for vaccinations: room X and room Z. These rooms were used for the application of the two vaccines. Only the military manufacturers in Moscow knew which of them was the placebo. Children in each class were randomized into two groups, X and Z, and were directed to the appropriate rooms. Each room was filled with twenty to thirty children at a time who were exposed for twenty minutes to an aerosol produced by a simple small fan with an attached device containing the vaccine or placebo powder. The colonels created the aerosols, and they kept strict watch so that members of my team would never have access to the powders. The material ("stabilizer" as referred to by the colonels) provided stability of the aerosols in the air, a part of the vaccine and used as a placebo, and was the great secret. The same stabilizer was intended for use in the aerosol application of the bacteriological weapon, and that was why it was so guarded. Within a very short period of time, the vaccination was finished and no side effects were observed. There were more than twelve thousand children registered in each of the two groups.

It should be noted that the detection and reporting system of infectious diseases in the former Soviet Union was quite efficient. After the vaccination was completed, local health personnel compiled a list of those who had been vaccinated without indicating to which of the two vaccinated groups the individuals belonged. All patients in the city diagnosed with typhoid fever were routinely hospitalized, and medical records of those who were on the list of those vaccinated were pulled out for analysis.

After ten months, we returned to Dushanbe. Our teams had the lists of those vaccinated. They were divided into two parts, depending on the type of a vaccine (X or Z) each individual had received. The evaluations were conducted jointly by the colonels and by members of my team. The number of patients diagnosed during the ten-month observation period was fourteen in one group and fifteen in the other. The outcome was clear even without decoding X and Z and without any statistical analysis; the vaccine did not prevent typhoid.

7. Back in Moscow

While writing a report on the trial to the Ministry of Health, I received an invitation from Dr. G. to discuss the outcome of our "collaboration" on the typhoid vaccine. Dr. G. was a leader in the development of the aerosolized vaccines at the Military Research Institute in Lefortovo.

Dr. G. and I knew each other during my fellowship in 1947–1950. The fellowship was in infectious diseases, epidemiology, and microbiology. General Boldyrev, the chairman of the Department of Epidemiology, to which I was assigned, was also a chief epidemiologist of the Soviet Army. The department did not have a laboratory for experimental work, and the chairman arranged for me to do my Ph.D. work at the Military Institute located in Lefortovo, a suburb of Moscow and a name connected with an infamous political prison located in the same area. I spent almost a year with military people in an atmosphere of oppressive secrecy, in a place where people working in the same room were not allowed to talk to each other about their work. One day, with the arrival of a new group of military scientists and an enhanced level of secrecy, I was asked to leave and was relocated to the Metchnikov Institute for Vaccines and Sera. I had to start my work from the beginning since I was not allowed by the Military Institute to take with me any materials or notes. At the Metchnikov Institute I finally found a proper environment and good advisors to start and complete my Ph.D.

In 1963 everything was different. A black limo (Volga) driven by a military chauffeur took me to the institute in Lefortovo, the same place where I had spent part of my fellowship. This time I was welcomed through the entrance with military guards and led to Dr. G's office. In the past, Dr. G. and I had had serious disagreements, but this time she was exceedingly cordial and charming despite her military attire. We were served coffee and pastries, and our conversation was warm and affable. But the upshot of the conversation was that I was not to submit a formal report of the trial results to the Minister of Health, or, at least, to delay it as much as possible. Among the reasons were, "You know how important this research is for the defense of our country, and at this time a negative report may be perceived as the wrong direction, and we will not be able to work on improvement of the aerosolized vaccines." I was also assured that I would not regret my cooperation, with particular appreciation from Generals Burgasov and Alexandrov.

With the support of these powerful people, my future could have been predetermined as a great success! In any place on earth, particularly in the former Soviet Union, a rational person would grab this attractive opportunity. Perhaps I was either irrational or blinded by ambition, thinking of myself as an honest scientist with an obligation to report the truth, irrespective of the consequences. I wrote a detailed report that included the above-mentioned difficulties in organizing the trial to the Minister of Health, Dr. Kurashev. The Minister had his own "accounts" with the Ministry of Defense and obviously used my report to make certain points. As I later learned, this report was also used by a powerful group of opponents and enemies of Generals Burgasov and Alexandrov within the Ministry of Defense.

Some episodes vividly illustrate the conditions at the Military Institutes of the type mentioned above and, particularly, interactions among these elite people of the Soviet society. I witnessed and was involved in at least one such episode. My supervisor was a female of high military rank, and she used to come late and go to her desk covered with only a few papers but all kinds of make-up and other feminine frills. Her day started with a few leisurely calls to some friends, and arrangements or appointments for later. One day her routine was out of character; she put on a lab coat and asked me to go with her inside the walk-in incubator. I was surprised since she never did any benchwork or handled bacterial cultures. Inside, she unexpectedly asked me, "Leonid, some people keep talking about anti-Semitism in our country and that emigration to Israel can be a solution of the problem for Soviet Jews. What do you think about it?" The lady was of Jewish origin, but she was far removed from Jewish issues, and I was surprised by her question and by her choice of the 37°C incubator for this conversation.

The explanation was obvious: The incubator consisted of two compartments with separate entrances, and I could sense that someone on the other side was listening to our conversation. Apparently she had an assignment from the security administration. Intentionally or unintentionally, her conduct was slipshod. At that time, in 1948, I was very much in favor of creation of the state of Israel and had started thinking of emigrating there, but those thoughts were concealed deeply in my mind. My answer to that thorny question was very clear, "No, I don't think we have anti-Semitism in our country, and I don't know anything about Israel. I am focusing only on my research." Perhaps I had not fully convinced the person on the other side of the incubator room of my loyalty and that was a reason for my exit from this institute.

Another story I learned from a colleague of mine was story about a quite talented female lieutenant colonel. Let's call her Mrs. X. It was rumored that this somewhat attractive lady was greatly desired by high-ranking military men despite (but perhaps, because of) her excessive use of make-up, ultrafashionable clothing, and imported perfume. She was married to a one-star general who was a serious scientist and a decent man much older than his wife. Eventually, she greatly contributed to his psychological and physical degradation.

According to a popular Russian joke, scientific people can be divided into three categories based on how they built their scientific career: some by using their brains, some by using their bottoms (hard-working people), and some pretty ladies by using another part of their body... It seemed that Mrs. X., who married the right man at the right time, did not belong to any of these categories. But there were others who believed she belonged to all three categories. She had received numerous degrees and awards and did not need anything more, but perhaps she just could not resist the attention of the generals and colonels; in their circles, having her at least once became a sign of manhood. There was one minor scandal when she became pregnant by Colonel L., a known Moscow playboy. This led to an abortion in a military hospital and the news leaked to the community. My colleague explained that her behavior sprang from her military rank, lieutenant colonel, which in Russian literally means "under-colonel." Perhaps this was malicious slander by a spiteful person, but allegations aside, the above episodes illustrate the characters of people and the group's attitude toward scientific integrity. Only success counts!

More than ten years later, to solidify the facts and for self-protection, I decided to publish the main data from the trial. I included them in a lecture prepared for an international meeting. To make it easier to pass censorship, I combined the data on the aerosolized vaccine with the results of other field trials on oral vaccines. I knew that I would not be granted permission to go abroad to attend the conference, so I asked Dr. Joo, whom I never met but conducted active scientific correspondence, to give the oral presentation on behalf of my group. And that is the presentation at the Isle of Man referred to at the beginning of this story. Long before the report was presented and published, the events had already taken their dramatic course.

8. Outcome

While I was busy with field trials and laboratory experiments evaluating other vaccines, news came that the Main Directorate No.7 of the Ministry of Defense was scrutinized, and both Generals Burgasov and Alexandrov were fired from their jobs and dismissed from the Army. I was told by some of the military scientists that my report contributed to their dismissal. I realized that these people would not be unemployed for long, particularly Burgasov, who had close connections with his former colleagues at Beria's former secret police network. One can only imagine the anger and hate of such a person for anybody who may have been responsible for his humiliation. There were rumors that Burgasov escaped from visibility into the world of fishing, hunting, and… heavy drinking. But my suspicion that he would reappear in the civil world was soon realized.

Suddenly the Minister of Health, Dr. Kurashev died, and the newly appointed Minister was Professor Petrovsky, a famous Russian surgeon. Soon thereafter, Deputy Minister Nikolaeva also died, and Petrovsky started looking for her replacement. Someone from among Burgasov's powerful sympathizers suggested him as replacement for Nikolaeva. Burgasov became Deputy Minister of Public Health and the Inspector General for Hygiene. The Metchnikov Institute for Vaccines and Sera, where I worked, fell under his command. It was obvious to me that Burgasov was not going to pass up the opportunity for revenge. The time came for me to pay the price for my naïve ambition and lack of caution in dealing with powerful people. So, the evaluation of aerosolized typhoid vaccine was a dangerous assignment, and perhaps only miracles would save me from deadly dangers during a long struggle for survival that ended only with my emigration from the Soviet Union in 1978.

The legend about the Sword of Damocles comes to my mind when I think about my life during the period of 1966 to 1978. Damocles, a courtier at the court of the fourth-century BCE Syracuse tyrant Dionysius, once expressed envy about the life of his ruler. Dionysius, in reply, proposed to Damocles that they exchange their places for one day, so that he would understand the price the king pays for power and luxuries. As Damocles was enjoying royal treatment at the banquet, he looked up and noticed a sword hanging by horsehair above his head. He lost his appetite and asked to be released from playing the role of the king. Unlike Damocles, I did not choose to play a king, but nevertheless, a sharpened sword hung over my head for almost twelve years.

CHAPTER NINE

Under the Sword of Damocles

"Whether 'tis nobler in the mind to suffer the slings and arrows of outrageous fortune, or to take arms against a sea of troubles, and by opposing, end them?"

Shakespeare, *Hamlet*

1. Inevitable Choices
2. Bacteriological Warfare Zealot
3. Public Confrontation
4. The Struggle Continued
5. Penalty

Fig. 32. Research Council at the Academy of Medical Sciences in Moscow: I am defending my Sc.D. dissertation.
Drawing by Edward Tabachnik

1. Inevitable Choices

The history of mankind abounds with spans of time when individuals, groups, and even nations did not have the freedom to make choices and, because of that, often faced their inevitable fate of destruction. Blessed are those who have had the opportunity to choose. Many people don't wish to take the trouble and prefer to have others make these choices for them. This was the case in the Soviet Union, where any sign of individualism and independent thinking was a cause for suspicion. Uniformity and subordination were the way of life. Although from a very young age I had a tendency toward independent thinking (perhaps genetically inherited from my ancestors), it was not my intention to be rebellious, either against the system or in my personal life. Nevertheless, the events in which I unintentionally became involved repeatedly caused me to face difficult choices. Some of these choices could have placed me in a very comfortable situation had I been able to ignore scientific and professional principles.

Early in my career, I decided to become an epidemiologist. I was very excited to be able to identify and address mysterious outbreaks of infectious diseases. As a physician and scientist, I derived satisfaction from my work that led to implementation of proper measures for saving the lives of many people. Some of these occurrences I was able to describe in publications; however, most of them were suppressed by the code of secrecy that surrounded infectious diseases in the Soviet Union. The Ministry of Health recognized my ability to do this work and sent me on a number of expeditions to analyze situations. Also, they engaged me in preparation of various Ministry documents, decrees, and instructions to manage and guide the fight against the infectious diseases, particularly in two fields of my specific expertise: enteric infections and vaccination. Subsequent organization of clinical (field) trials with typhoid vaccines ultimately involved me with the military establishment, which was readying for bacteriological warfare.

It was not my choice or my intention to confront the activity of rogue individuals working on bacteriological warfare, but it just so happened that the results of my studies kept coming into conflict with their plans. I had to choose between covering up objectionable results or reporting them candidly and bluntly. In other words, I could either hide or stand up! My professional pride and my ego (and perhaps some arrogance) made me to choose the latter, which led to a confrontation with some powerful and notorious people. One in particular, General Pyotr Burgasov, hounded me for years.

2. Bacteriological Warfare Zealot

The city of Sverdlovsk at the Ural Mountains (Yekaterinburg now and before the revolution) is the place where Tsar Nicolas II and his family were murdered by the Bolsheviks in 1918. On April 2, 1979, this city once again drew the attention of the world. A cloud of aerosolized anthrax bacilli appeared in the air at the outskirts of the city after a mysterious underground explosion connected with the so-called Town No. 19, the code for the super-secret facility built deep underground in 1946 for the purpose of developing and producing bacteriological weapons. The only connection with the outside world was through an underground railroad leading to another military installation called Town No. 32. It was rumored that this tunnel was blown up by an explosion in 1979 when a barrel filled with anthrax spores being shipped to a storage or testing facility suddenly burst open. Another rumor, perhaps more reliable, held that the bacterial aerosol escaped from a newly built and improperly installed drying system in Town No. 19. Another account of the accident was by technicians who were culturing anthrax in huge tanks changed shifts, and someone forgot to replace a clogged bacterial filter.

For many years Soviet authorities covered up this episode and presented it as a natural accident of an anthrax epidemic and created a complex scheme of disinformation. It was not until 1992 they acknowledged that an accident did occur and then only in part, when Yeltsin told the American president, "You know, Mr. Bush, we are still cheating on you. We promised to eliminate bacteriological warfare, and although some experts did all that was possible for me not to learn the truth, I got them..." In 1992, to comply with the International Convention (signed by the Soviet Union in 1972), Yeltsin issued the Presidential Decree that banned the development, production, or storage of bacteriological and chemical weapons (No. 390, April 11, 1992). Also, in 1993 in an interview with the newspaper *Komsomolskaya Pravda* on May 27 Yeltsin again admitted that the cause of the epidemic was military development; however, the whole truth about the past experience still has not been officially revealed. For example, the Russian authorities have admitted that sixty-four individuals died from anthrax as a result of the accident in Sverdlovsk, but some experts in the field insist that the actual number of very carefully concealed deaths was 10–20-fold greater, in the range of 1,500 to 2,000. The cover-up continues in Russian newspapers and in the last Burgasov interview in 2006 (quoted below).

The episode involving anthrax in the Sverdlovsk area provided first evidence of a broad, multi-institutional system in the Soviet Union with thousands of employees preparing for bacteriological warfare. It is not the purpose of this story to describe the bacteriological war program of the Soviet Union. This was well-presented in the book *Biohazard* by Ken Alibek and other publications. It must be noted, however, that initially these efforts were under two Chief Directorates (No. 7 and No. 15) of the Ministry of Defense, but later many more operational systems were established, in particular the *Biopreparat* (1972), a civilian network of research and production employing more than thirty thousand (by some accounts fifty thousand) people. Although the names and administrative structures changed, the same groups of people moved from one place to another to work toward the same goals. One of these people was General P.N. Burgasov, and this story is about my interactions with him.

A few biographical facts define Burgasov. From 1950–53, he worked for L.P. Beria, the notorious associate of Stalin, who, along with overseeing and directing the secret police and various security entities, since 1945 had been in charge of developing weapons for mass destruction (WMD). Burgasov provided information on the progress in bacteriological warfare to his boss and directly to Stalin. In a power struggle after Stalin's death, Beria and his top lieutenants were executed in 1953, but Burgasov survived and became the deputy chief (and chief, according to some sources) of the Chief Directorate No. 7 of the Ministry of Defense (one of two directorates in charge of preparation for bacteriological war) until 1964 or 1965 when he was discharged from the Army. By his own statements, from 1958–63 he was the "scientific deputy commander" of Town No. 19 during the anthrax epidemic in the city of Sverdlovsk facility. Subsequently, for another period of twenty-one years (1965–86), Burgasov remained a prominent personage in the development of bacteriological warfare as the Deputy Minister of Health and Sanitary Inspector General.

Almost until his death in September of 2006, Burgasov continued to give interviews, touching on his important past, and he never missed an opportunity to strew misinformation on the subject of the Soviet Union's bacteriological war program. Perhaps, his last interview with a Russian newspaper, *Moscovsky Komsomolets* (April 7, 2006, by D. Melman), might help to better understand the mentality of this man. Here is a quote from that interview related to an episode of illness that he suffered.

The reason I recently was in the Kremlin Hospital is that I had swollen joints. They brought me to the ward and left me there alone. I started walking to the bed, but fell, could not get up, and for half an hour nobody was paying attention at me. Then a young man came and asked in a very rude tone, "Hey, why are you laying on the floor?" In such a tone to me—to an academician, general, former deputy minister! I said, "I fell and just cannot get up." Finally they placed me on the bed, and then a nurse came and I asked her to take away a urinal from under my bed. She replied, "I am in charge for patients' treatment, not urinals, you'd better call for the appropriate help." I thought to myself, "You, a piece of shit, in my time I would not let you get even close to the hospital, and now you are talking to me like this. It hurts…."

Burgasov's own words reflect a longing for his powerful past, typical of some Russian individuals who were once at the top and were able to make life and death decisions (and they did) concerning people placed under their control. Burgasov was one of them, and in his time he would not have merely fired the nurse but would have sent her to the Gulag Archipelago. It would not have been for poor performance, but for being disrespectful—to him! In regard to the medical services and attitude of the medical personnel in Russia, the situation now is not much different from when

Burgasov was the Deputy Minister of Health (not just "deputy minister," as he stated in his complaint). Then medical professionals were selected for such places like the Kremlin Hospital not so much for their clinical skill but rather for their political past and their loyalty. Perhaps Burgasov was unable to see that he was now paying the price for his own activity in the past.

In spite of Burgasov's high rank and titles, I saw him as a person of a low social order and quite a primitive scientist and microbiologist. But I must give him credit for being a master of misinformation. In 1979, Dr. M. Meselson from Harvard University invited him for a lecture tour in the U.S. In his lectures Burgasov presented "evidence" that the outbreak in Sverdlovsk was caused by illegal consumption of infected meat and had nothing to do with the military. His explanation was convincing to the *National Academy of Science* and to the *Science* journal. The media seized the opportunity to point to the U.S. government's paranoia relating to WMD in other countries and expressed relief that, fortunately, the Soviet Union was not participating in such activities. Burgasov was still promoting the same lies in our time even though the whole truth became evident from many publications.

Yes, Burgasov, in the past a close associate to L.P. Beria, the most brutal head of the secret police and security organizations in the history of Soviet Union, had the power to send anyone to the Gulag. From 1963 until my emigration from Russia in 1978, I was a target of Burgasov's displeasure. He became my sworn enemy over this period of time. As described in the previous chapter, "Dangerous Assignment", it happened during 1963–64 after the field trial with aerosolized typhoid vaccine, when I insisted on proper organization of the trial to generate objective results. His anger against me was intensified after I refused to "sweep under the carpet" the results showing the lack of efficacy of this vaccine, developed under the Chief Directorate No. 7 of the Ministry of Defense.

In fact, the military creators of typhoid and other aerosolized vaccines never resumed such programs even after they returned to power and had the ability to do it. The reason, as I learned, was that the enhanced doses of these vaccines caused severe reactions in some of the "volunteers." It remains unclear, however, whether the reactions were caused by the specific vaccine components (bacterial antigens) or by the stabilizer needed for maintaining the aerosol suspended in the air. This super-secret stabilizer was developed not only for vaccines but also for bacteriological weapons. At that time, it was made from sheep fur, or, more accurately, from shredded and grained high-quality white felt imported from Mongolia. The contents of the stabilizer might have been the cause of allergic or hypersensitivity reactions. Later it was replaced by nanoparticles of polymers used to "weaponize" the bacteriological agents. If the military had lost all interest in aerosolized vaccines, why had Burgasov continued his hunt for me?

The explanation goes beyond the annoyance that I caused with the aerosolized vaccine. Once again, without any intention on my part, my work conflicted with Burgasov's plans. This time, Burgasov and his associates developed a new strategy for using vaccination to protect the army and the population against bacteriological weapons. It was to be a systematic annual mass vaccination against potential bacteriological warfare agents such as botulism and gangrene. By Burgasov's own admission made in the above cited 2006 interview, he had a goal to vaccinate the whole country against botulism, but to deliver it in such a way that no outsider would notice and foreign intelligence services would have no inkling that a mass vaccination against such infections had taken place. As he triumphantly stated, they incorporated botulism toxoids (neutralized toxins) into an existing "polyvalent vaccine" without disclosing it on the label.

While admitting this highly unethical practice that would affect millions of Soviet citizens (he did not view this as immoral), he still did not tell the whole truth. The only information provided on the original label was "typhoid-paratyphoid poly-vaccine." At that time, twenty to thirty million people in the Soviet Union were vaccinated against typhoid annually, providing the opportunity to stage a mass vaccination against other infections by secretly incorporating additional components into a typhoid vaccine. The problem was that such devious inclusion of the botulism toxoid (and other components) was possible with only one type of typhoid vaccine, called the "chemical poly-vaccine," that contained antigens extracted from bacteria rather than whole bacterial cells, and aluminum hydroxide, a necessary component for the toxoid adsorbency. With more than twenty million people to be vaccinated annually, all obstacles had to be removed, and it just so happened that I was one of those obstacles. Again, I found myself in the wrong place and at the wrong time!

3. Public Confrontation

A large, beautiful building the size of a palace was built on Solyanka Street in Moscow in the nineteenth century as a club for nobility. In Soviet times it became the headquarters of the Soviet Academy of Medical Science. Although the building was only two stories high, it was as tall as three- and four-story buildings on the same street. A wide, carpet-covered marble staircase led from the entrance to a large lobby on the second floor. Straight ahead was a magnificent ballroom converted into a conference room. The richness of the past radiated from the parquet floor, the marble columns, and the crystal chandeliers. This is where sessions of the Research Council of the Academy usually took place. Academician (member of the Academy) was the highest rank given to the most prominent and politically correct scientist. The Academy awarded two levels of scientific degrees in medical science, Candidate of Science (equivalent to Ph.D. in the U.S.) and Doctor of Science (ScD). The latter was only given to an established scientist for leadership and the development of new directions and/or new methodology.

On October 14, 1966, this place was to be the site of a momentous event that attracted more people than the building could hold. The conference room, the grand hall, and even the staircase was filled with scientists and medical professionals from various Moscow institutions, all attracted by the anticipated spectacle reminiscent of a public execution. The main characters of this drama were P.N. Burgasov, the all-powerful Deputy Minister of Health, and the victim of the execution, L. Heifets, who was to present the defense of his ScD dissertation.

The session started with my twenry-minute presentation, followed by reviews of three official challengers, most prominent scientists in the field of epidemiology and microbiology. All three reviews were very favorable and stressed the innovative approach of my research, particularly in regard to evaluation of the vaccines. After I responded to some minor comments, the chairman announced that in addition to the critiques presented by the reviewers officially appointed by the Research Council, a written review had been received from the Deputy Minister of Health, P.N. Burgasov. This was read, and I was given the opportunity to respond. Members of the Council and I had been given this letter in advance of the session.

Burgasov's letter was arrogant in tone and chaotic in structure, condemning me for daring to confront the Ministry's (Burgasov's) policies. By taking advantage of the obviously insufficient clarity of the letter, I formulated my response to his five specific objections using some of his own phrases. I classified them as follows: two were misinterpretations (he had overlooked some data presented in the text); one was an argument against my priority in methodology (which I demonstrated by showing appropriate publications); and the last two were arguments against my conclusion that the "chemical poly-vaccine" was the least effective among the typhoid vaccines.

My dissertation was much broader than the items addressed by the author of the letter. I analyzed the first experience with the controlled double-blind trials in the country and presented data on post-vaccination anti-typhoid immunity (quantitative assessment of protection, length, effect of different vaccination schedules, etc.). I presented a summary of five large-scale trials conducted during the period from 1959–1965 with total enrollment of 900,000 people. In these cohorts, 820 cases of typhoid were diagnosed. The trials were planned and conducted after lengthy discussions and were reviewed and approved by the Ministry of Health (before Burgasov). The results of the studies were published in many articles, including in Russian journals, the Bulletin of the World Health Organization (WHO), and other international journals. Just before Burgasov became the Deputy Minister, the Ministry of Health issued a series of documents (Collegium of May 7,1964, Decision of September 14, 1964, and the Decree of January 9, 1965) approving the results of the field trials, with recommendations and instructions for implementing the findings of these trials into practical applications for vaccination throughout the country.

In my reply to Burgasov's letter, I tried very hard to keep an academic tone and to restrain myself from expressing too much sarcasm regarding the absurdity of his comments. I stressed that his critique addressed only a minute part of the work, mainly the conclusion about the low efficacy of the "chemical vaccine." I confronted Burgasov's opinion on potential benefits of the chemical vaccine with facts—massive statistical data never presented before and for the first time derived from a comparison study. In two large-scale trials (one of them, trial #5, was a six-arm study), this vaccine protected only 60–70% of those vaccinated for a period of less than one year, while other vaccines provided two (sometimes three) years of protection with an efficacy rate of 80–85%. I sensed that I was winning from the reaction of the audience. The conference was over, and the audience waited in silence for the result of the secret ballot. Finally, the secretariat emerged to announce the results of the vote of the Research Council: *pro—16; con—0!*

The entire building exploded in applause! Victory! For the audience, many of whom did not know me personally, this event marked a triumph of science over bureaucracy and administrative interference in science by Ministry officials. Alas, this celebration was premature. People underestimated the power of the administration under the rules of Soviet Union tyranny. It was just the beginning of the struggle, for me personally and for the scientific community, to remove political correctness from scientific assessment. Not long after the above-described event, the Research Council of the Academy was dismissed by a decree of the Minister of Health—a signal of what was to come.

4. The Struggle Continued

Scientific degrees (Ph.D. and ScD) were awarded in the Soviet Union only with the approval of the Supreme Attestation Commission, which is still in existence in Russia. This Commission reviewed the materials on public defense presented by research councils of the universities or research institutions and assessed the political background of the candidate. The Commission is a large, complex, and powerful organization. It consists of a number of expert committees for various specialties, and each has its own "trusted" reviewers. Recommendations by these committees are subject to approval by the Plenary Session of the Commission. The process of approval (focused on political correctness) is controlled and supervised by the executive group called Presidium of the Commission.

My dissertation was directed to the Committee on Epidemiology on October 26, 1967 (one year after the public defense), and the decision was made "to decline," based on a negative review presented by a well-known associate of Burgasov, Dr. Bezdenezhnych. His arguments were similar to those in Burgasov's letter. Numerous positive reviews submitted to the Commission by various institutions and prominent scientists were ignored.

I complained to the Commission and insisted that the dissertation be analyzed by a broader group of scientists beyond epidemiologists and suggested that it be passed on to the Committee on Microbiology. This suggestion was accepted after several meetings with people on the Commission whom I perceived as potential antagonists of Burgasov. This expert committee collected a number of additional reviews and held two sessions, on April 4, 1968 and March 27, 1969. The final and unanimous decision was a positive recommendation! So, I achieved an unprecedented situation: two expert committees with opposite recommendations.

On April 25, 1969 the vote of the Plenary Session of the Supreme Commission was split, and there was no decision. I realized that victory was not yet sealed, so I did not show up on April 24, 1970 for the next Plenary Session. Instead, I insisted that the two expert committees hold a joint session to resolve their differences. Again, I had numerous private meetings with potential antagonists of Burgasov, in which I emphasized that Burgasov was using his position to pressure the independent Supreme Commission! I stressed that he had organized a secret meeting of the Ministry's Collegium on October 9, 1969 with the purpose of condemning my work and dismissing previous decisions of the Ministry. Eventually, on April 28, 1972, the Presidium of the Supreme Commission granted a joint session of two committees; it was another unprecedented event in the history of this organization!

At that time, the Supreme Commission received approximately twenty positive reviews on my work from prominent scientists, societies, and institutions, and there were still only two negative reviews—by Burgasov and Bezdenezhnych. In addition, a very strong argument in my favor emerged. The same two opponents, Burgasov and Bezdenezhnych, published a book entitled *Practical Immunology* in 1969. Feeling completely unassailable, they borrowed almost unaltered text (pages 77–86 and 144–149) from my dissertation without any reference to my authorship. Astonishingly, the borrowed text included statements that they had disparaged in their critical reviews. These facts, along with clear evidence of plagiarism, provided substance for the case that I presented to the joint session of two committees. Members of both committees were outraged! On May 18, 1972, the secret ballots (once again unprecedented) of the joint session were positive: *pro—27; con—1.* Another victory, and after six years of fighting, I finally received my ScD degree!

Another victory within the same struggle was the publication of a monograph that summarized the data from my dissertation (1968, Medizina). Twice (in 1966 and in 1967) Burgasov recommended that the medical publishing house, Medizina, not print the book. Mayevsky, the director of the publishing house, sent the last galley to Burgasov for his final opinion. The response was the same as before, with a reference to his review about my dissertation. I complained about harassments by Burgasov to Petrovsky, the Minister of Health, and was honored with a response from the Minister stating that I had the tendency to undermine a respected member of the Ministry's staff. The publisher, as an independent organization, complained to the Central Committee of the Communist Party about the pressure from Burgasov and his interference. Mayevsky told me that it was in consequence of the recommendation of this higher authority that the book was published. It was a black-covered book with the title in red and white lettering and soon became referred by many as "The Black Book." It was not displayed at the book kiosks in the Ministry of Health building, and anybody who wished to purchase one received a copy from under the bench.

5. Penalty

The scientific faculty of the Moscow Mechnikov Research Institute for Vaccine and Sera in Moscow, where I worked until 1969 as head of the department (laboratory) for vaccines evaluation, supported me in my struggle by issuing needed letters and documents. This was in spite of the fact that the Institute was under the direct authority of Burgasov. Much of the credit belongs to the Director of the Institute, Ivan Feodorovitch Michailov, who, after many years of working together, became one of my good friends. He was an extremely bright person and a talented microbiologist. He had a great sense of humor and a deep knowledge of literature and art. He was an excellent artist painting in oil and had a very unusual talent: he could memorize a page from a book after a single glance at it. These refined qualities contrasted with his appearance, particularly with his Slavic-type round face, which, in his opinion, was stereotypical of a simple Russian peasant. He would make jokes about his "primitive" face, stating that with such a face he had to be treated by the higher Russian authorities as a person who belonged in their circle. At the same time, he hardly could hide his skepticism of the Soviet system and was openly critical of people with conformist tendencies, so common for the *Homo Sovieticus* type of individuals. He knew that this alone, plus the fact that he was married to a Jewish woman, would prevent him from being accepted in "high circles."

Ivan was a tall man with broad shoulders and had the appearance of a strong and healthy person, which happened not to be the case. As a tank driver during the Great War with Germany, he was wounded, received burns, and was left with pronounced limp. Wherever he went he immediately attracted vast attention. After the war, he attended the Military Medical Academy in Leningrad, where he received his MD degree and, immediately afterward, his Ph.D. and ScD degrees in microbiology. Michailov's most distinctive characteristic was his belief in honesty, which he demanded from his staff and faculty, even in the smallest of details. He hated for anyone to complain about colleagues and thwarted most attempts at undermining others, so common in academic institutions. This type of decency was rare among the ranking individuals in the Soviet Union milieu. I was very fortunate to know this man and honored to be one of his closest associates.

Burgasov knew that I had the support of Michailov and the faculty of the Mechnikov Institute, and he was looking for the right moment to penalize both the Institute and its director. It was not long before that opportunity presented itself. Losing the battle on scientific grounds did not distract Burgasov from his plans. Ignoring the scientific data and previous decisions by the Ministry of Health, he issued an order for the development and production of only one type of the typhoid vaccine—the chemical poly-vaccine—for mass vaccination of the population. Soon a new vaccine was developed under this label which contained toxoids of botulism, gangrene, and tetanus and was targeted for use in an annual vaccination of twenty to thirty million civilians and military personnel.

Thirty years later, according to the 1998 catalog, Russian industry began manufacturing a product containing neutralized toxins (anatoxins, or toxoids) against botulism (three types), tetanus, and gangrene (two types), but this time under the correct label "Sexta-anatoxin," and this time, no mention was made of a typhoid component. It is hard to imagine an indication for broad application of this vaccine other than as protection against the toxins used as bacteriological weapons, especially the version of vaccine not containing a tetanus component. Perhaps the purpose for manufacturing this vaccine during our time was to have it just in case...

As a leader in the field, the Mechnikov Institute received, in 1968, an order to study and test the so-called "typhoid chemical poly-vaccine" in human subjects. The Research Council of the Institute was outraged with this development, especially after we learned that preliminary testing on animals and "volunteer" soldiers by the military indicated an excessively high rate of local and general side effects. No one on our faculty wanted to be involved in a program obviously connected to bacteriological warfare, but no one dared to openly oppose it. Nevertheless, we had good reasons to oppose it on the grounds of insufficient scientific development of the product. The Research Council of the Institute voted to reject the directive from the Ministry to test the new vaccine. This was a rebellion! It was amazing to observe that the leading scientists of the Institute had enough courage to take this dangerous stand on the basis of ethical and scientific principles. In 1969 this was a unique stance in the Soviet society! How proud I was to belong to this courageous group of scientists.

Burgasov anticipated this outcome and perhaps even provoked it. It gave him a good excuse to send an inspection team to review the Institute's performance. The purpose and anticipated outcome of the inspection was obvious: the Institute was restructured, about twenty laboratory heads and other leading scientists lost their jobs, and Michailov was removed from the directorship. They could not simply fire a person who was known as a war hero. He was given a job as the director of a research laboratory in another institution, but he could not overcome the humiliation and soon died from a heart attack. I was not fired, probably because it would have been too obvious that the Institute was penalized because of my activities. My laboratory was closed, and I was given a desk in somebody else's office. The time came for me to move to another field, to another job, and start secret preparation to emigrate from the country in which I no longer belonged.

Finding a job presented a very difficult problem. Everyone among the directors of institutions in the field knew me, but they were all afraid of the repercussions from Burgasov if they showed any rapport with me. Finally, I approached some relatively low-ranking people in the Ministry of Health whom I had developed trust with while conducting field trials during the previous administration. Many of them despised Burgasov and his style. And so, quietly, right under Burgasov's nose, I received two offers to work as a microbiologist. One offer was at the VD Institute, and the other at the TB Institute. I accepted the TB Institute, since VD was a classified topic, which I wanted to avoid. From 1969 until my emigration in 1978, I worked as a microbiologist at the Central Institute for Tuberculosis, trying to maintain a low profile and avoiding anything that might be considered a state secret. I tried to be especially cautious and avoided appearing proud after publishing my "Black Book" in 1968 and obtaining my ScD degree in 1972. The Sword of Damocles was still hanging over my head.

The twenty-year period of my life from 1958 to 1978, between the ages of thirty-two and fifty-two, was an amalgam of excitement, scientific achievements, fight for survival, humiliation, disappointment and satisfaction, defeats and victories.

I consider the years between 1958 and 1965 the most productive and exciting period of my professional life. Organizing a team of highly dedicated professionals and devoted friends was, by itself, a great achievement in the corrupt state of affairs in the Soviet Union. I owe to these lifetime friends (many of whom are not with us anymore) much more than just thanks. They made my life meaningful, and to date, this experience is still etched in my mind. Organization of controlled trials at that time, and the results obtained during this period of hard work, led to well-received publications that made us all proud and happy. We were sequestered in our own realm of basic decency within the vast, hostile Soviet system.

The fights, the politics, the manipulations, the need to maneuver to survive in that environment took so much of our time, but it was inevitable. The indifference of the leading authorities toward the health of the people of the country, the dismissal of the results of thorough research for the sake of their own ambitions, growing government-sponsored anti-Semitism, and the fear that my children would not be able to develop the skills (as I did) to survive in this hostile environment, brought me closer to the difficult decision to emigrate.

During those long years of my life under the Damoclean Sword, I was thinking and preparing for emigration from the Soviet Union. One of my concerns was that I did not want to be viewed by friends and colleagues, or adversaries, as a person for whom emigration was a reaction to misfortune or failure. But with the successful publication of the book and, having obtained the ScD degree, I felt indomitable.

CHAPTER TEN

Code Name "Green Eggs Project" and Escape from Russia

"Do you like green eggs and ham?...
I do not like them here and there,
I do not like them anywhere."
Dr. Seuss, *Green Eggs and Ham*

1. Green Eggs and Freedom
2. Green Eggs and Condoms
3. Green Eggs and Vodka
4. Farewell, Russia

Fig. 33. Special meeting of the Sokolniki Party District Bureau of Moscow: my expulsion from the Communist Party membership and condemnation. On the wall is a picture of Lenin and a slogan citation from Karl Marks. *Drawing by Edward Tabachnik*

Fig. 34. "Green Eggs". On the left, top to bottom:
- Prof. A. G. Khomenko, director of the Central Institute for Tuberculosis (TB Institute), photo of 1994;
- I am at the start of work at the TB institute on the "Green Eggs" project (1970);
- On the right – 32 years later, with two Russian scientists at the Yekaterinburg TB Institute in 2002. Two of us are holding bottles with dry powdered culture medium (L-J) for cultivation of tubercle bacilli; and
- I am at the same place with a bottle of "green eggs" powder (2002)

Fig. 35. Farewell to Moscow:
- Michael and Helen with the newborn son Boris, getting ready for emigration (1977);
- Dr. Guramy Arabidze, a loyal friend, who visited me at my office in the TB Institute at the time when I applied for emigration (1978);
- The section of the Red square with the St. Basil Cathedral; and
- The main part of the Red Square with Lenin's Mausoleum on the left.

1. Green Eggs and Freedom

To escape from the Soviet Union to freedom in the 1970s was just a dream. Any attempt for legal emigration to the West could easily end up in exile to the Siberian Gulag Archipelago in the East. Everyone with clearance who applied for emigration at that time was refused and often risked losing his/her job. Expiration of the secrecy clearance required a period of ten years. After taking a new, nonsecretive job at the TB Institute, I had enough time to develop a plan for my safe emigration—to make sure that I went to the West and not to the East!

The major problem I faced was that almost everyone who applied for emigration at that time was forced to quit his or her job while they waited for permission (or refusal) to emigrate. To be unemployed in the Soviet Union was dangerous, especially after one had received refusal to emigrate. A person could have been accused of being a "parasite," a crime leading to incarceration in forced-labor camps of the Gulag Archipelago. Few exceptions were made for high-profile professional individuals without any records of antigovernment activities.

I was known as a troublemaker, but only in the professional aspect. As a consultant to the Ministry of Public Health, I used to demand proper actions in the area of infectious disease control. At the same time, I was never accused of being politically incorrect. Having this background, I only needed to produce something so good and impressive that in case I requested emigration, the head of the TB Institute would not dare fire me without creating a scandal and legal problems. The challenge was, what could an average scientist in the field of tuberculosis in Russia invent at that time so that it would be extremely visible?

After years of trying different avenues, I devised a plan with the code name "Green Eggs Project." This plan had to be related to my professional work in the field of tuberculosis, and, therefore, the project could also have been titled "Green Eggs and Tuberculosis."

Tuberculosis in the Soviet Union was not only a health problem but also a political issue. The Soviet authorities identified tuberculosis as a social disease of poverty and social injustice. It was therefore considered a disease of the capitalistic society. According to this ideology, tuberculosis should inevitably have been eliminated from the Communist Society of the Soviet Union. Reality did not prove this expectation, and therefore the real data reflecting tuberculosis prevalence was considered one of the state secrets. At the same time, the authorities seriously supported any reasonable measures of research in tuberculosis.

One of the key elements among the tuberculosis control measures was the bacteriological diagnosis and monitoring of tuberculosis and patients' response to therapy, including detection of drug resistance. Unfortunately, even now, the importance of this tool for proper selection of a drug combination to treat patients is not fully recognized around the world. In Russia in the 1970s, bacteriology was respected as one of the most important elements of the tuberculosis control system, and TB laboratories were in every district of the country.

Bacteriological diagnosis of tuberculosis and the tests to detect drug resistance require cultivation of tubercle bacilli. The most traditional medium for such cultivation is made from eggs mixed with a variety of reagents (salts), with addition of a malachite green dye. This mixture, when coagulated with heat in tubes, produces green solid slants with a smooth surface ready for cultivation of the tubercle bacilli. This recipe is called Löwenstein-Jensen medium (or L-J). I called it the "green eggs medium."

The problem was that the ingredients (salts) to make this medium were not always available, and even qualified microbiologists in the local laboratories could not follow the correct composition of the medium. It seemed the only solution was a centralized production of this L-J medium, as it was done in the West. It was impossible in Russia for the very simple reason that the Soviet industry could not produce standard screw-capped glass tubes.

My "Green Eggs Project" was dedicated to resolving the problem of centralized manufacturing of the L-J medium differently. The general idea was to manufacture a dry, sterile powder made from eggs and all other ingredients (salts) in large bottles and ship them to the local laboratories. The laboratories would only have to dissolve this powder in water, distribute the mixture into the tubes, and coagulate the medium in a slanted position of the tubes. It sounded simple, but it proved to be quite complicated.

Within a period of about three years I collaborated with a group of scientists in the Kyrgyzstan Republic who had been developing a powdered L-J medium, after which I organized its industrial production. To prepare such a medium, Dr. E.A. Finkel, a prominent microbiologist, and her colleagues in Kyrgyzstan suggested a process called lyophilization, or drying from a frozen state. Coordination of their effort with groups of physicists and engineers from other areas resulted in the development of a quite sophisticated, but realistic, methodology.

The next step was to transfer this methodology into industrial technology, which meant finding a place, organizing a team to do the work, and obtaining the necessary machinery. I chose the city of Tumen in Siberia for two reasons. One was the city had a Microbiology Research Institute that had been looking for an opportunity to get involved in a significant project. In addition to having sufficient space to organize production, this institute had a number of qualified microbiologists and engineers. The second reason was the availability of a substantial egg supply from a large state chicken farm in the District of Tumen.

After the technology was developed, the Ministry of Health purchased several lyophilization systems from France, and within one year, there was enough manufacturing of lyophilized medium to supply the entire country. I was officially recognized for my achievement, and the director of my Institute, Professor Alexander Khomenko, awarded me with a bonus (twice-monthly salary). And so, the time was now ripe. Two weeks after receiving the award, I requested an employment certificate from the director of the Institute. This certificate was necessary for submitting an application to the Emigration Office (OVIR).

The Director of the Central Tuberculosis Research Institute, Alexander Grigorievitch Khomenko, was my age and had received his MD degree at the same time. (He graduated from the Medical School in 1949 in Kharkov, Ukraine.) Other than these similarities, our professional paths and lives were completely different. To ensure his successful career, Khomenko skillfully used his status as a person of Ukranian ethnicity and a trusted member of the Communist Party. In addition, he was talented. He received his Ph.D. in 1955 and his ScD in 1965 without any obstacles. He also held high academic positions in the Ukraine, followed by his appointment in 1973 as the director of the Central TB Institute in Moscow, a position he held until his death in 1999. Combining his high position as a director of the leading TB Institute with his diplomatic skills, Khomenko developed good relationships with the health-care leaders in all fifteen republics of the Soviet Union, thus establishing himself as a top TB expert in the USSR. He was among the few scientists allowed to travel abroad to participate in international conferences. Besides being an official representative of the country, he showed, at the same time, remarkable capabilities of interactions with the Western scientists, giving them the impression of his being a free-minded scientist and physician. They did not know that Khomenko's activities, as of many other successful Soviet representatives, were based on a simple principle of complete separation of deeds, words, and thoughts, as well as separation between what is done or said internally and what is presented abroad.

One typical example of this is a story Khomenko told me many years later at one of our meetings in Paris after the disintegration of the Soviet Union. It was an issue of Russia accepting the so-called DOTS strategy (Directly Observed Therapy Short course) proposed by the World Health Organization, which was vigorously opposed by the Russian medical society. Khomenko's skepticism about application of this strategy to Russia was no different from those of other Russian experts, but he said, "It is silly to fight against the WHO; after all, they are offering a lot of money, and it would not affect the whole country and would not change the overall Russian strategy. My institute needed only to run a small site observation to show the benefits of the WHO strategy. After all, we desperately needed the foreign currency." And so he did, and he received not only money but also recognition from the WHO and from some Western experts as the only Russian TB expert who understood the importance of implementing the WHO strategy in Russia.

Contrary to the impression of some observers, my relationship with Khomenko was not bad at all. He respected my scientific views and achievements, and once he even took me on an expedition to analyze the TB situation in Kyrgyzstan. At the same time, he was very cautious to not show any positive attitude toward me because of my problems with the powerful Deputy Minister of Health, Pyotr Burgasov.

Khomenko was shocked when I told him about my decision to emigrate, and, as expected, suggested that I resign first. I refused, stating that I would resign only after obtaining the emigration visa. I also stressed that after having given me a reward for doing a good job, it would be quite difficult for him to fire me for not being productive, as this was usually the excuse given in such circumstances.

I would say now that his reaction was rather modest when compared to similar incidences in other places. Khomenko was not in very good health, and perhaps he had some heart or kidney problems. His face was often very pale with signs of swelling. In part, because of his health conditions, he often tried to avoid any conflict; however, the main reason for his relatively modest reaction to my request was more political. It is important to stress that he definitely valued his good reputation abroad. I knew that and found it to be very helpful in my goals. He anticipated that eventually I would emigrate, and he did not want his Western scientist friends to get the impression that he was a typical Soviet bureaucrat.

Khomenko did what he was supposed to do, as he told me about fifteen years later, when we met at a scientific meeting in Dubrovnik, Yugoslavia. He came to the microbiology section to meet with me and to attend my presentation. We met as old friends, with hugs, as is common among the Russians. After that, we had a few more friendly meetings at scientific conferences in Paris and, at times, even corresponded. There was a good reason for being friendly with Khomenko and even to be thankful to him. After all, in the past, regardless of motivations, he had avoided informing my sworn enemy, the Deputy Minister of Health Burgasov, of my intention to emigrate, which could have sent me to the East instead of the West.

My struggle to obtain the necessary documents without quitting my job continued for three months, along with a series of complaints from me and negative responses from different state offices. My patience, as well as my acquaintance with the system, was rewarded. I finally received the employment certificate and applied for emigration with my younger son, Herman. Four months later, we received our emigration visas, thus paving a road for my older son, Michael, and his family to follow. For a period of almost eight months, until my emigration in October 1978, I was employed, e.g. protected from potential imprisonment as a "parasite"! For that, at least in part, I should be thankful to A.G. Khomenko.

When we met in Dubrovnik in 1985, Khomenko told me that centralized production of the dry L-J medium continued successfully. At that time I had already become an American citizen. Thanks to the Green Eggs Project, I was a free man.

In 2001, the first time after emigration, by invitation from the Euro-Asian Educational Institute, my colleague Dr. Michael Iseman and I visited several cities in Russia. During this trip we had an opportunity to witness use of the dry L-J medium in several cities, including Yekaterinburg. This was the medium that I had helped develop many years ago, but, of course, my name was omitted on the label, because back in the 1970s I did not want my name associated with any patents that could pose a potential obstacle to receiving the exit visa. Subsequently, my name was not mentioned in a monograph about this medium published by Dr. E.A. Finkel. A scientific report on multicenter evaluation of this medium, published in a Russian journal in 1986, included as authors a large group of prominent individuals, including A.G. Khomenko, but again, without even mentioning my name.

2. Green Eggs and Condoms

The lyophilization process, which was the basis for manufacturing the dry L-J medium, consisted of two major steps: freezing the egg-containing suspension in 500 ml bottles and drying by vacuum under steadily increased temperature. Each phase was done in two different instrument settings. One concern was to keep sterility of the L-J medium. The bottles could have been sealed during freezing with conventional cotton stoppers, but it would have been too difficult to open them quickly after they were placed inside the drying apparatus. Someone suggested using condoms instead of stoppers. They had to be pulled down on the bottlenecks after wiping the bottlenecks and the outer surface of the condoms with alcohol. Opening the bottles inside the vacuum system was easy; we simply cut the top of the condoms with sterile scissors.

The "condom technology" was originally developed long before the Green Eggs Project, for lyophilization of a different product at the time when I worked at the Metchnikov Institute for Vaccines and Sera. The inventor of this technology was a laboratory technician named Victor Bulk, an expert in the field, who later became a faculty member after defending his Ph.D. This man, who was in his late thirties at that time, was of Gipsy descent. He was tall, slim, with black hair and dark skin. He had a great sense of humor and invention of the condom technology was just one of his jokes. Often in a small group he would tell jokes; some of them were of his own creation. One of his jokes regarding the Soviet dictator Joseph Stalin follows:

Joseph Stalin wakes up with a heavy hangover, grabs a pipe, stuffs it with tobacco, and inhales a couple of times. Not feeling any better, he takes the telephone and requests his switchboard, "Give me Molotov." (*A special twist to the story was added by Victor's ability to imitate Stalin's far-from-perfect Russian with a heavy Georgian accent.*)

Stalin:	Vyacheslav Michailovitch, some say that you stutter even when talking about our Party ideals. Is it true?
Molotov:	Comrade Stalin, sorry, but I have always been truthful with the Party and never concealed this defect of my speech from the Party.
Stalin:	Okay, but just keep in mind what people say. Stalin makes another call to Kaganovitch.
Stalin:	Lazar Moiseevitch, some people say that you are a Jew. What can you say about it?
Kaganovitch:	Comrade Stalin, I have always been honest with the Party and clearly indicated in my file that I am of Jewish descent.
Stalin:	Yes, but just keep in mind that people are talking about it.

After these short conversations, Stalin suddenly felt much better, rubbed his hands, and said loudly to himself, "Well, now I can do some productive work, like deciding about the death sentence for another hundred enemies of the people."

Telling such jokes was dangerous, and the teller could easily end up in the Gulag Archipelago, but nothing of this sort ever happened to Victor Bulk, and there were two possible explanations for that. One was that there were no KGB informers in the audience, and the other was the possibility that Bulk himself was assigned by the KGB to tell such stories with the purpose of provoking similar stories from someone in the audience. The latter was denied, then and now, by those who knew Victor well, which leaves us with the pleasant conclusion that there were no KGB informers among those who listened to Victor's jokes.

At the time of Bulk's invention, we used approximately fifty condoms per week, and they could only be obtained from the local pharmacy. The customers in Russian pharmacies did not have direct access to any product and to purchase anything one had to ask the clerk, most often in the presence of a crowd of people waiting in line. It was a problem to assign someone in my laboratory to the pharmacy. Only one technician in my laboratory volunteered to take this assignment. It was an elderly woman by name Anna Vasilievna Kurakina, a short, stocky person with severe myopia who wore very thick glasses. She was a peasant, poorly educated, and was very proud of being accepted as an equal and being treated with respect for her hard work. Once every week, this strange woman would go across the street to the pharmacy. She would approach the clerk and very loudly say, "I need fifty condoms." And after paying with cash she would say, "Please give me a receipt; after all these condoms are not for personal use, but for our research." One can only imagine the reaction of the people waiting in line.

When the production of the powdered L-J medium began in Tumen, implementation of the condom technology created several peculiar situations. The supply of condoms needed for production was so large that they had to come directly from the rubber factory. The city officials visiting the Institute became targets for practical jokes by the technicians, who would secretly place a few condoms into the visitors' pockets, subsequently to be discovered by their wives. As with anything else in the Soviet Union, the local pharmacies often experienced a lack of proper supplies. It was not long before the local population learned that the only place in the city where condoms were always available was the Microbiology Institute. At that time the typical Russian/Soviet proverb "Tell me what is in your pockets, and I will tell you where you work" became the motto of the Microbiology Institute employees. The request for condoms from the Institute tripled within a year without any increase in the L-J medium production. The people of Tumen had a better supply of condoms than any other city in the Soviet Union; however, how this situation influenced the birthrate and prevalence of venereal diseases in the city of Tumen remained a mystery.

3. Green Eggs and Vodka

Above I described how collective efforts of several groups of scientists resulted in the formulation of a powdered L-J medium for cultivation of the tubercle bacilli. The local laboratories around the Soviet Union who received this powder had to only add water, distribute the suspension in the tubes, and coagulate the medium. The crucial step in my assignment was to find a place to manufacture the medium for the whole country, a place that would be close to the source of a significant supply of eggs.

I chose the city of Tumen in Siberia for this production. When I arrived in Tumen, the staff of the local Institute treated me with the utmost respect and appreciation. The assignment of the medium production was going to save this Institute from anticipated closure. They even gave a party for me at the home of one of the employees. Everyone was very excited at this party, especially when hot dogs were served. "Masha, where on earth did you get these?" everyone asked. "We have not seen any meat products in our grocery stores for almost a year." Yes, the groceries of the city were quite scarce, and, paradoxically, were not only lacking meat, but also chicken and eggs, despite the large chicken farm that was nearby.

One of the reasons for choosing Tumen as a site for production of the medium was the location of this large chicken farm. There were rumors that a substantial proportion of eggs produced on that farm failed to be shipped out, due to problems of transportation. My goal was to convince the local authorities to commit most of the egg production to the large-scale manufacturing of the L-J medium.

No one except the Secretary of the District's Communist Party could make such a decision, and I was faced with the problem of obtaining his favorable decision. The administration of the Institute informed the Secretary about the recent successful development of a new product and invited him to visit with their adviser from Moscow who had helped them with this accomplishment—me. We began the necessary preparations for this important event, and the plans for the Secretary's visit were elaborately detailed. One detail was the serving of vodka, a common element of any meeting in Russia—whether to serve it, how to serve it, and at what moment to serve it.

Vodka consumption in Russia always played an important role, not only in social and personal interactions, but also in politics and the economy. A drink always accompanied any important meeting, deal, or arrangement. Anyone in a group who does not drink is usually ostracized. Appreciation of vodka consumption as a part of the tradition and culture could help in resolving difficult problems. On the other hand, underestimation of the importance of this issue could be disastrous.

There were at least two vodka consumption related large-scale disastrous episodes in the history of Russia. With good intentions, Tsar Nicolas II, during World War I, decided to abolish vodka production. This made the Russian people so unhappy, and the monarchy so unpopular, that according to historical accounts, it is considered as one of the causes of the Russian Revolution of 1917. Another example is from more modern times. In the Soviet Union, the government had a monopoly on vodka production and distribution, and the revenue constituted about twenty-five percent of the budget. After taking over the leadership of the country, Gorbachev decided to diminish consumption of vodka in the country because he thought it interfered with productivity in the workplace. This anti-alcohol campaign made him extremely unpopular. Most of the vodka production went to bootleggers and led to the rise of the organized crime. Apparently, Gorbachev did not learn a lesson from the prohibition era in the United States or from Tsar Nicolas II in his own country.

I knew well the history of Russia and always appreciated vodka consumption as an element of social life, especially after my experience living in the Far North, where I learned how to drink 95% alcohol and still remain conscious. So, I was ready for a new challenge!

The Secretary, a stocky man (just imagine Yeltzin's appearance when he was young), came to visit the Microbiology Research Institute. As the "representative from Moscow" I was responsible for explaining the problem to the boss.

With a smile of superiority on his face, the Secretary said, "So, I have been told that a great discovery has been made here, and that our Oblast (District) is about to save Russia from tuberculosis. Please, doctor, explain to me in lay language, what is this all about?"

The Secretary and I were sitting at a table across from each other; standing around was a group of microbiologists and administrators of the Institute. The following dialog took place.

I: Well, this 500 ml bottle contains a standardized medium developed in this Institute of your district. It will help the rest of our great country deal with tuberculosis through better diagnosis and better drug administration. It will generate revenue for your institute, and production will guarantee substantial employment in the city of Tumen.

Secretary: That is good, but what do you want from me?

I: You see this powder in the bottle? This medium is made from eggs, and you must make the decision to commit a substantial proportion of local egg production for manufacturing this medium.

Secretary: Oh, no! I cannot do that! I am supposed to feed the people. That is what the eggs are for! Not for tubercle bacilli. Oh, no!

I: But, as everybody knows, the eggs produced at the local farm are getting rotten because they are not being shipped in a timely manner.

Secretary: That is true, but that is the fault of the Minister of Transportation, not mine. I am responsible for the production of the eggs, and the high efficiency of our farm is well recognized.

For a few moments dead silence dominated the room. Suddenly I remembered another argument that I had prepared in advance but almost forgotten. I knew from my many years of research in the Soviet Union that any project could be justified if it contributed to the military strength of our Great Motherland. And so I continued our dialogue:

I: Comrade Secretary, here is another facet of the issue that I did not have a chance to mention before, the production of this powder may become a great contribution to the defense of our country.

Secretary: You cannot catch me on that, doctor. I am familiar with such arguments from the scientists who are eager to get funding for their research. How can this medium have any military importance?

I: But you do remember, Comrade Secretary, how during the Great Patriotic War, especially in 1943–45, so many lives in the army and in the population were saved thanks to the egg powder provided to us from China.

Secretary: Oh, yes, I remember that. I was on the front, and every day the soldiers in my platoon were making scrambled eggs from this powder.

I: Comrade Secretary, what you see in this bottle is an egg powder! By manufacturing this medium you can produce a great reserve of food for the future time of war, and not a single egg in your farm would be wasted. You can even increase production of eggs. You know that a well-preserved food supply is an important element of success during the war.

Secretary: You are saying that it is an egg powder, but why is it green?

I: A completely safe green dye is added to it just for better preservation. Otherwise it is just an egg powder. I suggest that we go from words to action; let's make a meal of scrambled eggs from this powder right now.

Secretary: Oh, you are a funny man, doctor, but okay, let's do it!

People in white coats around us, relieved after a period of tension, suddenly became very active. In no time, an electric stove with a pan, butter, and water appeared on the table, as well as two plates, forks, and four glasses. I also noticed another bottle, obviously not water, in the hands of one of the technicians.

Water was added to two of four glasses and to the bottle with the dry L-J medium. The egg powder was easily dissolved and the contents of the bottle poured onto the hot pan. In a few minutes we were served a meal of scrambled eggs, which appeared quite green on the white plates. The Secretary said that he would watch me eat first, but the important decision that he had to make required a drink before the meal. That was the signal for the technician with the mysterious bottle in his hands to pour two remaining glasses. Actually, I already knew from the fact that the other two glasses were filled with water that the drink in the bottle was not the traditional 40% vodka used in other parts of Russia (for example, in Moscow) but rather a 95% (190 proof) spiritus. Obviously this was a test. I proposed a toast for the success of the new factory, and swallowed 150 ml of the spiritus, followed by water. The Secretary was impressed. He did not know that before becoming a Muscovite I spent seven years in the Far North, where 95% drinking spiritus was common and one had to learn how to drink it if you wanted to be accepted socially.

The Secretary said the traditional *"Na Zdorovie,"* and after swallowing the drink he started eating the meal. He said, "You were right, doctor; it is not bad, though a little bit salty." We had a second drink, finished the meal, and…the Secretary signed the document, which had been prepared in advance and had now been placed on the table in place of the empty plates and glasses. Thus, the way for industrial production of the green egg powder was opened.

And so, my dear Dr. Seuss, I will not eat green eggs with ham, and I will never eat ham, but I did and will again (if necessary) eat green eggs alone, under the condition that this meal is served with vodka.

Na Zdorovie, my dear comrade, Dr. Seuss!

5. Farewell, Russia

Fear, uncertainty, and tension were the dominant emotions during my last few months in Moscow, although I pretended to be happy, confident, and without any serious concerns. In early 1978, my good friend Dr. Guramy Arabidze visited me at my office in the TB Institute, and we reminisced about our work together in 1960 during our expedition to Africa. His visit was very supportive. He was brave to openly spend time with me, knowing that I had applied for emigration. He was also amazed that I was smiling and joking. He said, "Leonid, how can you do that while you are in such danger?" I explained that my outward demeanor and my internal mood were part of my survival strategy; at a time when most people were reluctant to be seen with me, I was very glad and grateful that there were a few like Guramy who did not hesitate to visit me, to shake my hand, and to wish me good luck.

At that time, my main concern was protecting my son, Herman, from being drafted into the Army. That would end any attempts to emigrate. Previously, he had been protected from mandatory military service because he was a university student; however, he had to resign from school in order to begin his application to emigrate. Information about his resignation was sent to the local police station and to the military draft bureau, so we knew to expect some visitors.

While my wife and I were at work, Herman spent most of his time behind locked doors studying Italian. One weekend, while Herman was out, two plain-clothed individuals came requesting that Herman come to the police station for a "conversation." I told them that he was out of town at the Caucasus Mountains getting mineral water baths for treatment of his spinal problems. They requested that he come to the police station upon his return to Moscow. Naturally, just as they left, Herman suddenly returned home. I looked outside to check and they were gone, but I was still concerned that our place was being watched. I instructed Herman to follow me at a twenty yard distance as we quickly left the apartment and headed toward the nearest subway station. I told him that I would check around, and if I saw anything suspicious I would scratch my head. That was the signal to stop following me and head off in a different route. We were trying to get to my friend, Dr. Ludmila Levina; we had previously told her that we might need her help. After changing subway trains and directions to make doubly sure no one was following, Herman reached Ludmila's place, where he stayed hidden for about six weeks. Then we moved him to my friend Mars Galiev's apartment, and then another month was spent in the Caucasus, at the Itkol Hotel, which was generously provided by my good friend Noah Bezirov. Directives to visit the military draft station kept coming, but we ignored them. Finally, in November of 1978, two armed men came to pick up Herman. But by then we were out of reach, already in Vienna. It was the grace of fortune that the right hand of the Soviet bureaucracy didn't know what the left hand was doing.

Another dramatic event in our lives during the waiting period and hoping for permission to emigrate was my expulsion from the Communist Party. My application for emigration could not be processed without first being expelled from the Party. For this I had to appear before a special Communist Party Committee in one of Moscow's districts. The committee consisted of about thirty members, mostly retired military and older KGB men. The members were seated at a long table, while the chairperson and I were seated at the head. The purpose of the meeting was not only to condemn my "betrayal," but also attempt to convince me to change my mind, and if I stubbornly refused, to provoke me into making anti-Soviet statements which would lead to criminal charges against me. One set of questions was: "Are you in disagreement with the policy of the Soviet Union regarding Israel? Do you consider Israel your motherland and not Russia? Is the purpose of your emigration to Israel to support the Zionist's aggressive strategy there? Are you against the Communist ideology at all? Are you planning to serve the capitalist society, you—a member of the Communist Party?"

My responses were very simple. They consisted of the same straightforward and repetitious answer: "I have no political ambitions, and the only reason for my emigration is strictly personal—to be with my mother because I did not give her enough attention while she lived in Moscow. I feel guilty because of that and want to be with her now because she is very ill." The major thing that made the members of the committee especially angry was that they couldn't provoke me to make a political statement. They were also annoyed by two suggestions that I made. One, I was not seeking expulsion from the Party, and therefore could they consider transferring me to the Communist Party of Israel? Two, instead of emigration could they just allow me to visit my mother in Israel and stay with her as long as she was alive, and then come back to Moscow, on the condition that my job would be saved? We all knew that it was a game, but I did not follow the rules. Rather, I pretended to take their concerns quite seriously. They still kept attacking me with labels such as "Zionist" and "traitor." My patience was waning, and I figured that the best defense was a good offense. So I said that in Israel I was not going to serve the capitalists but the patients, as I had done during my whole life. I reminded them of my record of working many dangerous assignments, investigating outbreaks of infectious diseases around the country, and risking my life during the mission in Africa on behalf of the Soviet government.

Then, with well-played anger and emotion, I pointed a finger at a few of the most aggressive members of the group, addressing each one individually. I said, "I understand that you are not very young now, but maybe you still remember your mother? Did you ever have a mother, or did you just emerge into this world by somebody's decree? Why can't you understand the feelings of a son who wants to see his sick mother at the time when she needs him the most? Why can't you, as humans and as members of the Communist Party, understand that?" With all these questions and statements I had co-opted their main weapon, demagogy. Perhaps they appreciated it. It played well, and I could see that it was not easy for some members of the group to hide a smile and keep a straight face. I was stripped of my Party membership, but without the usual "traitor" or "Zionist sympathizer" labels that could have spelled danger. This was rather unusual.

After another series of games that I played to keep my job, I finally received a phone call from the Emigration Office (OVIR). In order to process my application further, I had to surrender my certificate of employment, that is, to resign. I argued that I could not afford to take this risk in case my application was refused. The woman on the other end said, " Listen, I can tell you that you will be permitted to emigrate, and the decision in principle has already been made. Resign from your position and bring the employment certificate to me personally. My name is Captain Evreinova." I had no choice, but I wanted to be sure. I submitted my resignation to the head of the personnel department, a lady with whom I had always had good rapport, and asked her to hold on to my letter until the next day. With the certificate in hand I rushed to the OVIR.

The OVIR office was located in a two-story building. The first floor was a waiting room where the applicants sat in anticipation of being called to the window. This was not an option for me. I had to see Captain Evreinova in person to find out if I was indeed being granted permission to emigrate, and only afterward would I hand over my certificate to her. Her office was located on the second floor and off limits to visitors. A policeman stood at the stairs leading to the second floor. I blended into the crowd of visitors to assess the situation. As I anticipated, in a couple of hours the inevitable biological process sent the policeman to the bathroom. I rushed to the stairs, ignoring the warning sign. Once on the second floor, I started walking down the corridor as though I belonged there. When I saw a woman in plain clothes, I asked her where I could find Captain Evreinova, who had asked me to come. In a few minutes Captain Evreinova, a very attractive young woman in a KGB uniform, approached me. She was surprised to see me on the second floor and definitely wanted me to disappear without attracting any attention from her colleagues. She pulled me to the top stair and said, "Yes, you already have permission, and you will get it in the mail in few days if you give me the certificate." Even in a uniform, what a pleasant woman she was! I shook hands with her and complimented her on her appearance. One needs to appreciate that it is hardly customary in Russia, even now, to make eye contact and smile at a stranger. Smiling to a KGB officer, complimenting her appearance, and shaking hands with her must have been a shock to Captain Evreinova. She was used to dealing with fearful applicants. My strategy was to impress her so that she would not forget her promise to expedite the documents. A light smile mixed with surprise appeared on her face. After all, she was a woman, and most women do appreciate compliments, especially when they are

genuine. I walked down the stairs with an expression of importance on my face, and the policeman did not dare stop me.

A few days later, Herman and I received our exit visas, documents given instead of passports to those who were stripped of their
Soviet citizenship because of emigration to Israel, since the Soviet
Union and Israel had no diplomatic relations. Our emigration
would also pave the road for my older son, Michael, and his family
to follow us under the international rules for unification of families.

Herman and I finally left Moscow at the end of October of
1978. Our departure was extremely depressing. We waited long
hours and overnight in the airport, going through humiliating luggage searches by customs officers. There was the agonizing uncertainty of actually getting through, and finally, the sadness of saying farewell to my wife, Sima. Only after actually landing at the
airport in Vienna did I begin to feel certain that we were out of the
grip of the KGB. During the last few months in Moscow my
biggest fear was the possibility of arrest. This fear was justified by
the possibility of Deputy Health Minister Burgasov finding out
about my emigration; he was my most powerful enemy.
Fortunately, nobody mentioned it to him. Most of all I was afraid
of physical torture, which was a common KGB practice. During
my last weeks in Moscow I actually carried vials of cyanide powder in case I was arrested. I destroyed these two vials only
moments before going to the airport.

Our arrival in Vienna eliminated this fear, but it still did not lib-
erate my mind from the heavy tension. I felt that Herman was also
somewhat depressed. Staying in a dilapidated hotel and walking
through the streets of Vienna turned out to be a gloomy experience. Once I lost my direction and started asking questions. At that
time my German was still good. There were only a few people in
the streets and one of them was a drunk. For some reason (maybe
because I was wearing a beret), he thought I was from Holland. He
told me, with evident pride in his tone, that he had been one of
Hitler's soldiers and had been stationed in Holland during the
war. He spoke of pleasant memories of that time.

Although we were in Vienna only for a short time, it added to
our overall experience of ominous dread. There were guards with
machine guns who were protecting Jewish emigrants from terror-

ists. There was the coldness of the Austrians and of some officials who handled our processing. One very unpleasant discovery was to see the number of "Jewish" emigrants with obvious criminal backgrounds and intentions. I wondered if the Soviet authorities had found a clever way to dump them off through emigration instead of using court and prison resources. It was also the first time we had seen such an abundance and variety of food and other goods, none of which we could afford. This contributed further to our depression and the feeling that we were second-class citizens and now refugees. All that changed when we arrived in Rome.

We were amazed at the friendliness and attentiveness of the Italian people. Our affairs were handled by a group of extremely pleasant and efficient Americans at the office of the Hebrew Immigrant Aid Society (HIAS). Herman and I settled in Ladispoli, a suburb of Rome, which was a resort in the summer but vacant in the winter. Local people, whose apartments the immigrants rented, were most hospitable. Local stores displayed signs in Russian, and the merchants tried to meet the needs of the newcomers. After the people at HIAS learned that Herman knew Italian (in addition to English), they asked him to work as an interpreter at the bank. Secretly learning Italian in our apartment before emigration paid off. Although he only spent one month working at the bank, his Italian was so good that when we visited other Italian cities, people actually thought he was a native of Rome.

I had to give a detailed account to HIAS about my past membership in the Communist Party. They were uncertain about whether I would get an American visa and suggested instead that Herman and I go to Israel. That was not our intention; I already knew that in Israel I would not be able to pursue a new career in my field. At the same time I did not want to deny my past. No more lies and no more *Homo Sovieticus* style! After all, I did not care what I was going to do in the free world. I started dreaming of going into the restaurant business. My hobby was cooking, and that could have become my new career. (Perhaps it was just a fleeting, self-indulgent thought.) At the same time, I felt the obligation to at least try to continue in microbiology or infectious disease medicine. Therefore, with such plans in mind, we managed to carry a typewriter along with our four small suitcases. I also had a specially prepared address book with the names of American scientists and institutions.

During the first few weeks in Ladispoli I wrote at least fifty letters and mailed them with my curriculum vitae to various scientists and institutions. In each of the letters I stressed that, in spite of my experience and professional certification from Russia, I wanted to make a fresh start. Some did not respond. Some said that they would keep my CV on file. Only two responded positively. One was for a residency in infectious diseases at the Johns Hopkins University in Baltimore. The other was a proposal of fellowship from Dr. Mayer Goren at the National Jewish Hospital in Denver. Without hesitation I chose Denver. I already knew about Dr. Goren from my correspondence with him, and I did not want to become a practicing physician again. Another point was the opportunity to live near the mountains and resume my hiking activities on American soil. But first we had to get American visas.

Eventually, we were invited for an interview at the American Consulate in Rome. It was a detailed but quite interesting and inspiring conversation with the American Consul, a very intelligent and elegant person with an Italian-sounding name. At the end of our conversation he said to me, "I know your story, not only from what you told me today, and I am making an unusual decision. Even without consulting with the State Department—and I could lose my job for this—I am issuing an American visa for you and your son. I wish you the very best in the United States." It was my birthday, January 5, 1979. One could not imagine a better birthday gift! People at HIAS could not believe it. They started speculating that we must have misunderstood what the Consul said; however, a few days later we got the American visas and we were on our way.

We arrived in New York on January 23, spent the first night on American soil there, and came to Denver on the twenty-fourth. Dr. Mayer Goren and his wife Ethel met us at Stapleton Airport and took us to the apartment they had rented for us. I asked Dr. Goren, "When do I start my work in your laboratory?" to which Mayer responded, "You just started today." Words fail to describe my feelings at that moment!

Six months after our arrival to the U.S., my older son Michael, with his wife Helen and two-year-old Boris, joined us in Denver. Michael had graduated from the Medical School in Moscow and started his internship there, but his medical diploma needed American verification to start his residency in the U.S. With Dr. Goren's help, I arranged for him to take the International Council Foreign Medical Graduates certificate test upon arrival in Denver. He passed successfully and immediately began applying for residency at different medical schools. Herman started classes at the Metropolitan College to receive his BS degree, and I started my new career, at the age of fifty-three, by conducting the most exciting research at the bench level in Dr. Goren's laboratory. We had all started our new lives in America; now, finally and with certainty, I could say "Farewell, Russia."

CHAPTER ELEVEN

"Discovering" America, First Impressions

"Success depends upon previous preparation, and without such preparation there is sure to be failure."
Confucius

1. Arrival to the U.S.
2. Mayer Goren, Mentor and Friend
3. New Friends
4. National Jewish Hospital in Denver

Fig. 36. Mayer Goren – a great scientist, mentor, and a friend:
- **Mayer as a chemist (1967);**
- **As a musician (1981);**
- **A gentle opponent, in discussion at the American Society for Microbiology (ASM) meeting (1986); and**
- **Attending my first in the US poster presentation at the ASM meeting (1981)**

Fig. 37. First interactions in Denver (top to bottom):
- The campus of National Jewish, left to right: my daughter-in-law Helen, Diane (Mayer's assistant), Mayer, his wife Ethel, myself, (behind is Michael holding little Boris), 1980;
- Boris between Mayer and me (1984);
- Taking Mayer to the high country; and
- We made it at 13,000 ft!

Fig. 38. New friends (left to right, top to bottom):
- Richard Bluestein, President of the National Jewish Hospital (1962-1982);
- Ann Bard, a caring friend;
- Harry Aschkinasi, Vice-President for development at the National Jewish until 1984;
- With Thomas Moulding, a staff physician at the National Jewish and a hiking companion; and
- Jack Goldman, a professional photographer and a friend of our family.

Fig. 39. From the history of the National Jewish Hospital in Denver (left to right, top to bottom):
- **Ms. Frances Wisebard Jacobs;**
- **Rabbi William S. Friedman;**
- **Dr. Werner B. Schaefer; and**
- **Dr. Gardner Middlebrook.**

Fig.40. National Jewish Presidents/CEOs after 1982 (left to right, top to bottom):
- Michael K. Schonbrun, 1982-1991;
- Leonard Perlmutter, 1991-1993;
- Lynn M. Taussig, M.D., 1993-2005; and
- Michael Salem, M.D., 2006- present.

1. Arrival to the U.S.

Safety! Promise for the future! Freedom! Fairness! Equal rights! Democracy! Pursuit of these aspirations defined those emigrants from the Soviet Union to the United States who were motivated by ideological rather than economic issues. My very first step on American soil gave me the confidence that most of our expectations would be met. My most intense awareness was that of being free, feeling free, liberated from mental oppression, from suppressed fear, from imposed obligations, free to make choices for the future, etc., etc. Feeling free is so overwhelming that it is beyond precise expression in the words of any language!

I experienced these feelings for the first time in my life even before entering the U.S. It was in Rome, when my son Herman and I walked through St. Peter's Square in November of 1978. Perhaps the architectural design of that place causes a feeling of being the center of attention, the feeling that nothing around could dominate you, not the Vatican, not the cathedral, not the buildings, not the columns surrounding the square. The unique architecture of this square is in dramatic contrast to the architecture of the Catholic cathedrals, where one is dominated by the surroundings and experiences a feeling of being just an insignificant part of the world.

There are many famous squares in the world, but their grandiose architecture seems to reduce a person to a state of insignificance. The most familiar to us was the Red Square in Moscow. This immense plaza reminded us of the Victorious Past (the Cathedral of St. Basil), next to it the historic place of public executions (*Lobnoye Miesto*), and also of the power of the Kremlin and the Lenin-Stalin dictatorship (Lenin's Mausoleum). St. Peter's was different. This square, bathed in the warm sun, enhanced our elation of being free in a free world around us!

The feeling of being a free person intensified when we arrived at JFK airport on January 23, 1979 and the next day, in Denver, Colorado. Subsequently, we learned that many Americans don't appreciate the freedom they have simply because they have not had our experience and often cannot imagine anything different.

In a Russian story, two journalists, an American and a Russian, are debating which country has more freedom, the U.S. or the Soviet Union. The American said, "You know, in my country I can demonstrate in front of the White House with a statement that the U.S. president is stupid and unfit. Can you do anything like that in your country?" The Russian responded, "Yes, of course. I can demonstrate in the Red Square in front of the Kremlin with a statement that the U.S. president is stupid and unfit."

One of our impressions in the U.S. was how little the Americans knew about the Soviet Union. This was reflected in questions we were asked, such as, "What is the climate in the country?" or "Do they have modern television systems?" Many American Jewish activists believed that our reason for emigration was that we were not allowed to practice Judaism. It was not very easy to explain to them that most of us (in fact, a whole generation) were deprived of any religious education for too many years to have any knowledge of religion and/or commitment to it. In fact, most of us were rather secular people who were only ethnically recognized as Jews. Economics (in quest of a better life) was not one of the primary concerns for those who went through many obstacles and took enormous risks by emigrating in the 1970s. Therefore, the often-asked question was, "If it is not for economic reasons and not a search for better life, then why go through the dangers of emigration to leave the country where you grew up?" A simple answer to these questions in regard to my personal reasons was, "There were many reasons, but the main reason for my family and me was because of the growing government-sponsored anti-Semitism, I did not see any future for my children."

In fact, it was much more than "not seeing any future prospects." I tried to explain to my new American acquaintances that it was a fear for our survival. Many Americans did not know that just before Stalin's death in 1953 a plan was developed to expel the Jews from all major cities (under the pretense of saving them from pogroms by angry Russian people) and send them to Siberia, with subsequent extermination. When Stalin died and Khrushchev (who was an active participant in the anti-Jewish plan) denounced him, a period of "post-Stalin thaw" provided hope that everything was going to change. These hopes came to an end in the late 1960s and especially in the 1970s when anti-Semitism was used as a tool to stimulate Russian nationalism, which required, as any other historically known nationalistic propaganda, a loathsome target. The new wave of anti-Semitism was also fueled by the success of Israel as the potential home for Jews and because of the successful wars against the Arab countries that represented the Soviet geopolitical interests in the Middle East. So again, we did not feel safe. On a personal level, I knew that I would soon lose my job and be degraded to the humiliating status of a second-class citizen.

Upon arrival to the U.S. our first impressions with regard to expectations, other than freedom, were much more complex. We learned that equal rights and fairness have been subjects of constant struggle among American people throughout the history of the country, with the greatest achievements possible only under unique U.S. conditions.

As did many other immigrants from Russia, we felt that the system for controlling immigration was too loose, with not enough measures against crime and criminals and not enough control over the anti-government activities of hate groups such as the KKK or neo-Nazis. We happened to be right in our view of this part of our first impressions. Still, many Americans don't understand how vital it is in the modern world to take measures that may require a very minimal and insignificant sacrifice in limiting some of our freedom, such as having a national ID card.

2. Mayer Goren, Mentor and Friend

More than thirty years ago, while working in Moscow as a scientist in the field of tuberculosis and translating advanced scientific reports into Russian for publication, I came across the brilliant publications by Dr. Mayer Goren. I perceived his work as an innovative approach to the biology of tubercle bacilli. Retrospectively, it's clear that he was a pioneer in what is now known as molecular biology, specifically the molecular basis of the immunity to tuberculosis. Unfortunately, he has not yet been widely recognized as a pioneer in this field. He was the first to combine a high level of expertise in the two fields of chemistry and microbiology. Because of my admiration for these works, I wrote him a letter with a few comments and questions. We continued our correspondence for a few years. As required, each of my letters was submitted in an open envelope to the Institutional Human Resources Department (under KGB supervision) for mailing abroad.

At first our correspondence was related to scientific matters only, but over time we began to include personal items as well. Initially it did not cause any suspicion by the KGB. After all, I played the role of an obedient Soviet citizen by not revealing my home address and by sending the letters through the institutional authorities.

In 1977 when I was preparing for emigration from the USSR, I decided to inform Dr. Goren of my intentions. My dream was to visit his laboratory and perhaps even work for him. Obviously I couldn't send such a message through the KGB censors. So in one of the handwritten letters I just added three Hebrew letters indicating "Shalom" to my signature, hoping that the censor would see it as a part of my signature. The trick worked! As I learned later, Mayer got the message! Only a brilliant and highly perceptive person such as he would have deduced that this little sign indicated my intention to leave the USSR. He had already received a recommendation letter from the famous TB expert Gardner Middlebrook, whom I had met in Moscow at the International TB Conference. He had also received a copy of one of my scientific papers through Middlebrook and translated by Roy Medvedev, a scientist who had previously defected from the USSR. At my meeting with Middlebrook in Moscow, I mentioned my correspondence with Mayer and my dream to visit his laboratory.

It was only after leaving Moscow in 1978 and waiting in Italy for the U.S. entry permit that I finally had the opportunity to communicate with Mayer openly. Based on the information I sent him, he arranged my acceptance in a fellowship program with Richard Bluestein, then President of National Jewish Hospital, and Dr. Reuben Cherniack, Chairman of the Department of Medicine.

Soon after beginning work in Dr. Goren's laboratory in January of 1979, a package arrived from Moscow marked "return to sender—the addressee could not be located." It was a package that Mayer had sent to me more than a year earlier as a birthday gift. It contained three records of Yasha Heifetz' violin compositions performed by Eugene Fodor, who was one of his students and also a friend of Mayer's, and he had autographed each record. Perhaps the gift was also selected because the composer's name was

Heifetz, much like mine. Apparently the KGB in Moscow had unsuccessfully spent a whole year trying to decipher secret messages hidden in the records.

My fellowship in Dr. Goren's laboratory was the happiest period of my professional life. I enjoyed exciting research under the direction of one of the world's leading scientists, long hours of hands-on experimentation at the laboratory bench—and all this without politics or bureaucracy! There was also a deep satisfaction with the results.

Within a year, under Dr. Goren's direction and in collaboration with Katsuyuki Imai, a visiting scientist from Japan, we completed a project, published a paper, and I received my first federal grant from the National Institutes of Health (NIH). During that period, Dr. Imai and I would begin our experiments early in the morning. Mayer would start his day at around the same time, but at home, playing his violin for an hour or more. He would arrive in the lab around ten o'clock and, having been inspired by his music, he would come in with new ideas. Then he'd often cancel what we were doing and start new, more exciting experiments. He seemed to derive energy and inspiration from both music and science.

From time to time on weekends, Mayer and his wife Ethel would host a chamber performance at their home. Mayer was a wonderful violinist, and we were lucky to enjoy these great performances. In music Mayer was also an innovative expert, rendering original interpretations in musical events throughout the city.

Mayer was also a devout scholar of Judaism and Jewish culture, and he had a strong influence on many of us in our commitments to Judaism. At the same time he was an example of tolerance to different views and peoples. Mayer respected and loved all people who were connected with him in one way or another.

Everyone who knew Mayer Goren was enriched by his influence. After having touched so many lives during his lifetime, he passed away on October 9, 2005 at the age of eighty-four. A detailed obituary about Mayer B. Goren by Franklin M. Harold and Patrick J. Brennan was published in the *Microbe* magazine in the June 2006 issue. Those of us who cherished our time with him will forever hold his memory within our hearts, and we all miss him greatly.

3. New Friends

A number of people became our new friends. They tried to under-stand our past and our expectations for the future, and they were extremely helpful in our adjustment to life in America. Besides Dr. Goren's constant care and help, I received ample attention from various people in the Denver community and from some of my colleagues at my place of employment, National Jewish Hospital (now called National Jewish Medical and Research Center). I can-not find enough words to express my gratitude to Richard Bluestein, Harry Aschkinasi, Jack Goldman, and Ann Bard for their help in our adjustment to the American society. I am indebt-ed to the librarian Ned Eig and my colleague in the TB laboratory Pamela Lindholm-Levy for helping me improve my English skills. Help and encouragement by these and many other people was essential for our adjustment in the U.S.

On January 24, 1979, the first day of our arrival to Denver, Dr. Goren took me to the office of the President of the National Jewish Hospital, as it was called at that time. The President, Richard Bluestein, welcomed me with congratulations for a safe arrival and the suggestion that I come directly to him if any problems arose. Such a warm welcome, combined with the openness and kindness by the head of this great institution, made this day a turning point in my life, and I will remember that day for the rest of my life. Richard Bluestein was an unusually kind person, always available to all employees of any rank, and a great leader, making National Jewish Hospital a place where people loved to work. He watched over my activities even after his retirement in 1982. Occasionally he and his wife Eleanor would invite my family to their home and to a number of social events. This attention from such a great man was important for us; we had come from a different world and needed moral support to settle in the strange environment of this country.

Ann Bard, employed at that time as a patients' representative, gave special attention to our family. Her professional skills, togeth-er with her kind personality, made this beautiful woman a confi-dante with whom I did not hesitate to share the episodes of my past life and current personal problems. We used to spend hours walking in the streets and talking about life in the Soviet Union, Jewish problems, religion, and even world problems. Ann and her husband Eli often invited me to parties at their home, and this gave me an opportunity to meet many people and learn about their lives and problems, as well as learn about "American social interactions." Ann also helped us to join the local Jewish community and become members of the synagogue. I would define Ann's character as "a happy person, no matter what." It was not surprising that a few years after she was widowed, she became close to another person of very similar character, Richard Bluestein, who was also widowed at about the same time as Ann. Coming from a country of different culture, I was impressed with the American style of keeping personal problems inside and not imposing them on others. In this regard, Ann appears to be an example (perhaps, even an extreme example) of this behavior.

Harry Aschkinasi, Vice President for Development at National Jewish Hospital at the time of my arrival, is known as an American war hero. A thirty-year-old lawyer from the Bronx turned U.S. Army lieutenant during the war with Germany, the major American newspapers (*New York Times, New York Post, PM*) published stories in June of 1944 about his unusual adventure. Harry happened to be in front of a German bunker (pillbox) at the German gestapo headquarters building in Cherbourg. The Germans hung out a white flag but changed their minds and kept firing. Harry started talking to them trying to convince them to surrender. One of the German officers in the pillbox, a captain, knew English well (he had lived in New York before the war) and responded that he would fight to the last man. Harry negotiated, saying that he would come to the pillbox just to talk, and he went alone (!) to the bunker. Inside the pillbox, this Jewish lawyer from the Bronx had several drinks of cognac with the Nazi captain, and after a thirty-minute conversation, he persuaded the Germans to surrender. As the media reported, Lieutenant Aschkinasi came out with "a bushel of prisoners." According to the *New York Times* report, Harry's sister Anna commented, " There goes Harry—talking again."

It is not a surprise that as a vice president for development at the hospital, Harry became known as one of the best experts in fundraising. I am proud and honored to be a friend of this most talented and modest man who advised me on many difficult problems before his retirement in 1984, and for many years thereafter. I am indebted to him for his essential help in my start-up research by soliciting a small grant from a private donor. Harry is a great artist and sculptor, and now, at the age of ninety-three, he continues his work in art. I am proud to have two of his paintings that he gave me for my new apartment. I feel blessed having such a great friend.

Dr. Thomas Moulding, a staff physician at National Jewish Hospital, was interested in understanding life in the Soviet Union beyond the superficial casual events. We would discuss for hours a broad range of topics related to international politics, as well as professional subjects. Tom remains one of the most knowledgeable clinical experts on tuberculosis. That was my first experience with open conversations sharing differences of opinion on political issues. Tom is a WASP—White Anglo-Saxon Protestant (he had to explain the meaning of it to me)—and it was most interesting to learn from a person who is quite open-minded on religious and ethnic issues.

At that time, I was quite ignorant about Judaism and religion in general, but I had had a good education in Russia on anti-Semitism, one of the issues that interested Tom. To my surprise, Tom told me about the prejudice against Jews among some of his relatives and those categorized as WASPs in general. He also educated me in the fact that the U.S. is far from being free from anti-Semitism.

In this regard, one story particularly impressed me. Tom was once a member of the admission committee at the medical school in Denver, and this committee was particularly instructed on how to limit the number of Jewish students, especially those coming from New York, where such measures were already in place. Technically it was not easy to identify a Jew since, already at that time, to avoid being accused of discrimination, one could not ask the applicant about his or her ethnic origin or religion. The guess was based on such elements as the last name, appearance, etc. All these discussions were not only educational, but also showed me a way to develop friendships with people of different background and opinions. Tom and I became close friends, and often my whole family was invited to join his at their mountain home. The most exciting part of our interactions was our interest in the mountains.

Quite often Tom would call me at seven o'clock or earlier on Sunday and ask, "Leonid, are you ready?" This meant we were going for another hike. Tom knew the mountains very well and even showed me some secret places where no casual tourists would go. I am very grateful to Tom for this unforgettable experience.

Jack Goldman, a well-known professional photographer and an active member of the Denver Jewish community, extended his friendship to us from the very first days of our arrival in Denver. Jack's family was originally from Poland, but he was born and lived in Germany. During the war Jack survived the hardship of the German extermination camps (Saxenhausen, Auschwitz, and Dachau). He was liberated from Dachau in 1945 by the American Army and came to the U.S. in 1946. In 1952 he married Margot, who had escaped from Germany before the war. Jack and Margot and their children, as an answer to the Holocaust, became committed to Judaism and support of Israel. Jack took an active role in bringing Judaism close to our family.

Shortly after our arrival to the U.S., Herman and I had the unforgettable experience of participating in the Passover Seder at Jack's house. Seder is a celebration that is particularly important to us as a symbol of freedom. Jack prepared Herman, who was twenty-two years old at that time, for his Bar Mitzvah. Later, he also prepared Herman's daughters Sarah and Abby for their Bat Mitzvahs. Through the years, Jack and Margot became our close friends and spiritual advisors, particularly to Herman and his wife Linda.

4. National Jewish Hospital in Denver

After emigration from the Soviet Union and while staying in Italy on the way to the United States (December, 1978), I received a message from Dr. Goren about my fellowship acceptance at the National Jewish Hospital in Denver. This acceptance came as a response to my desire to have a new start in my scientific career in the U.S. regardless of my previous achievements and titles back in the Soviet Union. Although to become just a research fellow is not a very high level in the scientific community for one at age fifty-three with a whole life of experience in medical research, I was thrilled with the opportunity to become employed in the U.S. from the very first day of my arrival. The most important part was not just employment and not just to continue to be involved in medical research, but an honor to become a part of one of the most famous scientific institutions called, at that time, National Jewish Hospital (NJH).

NJH has a remarkable history and fame as one of the best American medical institutions. It was established in response to the tuberculosis epidemic in the U.S., when hundreds (perhaps even thousands) of TB patients were arriving in Denver in the 1880s and 1890s with hope that the clean air in this mountain area would help them overcome their illness. Many of these patients were recent Jewish immigrants from Russia who contracted tuberculosis in New York, Chicago, and other large American cities. It is remarkable that while in Russia the prevalence of tuberculosis was very low at that time (tuberculosis cases were not reported there until the 1960s), the epidemic of this illness in Europe was extremely high (it was called the white plague) and was on the rise in the U.S. in large urban centers and on Indian reservations. Denver's dry climate and high altitude attracted people seeking relief from all kinds of illnesses, and it became a place of growing prevalence of tuberculosis. Denver became what the media labeled a "mecca of consumptives." New arrivals, mostly poor people, crowded the city and often died in streets without being able to receive any medical help or general assistance.

Denver was founded in 1858 as a supply settlement for Rocky Mountain mining camps, with most of the population (about 35,000 in the 1880s) consisting of people involved in the mining of gold and silver, many of whom were adventurers and characters of the "Wild West." In 1876 Denver became the state capital when Colorado was admitted to the union as the thirty-eighth state. Most of the business activities in town flourished by serving the needs of the miners bringing gold and silver in exchange for various services provided to them. The attention of the public and newspapers was rather focused on stories related to cowboys; gunmen and outlaw adventures competition among the six famous bordellos and other events in the "red lights streets"; and tragic events related to the silver crisis, such as stories about Mr.

Tabor's enterprise crash in 1893 or the personal romantic story of Baby Doe Tabor.

Under these circumstances the problems with large numbers of TB patients arriving in Denver did not appear to be in the focus of society. Even publications in our time (for example, booklets by Caroline Bankroft) and various Internet sources on the history of Denver and Colorado mention many events of the past, but not about the history of TB in Colorado or about the National Jewish Hospital and its foundation.

Despite the background of public indifference toward a devastating public health problem in 1880s and 1890s, the Denver Jewish community perceived the situation of TB patients dying in the streets as intolerable and initiated activities that led to the establishment of the National Jewish Hospital. Along with a substantial number of members of the community who were involved, two individuals, Mrs. Frances Wisebart Jacobs and Rabbi William S. Friedman, deserve special tribute for initiating these activities. Mrs. Jacobs, labeled later as Mother of Charities, was a compassionate person deeply concerned with the social problems of Denver, such as sickness and poverty. She became the founder of the United Way, the Ladies' Relief Society, and other charitable organizations. One of her concerns was the problem of the indigent patients suffering from tuberculosis and the need for a place for them to be treated. Unfortunately she died in 1892 before her dream of having a TB hospital in Denver was realized.

A man of action, Rabbi Friedman, promoted the idea that concern for the sick and indigent had always been an element of Jewish tradition. He initiated fund-raising for establishing a specialized TB hospital by addressing the tragic situation with tuberculosis patients in Denver in his Rosh Hashanah sermon in 1889. This speech can be called famous because it was (and is today) rather unprecedented that a sermon by a rabbi or any other clergyman would focus on the TB problem. This speech was followed by his other presentations at public gatherings appealing to the need for a TB hospital in Denver. Later rabbi Friedman became one of the first presidents of NJH; he served for fifteen years until his death in 1944.

The funds were collected within the Jewish communities of Denver and other cities, and the first hospital building was constructed in 1893. Unfortunately the hospital did not open for six years after its construction because of the financial problems caused by the silver crisis of 1893. Finally in 1899 the hospital began admitting TB patients, thanks to the Jewish charitable organization B'nai B'rith (Sons of the Covenant), which provided financial support for at least fifty years and also organized fund-raising events at many Jewish communities and organizations around the country.

NJH became a unique hospital in the U.S., providing free admission to indigenous TB patients for about fifty years. From the very beginning, NJH was proclaimed as a nonsectarian organization. Subsequently, the hospital has been receiving financial support not only from Jewish groups and communities but also from a large number of Christian and secular organizations and private donors. The hospital has changed its name over the years; it was renamed most recently National Jewish Medical and Research Center. Since July, 2008, it is called National Jewish Health. The word "Jewish" has remained in the new titles as a tribute to the role of the Jewish community in starting this institution and its continuing financial support, although only a small number of employees and patients were (or are) Jewish.

The history of the early years of confronting tuberculosis in Denver is addressed in detail by Dr. Jeanne Abrams in her book *Blazing the Tuberculosis Trail*.[12] According to this monograph, three more institutions (sanatoria) to address the problem of tuberculosis in Colorado were subsequently opened: the Jewish Consumptives' Relief Society (JCRS) in 1904, the Evangelical Lutheran Sanatorium in 1905, and the Swedish National Sanatorium in 1908.

Similar to the National Jewish Hospital, the JCRS was also established by the efforts of the Jewish community. Besides Mrs. Frances Weisbard Jacobs and Rabbi William Friedman, mentioned above, historic records also emphasize the roles of Louis Anfenger and Dr. Saling Simon in establishing NJH. Particular efforts in establishing both the NJH and the JCRS were attributed to Drs. Philip Hill Kowitz, Charles Spivak, and Zederbaum, and with the support from Louis Robinson, Abraham Judlovitz, Simon Quiat,

Rabbi Kauvar, and Rabbi Idelson. The JCRS alone took care of more than ten thousand patients during fifty years of recorded activities. As mentioned by Jeanne Abrams, current director of the Rocky Mountain Jewish Historical Society, "Denver was the only city in America to boast two Jewish-based sanatoriums, the National Jewish Hospital and the Jewish Consumptives' Relief Society." A motto at the entrance of the B'nai B'rith building (still in existence) of the National Jewish Hospital is carved: NONE MAY ENTER WHO CAN PAY—NONE CAN PAY WHO ENTER.

There were ups and downs in the activities of NJH. In the 1950s, after introduction of antimicrobial therapy, the TB epidemic began to subside, but the number of patients coming to the hospital was greater than ever. There were seven floors of wards in several buildings for TB patients who stayed in the hospital for a period from six months to two years, and the popularity of the institution widely spread around the world. Over the years, NJH attracted a number of very prominent physicians and scientists, and various research programs started, along with the continuous care of the patients. The main focus of research during the early years was on tuberculosis, and over the years it expanded to many other fields, such as other lung diseases, asthma and allergies, pediatric problems, cardiology and cardiac surgery, clinical immunology, and molecular and cellular biology. A number of prominent scientists and physicians have been guiding the work that generated recognition of NJH as a pioneer in medical research, nationally and internationally.

Work in the field of tuberculosis and tuberculosis-like illnesses caused by so-called nontuberculous mycobacteria or (NTM) by Gardner Middlebrook, Mayer Goren, Harry Corper, Maurice Cohn, Paul Davidson, Thomas Moulding, Werner Schaefer, Kenneth McClatchy, Marian Goble, Patrick Brennan, Pattisapu Gangadharam, and Michael Iseman brought NJH to worldwide recognition as a most advanced institution in the field. I had a chance and the honor to work and interact with some of these extraordinary people. Research by a number of microbiologists, particularly by Middlebrook, Shaefer, Goren, and Brennan, built the basis for modern understanding of the biology of tubercle bacilli and related mycobacteria, and this knowledge contributed greatly to the progress in combating infections caused by these organisms.

Gardner Middlebrook (1915–1986), a prominent scientist and a most advanced expert on tuberculosis, came to Denver from the Rockefeller Institute (1945–1952). He worked at NJH in Denver from 1952 to 1964 as the Director of the Division of Research and Laboratories. He was a microbiologist, but his expertise extended much beyond microbiology. Middlebrook was one of the first in the field who understood the problem of drug resistance, and, based on his early research in 1946, he pioneered the idea of combined use of the antituberculosis drugs to prevent emergence of drug resistance. This idea was implemented in the early clinical studies of 1953 at a time when the first three antituberculosis drugs became available (Streptomycin—1944; PAS—1946; Isoniazid—1952).

Middlebrook guided a broad range of research on microbiology and immunology of tuberculosis, as well as TB diagnostic laboratory procedures. Among his sparkling achievements were the development of an agar culture medium for detection of tubercle bacilli in a patient's specimen, methods for determining which drugs the patient's bacteria were resistant to, and the proper drug selection for the therapy of an individual patient. His "swan song" in this area was development of a semi-automated liquid medium system (Bactec-460) for rapid bacteriological diagnosis of tuberculosis and rapid detection of drug resistance of the isolate. It is ironic that only now, after many years since Middlebrook's revolutionary discoveries and inventions were made, the medical communities outside the U.S. are trying to implement these tools for improving their TB control programs.

I met Dr. Middlebrook in Moscow during the International Congress on Tuberculosis in 1972. I was deeply impressed with his personality and his presentations. Even his appearance and manners were in contrast to those of the Russian scientists, and in my mind I defined him as a man of "shiny brilliance." At a meeting of one of the sections of the Congress, following a mediocre presentation by a Russian scientist, this tall and slim man wearing a navy blue blazer stood up. With sparkling dark eyes and a penetrating gaze, he approached the blackboard and silently wrote some calculations related to the number of tubercle bacilli in a diseased lung tissue. Without hesitation he pointed out the absurdity of the data presented by the Russian scientist, who was considered an authority, just because he was a director of one of the TB Research Institutes.

The administration of the Congress asked me, as one of the few people who knew English, to escort Dr. Middlebrook and Dr. David (from the Brigham Hospital) during a boat tour on the Moskva River that was provided for the foreign delegates. This gave me an opportunity to establish contact for future communications. To avoid undesirable supervision, I invited the two guests to the upper deck that was empty because of the windy weather, and we had the opportunity for a quite open discussion, which they appreciated. Middlebrook expressed deep interest in my research on activity of various drugs against tubercle bacilli residing within macrophages and asked me to send him the paper when it was published. Subsequently when he received a reprint of my paper published in a Russian journal, he forwarded it to Dr. Medvedev (a famous Russian scientist and dissident who had defected to England a few years before) for translation into English. He then distributed it to a number of scientists and also sent a copy of this reprint to Dr. Goren at the National Jewish Hospital with a letter about meeting with me in Moscow. I was told that Middlebrook's recommendation was essential for Dr. Goren's decision to invite me for fellowship at the hospital. After coming to the U.S. in 1979, I did not have a chance to meet Dr. Middlebrook. At that time he worked at the University of Maryland School of Medicine, retired in 1981, and died at age seventy in 1986 in Davis, California.

Over a period of more than one hundred years of existence, NJH has adjusted its profile to meet the changing needs of society's health problems. The situation changed after the discovery of streptomycin by Zalman Waksman in 1945 (at Rutgers University) and after the decline in the prevalence of tuberculosis in the country. Over the years the focus changed to asthma and other problems. When I came to Denver in 1979, only a small group of scientists and physicians were still involved in TB research, and I was told that there was not much opportunity for me as an expert in TB because it was not a problem here anymore. ("You came to the wrong place at the wrong time.") This assessment happened to be wrong, as was proven during the following years.

In the meantime, to meet the situation I spent a year and a half in a fellowship on molecular biology in Dr. Goren's laboratory, published a paper with him in this field, and received my first NIH grant. In 1980, the director of clinical laboratories, Dr. Kenneth McClatchy, offered me a job as a director of the Mycobacteriology (TB) Laboratory, a position in which, to this day, I continue to work. While the prevalence of tuberculosis in the U.S. is dramatically declining, TB epidemics around the world represent a growing problem, particularly because of the association of TB with the HIV epidemic and the spread of drug-resistant TB strains. A group of TB experts at NJH is becoming involved in the education, training, and consultation for countries with a large burden of these epidemics. At the same time, the involvement of NJH, both in medical and basic research, is widening in areas of medical care in a growing number of health problems. Plans have been announced to use personalized medicine, with its modern technologies, to address asthma, allergies and immunological disorders, chronic obstructive pulmonary disease, heart disease, and lung cancer.

For more than a century of existence, National Jewish has been a prestigious place to be employed, and many scientists and physicians vie for appointment to join the faculty. This is the reason this institution has scientists of the highest possible expertise and qualifications. Revenue of this non-profit organization comes from three sources: patients, research grants, and charitable contributions. One of the requirements for the faculty is to provide full salary coverage from external sources, either payments for patients' services or research grants. Often times, it is difficult to meet this requirement, and this is the reason that some faculty members move to other places with lesser demands. In other words, "survival" at this institution is not an easy task. I was lucky to keep receiving grants over the years from NIH and industry to support about 40% of my salary, with the remaining 60% coming from my services in the clinical TB laboratory.

Contrary to the general predictions that the role of the TB laboratory would diminish, I saw a different picture and started expanding the range of diagnostic services, both by the number and by introducing new tests and procedures, and the laboratory received status as a Reference Laboratory. With the decline of TB prevalence in the U.S., we focused on so-called nontuberculous mycobacteria (NTM), which often causes much more severe illnesses than tuberculosis. In addition, most recently, with the growing worldwide epidemic of drug-resistant TB, this laboratory became a popular place for verifying the results of testing by other laboratories. The revenue of the laboratory has been steadily growing over the years from $60,000 in 1980 to $3 million this year. In recognition of developing these services, in 2004 I was given the Lifetime Faculty Achievement Award. It is a great challenge, honor, and very exciting to continue this work while approaching the thirty-year mark of my employment at this most advanced American medical and research institution.

CHAPTER TWELVE

Thirty Years Later, More "Discoveries"

"Only those who dare to fail greatly can ever achieve greatly."

Robert F. Kennedy

1. Jews in America, Perception of a Russian Immigrant
2. Commissars in America (Déjà vu)
3. Back to Russia: Visiting Russian "Weapons Scientists"
4. Lessons from the Past, Survival Tips
5. Not "Russian" Anymore

Fig. 41. Professional friends (left to right, top to bottom):
- D. A. Mitchison (England) and J. Grosset (France);
- Hajime Saito in a Karioki Bar (Japan);
- Kathy Eisenach (Arkansas, USA);
- Gaby Pfiffer, Baroness von Altenshoffen (Switzerland);
- Francoise Portaels (Belgium); and
- Chantal, Marquise de Chastellier (France).

Fig. 42. Major achievements in the US:
- **Family gathering in the US, left to right, sitting - Herman, my mother, Boris on my lap, my sister Galina, Michael, standing - my brother-in-law Edward, his mother Rivka, and Helen (1980);**
- **Grandchildren, left to right – Solomon, Boris, Abby, and Sarah (1980);**
- **Receiving the Faculty Lifetime Achievement; Award at National Jewish (2004)**

Fig. 43. In the city of Irkutsk In Siberia, June, 2007:
- On the left - an ultra-modern Diagnostic Center equipped with imported technology of highest standards, on the right - TB laboratory with standards of 1960s (not a part of the Diagnostic Center);
- A lecture on TB in the Medical School to the faculty and physicians of the city.

Fig. 44. Impressions from the last trip to Russia in 2007 (left to right, top to bottom):
- With a group of TB leaders in Russia at the banquet during the All-Russian TB Conference, July 8, 2007;
- At the Amur River in Blagoveshchensk, border with China;
- Tsar Alexander III, Lenin, Kolchak – all three in the same street of Blagoveshchensk; and
- Lake Baikal in the Irkuts Oblast.

Fig.45. Russian affairs today (left to right, top to bottom):

- I am with a patient that had MDR-TB, small town in the Sverdlovsk Oblast at Ural Mountains (2001);
- Russian hospitality: lunch with drinks at every occasion, in Sverdlovsk Oblast. I am in the center and to the right from me is the famous Russian microbiologist Dr. G. Mordovskoy and to the left is Dr. M. Iseman (2001);
- At a Conference in Moscow with Dr. V. V. Erokhin (in the center, director of the TB institute in Moscow where I used to work) and Dr. A. K. Strelis (director of the TB institute in Tomsk in Siberia), 2005; and
- Microbiologists from Yekaterinburg on training in Denver - Drs. E.A. Karelina, A. N. Kornienko, M. N. Zueva, and M.A. Kravchenko (2002).

1. Jews in America, Perception of a Russian Immigrant

Jewish emigration from the Soviet Union in the 1970s, either to Israel or to the U.S., was an unprecedented development in the history of the USSR. It was born from the combined effect of the establishment and development of Israel, increasing anti-Semitism sponsored by the Communist regime, and the awakening of self-identification and self-consciousness of Russian Jews. The change of mind by the Soviet government to allow the Jews to emigrate would not have been possible without the tremendous efforts by the American Jews ("Let my people go!") who mobilized government and non-government representatives and groups, Jewish and non-Jewish, to press the Soviet authorities. So we owed the American Jews for our freedom and opportunity to come to the U.S. Upon arrival to the U.S., the Russian Jews realized that they finally had a choice for their subsequent identity. They did not have to be marked as Jews anymore, but most decided to become part of the American Jewish community, whether in a religious or simply an ethnic sense. Most of the immigrants were quite ignorant about Jewish history in general, as well as about Judaism. Most challenging for the new arrivals was learning about the fascinating history of American Jews, whose presence in the U.S. became unique through integration into American society rather than remaining as "guests," which was the case in many other countries.

Even before the Holocaust, anti-Semitism in almost every European country and Russia was a driving force for Jewish emigration to America. The overall impression among those who remained behind was that the countries of the North American continent, particularly the United States, were a haven where Jews could reside in an environment free of anti-Semitism. Although no violent anti-Semitism of the European style (such as the massacre in York, pogroms in Russia and the Ukraine, or violent expulsion from a country or from its certain regions) ever happened in the U.S., anti-Semitism in a milder form did take place, with ups and downs over a period of time. Jewish immigrants at any given historical period did not always understand the reality of this situation in the U.S. That applies to the recent wave of emigration of the Soviet Jews as well. Learning about the Jews in America and obtaining information that was not available or not accessible in the Soviet Union was an important part of our adjustment to the new country. Because of our background, our perception regarding the lives of Jews in the U.S. may be different from that presented by the American authors.

The subsequent description, both in the historic and current perspective, is a reflection of the predominant views of Jewish immigrants from Russia on Jewish life in this country. One of the widely spread opinions is that Jews represent an influential group in the American social and political life. I believe that this is inaccurate, particularly by noting that Jews represent only between 2–2.7% of the American population. This number includes both religious groups (orthodox, conservative, and reform) and those who identify themselves as Jews only ethnically or "unaffiliated." This estimate does not include individuals raised as Jews but converted to other religions (about 10%). The diversity of the Jewish population in the U.S. is also enriched by about 15% who converted to the Jewish faith from other religions. It is obvious that Jews are a relatively small group in this country compared to large Christian groups. (About 51% of them are Protestants, 24% Catholics, 7% members of the black churches, and only 16% are unaffiliated.)

Jews faced controversies from the very early settlement in this country. According to the official records, when they first landed in New Amsterdam in 1654 (that later became New York), the first twenty-three Dutch Jews immediately faced a problem: the governor would not allow the Jews to settle in this Dutch colony. He was forced to admit them only under orders from the government in Holland after a petition from the Jewish community in Amsterdam. This episode set a precedent for all subsequent years of Jewish history in America—to fight against discrimination and to be recognized as equal to other American citizens. That was the most important difference from the history of Jews in Europe or Russia, where fighting for their rights was not an option.

Ten years later when New York became part of the British colony, a small Jewish community had to fight again to overcome restrictions imposed by the new administration. In 1787 the U.S. Constitution guaranteed the Jews equal rights on a federal level, but in subsequent years some states continued to forbid Jews to hold an office. The state of Maryland continued this discrimination until 1926 when, after years of debates, a special "Jew Bill" was passed.

Jews participated in the war for independence, fought on both sides during the Civil War, and behaved in any other events no differently than other Americans. Nevertheless, it did not save them from occasional episodes of anti-Semitism. For example, in 1862 Ulysses S. Grant issued an order requesting expulsion of Jews from Mississippi, Kentucky, and Tennessee. The Jewish community protested, and President Lincoln commanded revocation of Grant's order.

A well-known eruption of anti-Semitism occurred in 1915 in Atlanta, Georgia, when Leo Frank was falsely accused of murdering a thirteen-year-old employee of his factory. This bigotry was eventually condemned by society, and a movie was even made portraying this story of mob anti-Semitism. (Frank was lynched in Atlanta.) This episode, although a rare expression of extreme anti-Semitism in the U.S., is often compared in literature to such events as the Dreyfus affair in France in 1894 and the Mendel Beilis Blood Libel Trial in Russia in 1913. In both cases, the falsely accused were completely cleared and acquitted. Official clearance of Beilis was particularly impressive because of the extremely anti-Semitic atmosphere in Russia. Captain Dreyfus was not only cleared, but was also promoted in his military rank. In the case of Frank's story, no punishment was imposed on the actual killers, and Frank was officially pardoned (!) but not until 1986.

It is important to mention that many intellectual Americans strongly opposed the bias against Leo Frank. An example is the attitude of Lyndon B. Johnson's family. At the age of seven, Lyndon witnessed how his grandfather and father, both political activists of that time, demanded clemency for Leo Frank. Even such a modest action triggered threats by the Ku Klux Klan of Texas to assassinate Johnson's family.

Between 1920 and 1940, with the highest level in the 1930s during the Great Depression, anti-Semitism was spreading in the U.S. nationwide, although without the Atlanta-type violence. The Ku Klux Klan had more than four million members in the 1920s. Henry Ford funded a newspaper promoting anti-Semitism and published a four-volume book, *The International Jew*. A prominent Jewish leader, Louis Marshall, threatened Ford with a suit and forced him to issue an apology to the Jewish community. The American Jewish community became active in responding to most of the events that had any anti-Semitic sentiments. Most of the Jewish communities and organizations were first in the nation with an immediate response to Hitler's takeover of Germany in 1933, with a large rally in New York, boycott of German goods, and other demonstrations.

At the beginning of the twentieth century most of the newly arriving Jewish immigrants to the U.S. were involved in blue-collar work: peddling, community services, and farming. In the 1920s and 1930s, most of the second generation of the immigrants started taking the opportunity to follow traditional Jewish aspiration for education. That created a fear in the society, particularly in New York and other large cities, that the Jews would dominate the higher education in the country. For example, the president of Harvard University proposed quotas for the number of Jews to be accepted, arguing that such a measure would prevent anti-Semitism on campuses. The Harvard University committee did not accept this proposal, but these quotas (about 10% by some sources) were unofficially implemented in the 1920s and 1930s in many universities, particularly in the private schools. By contrast, during the same time period in the Soviet Union, any quotas on accepting Jews to the universities, previously imposed by the Tsars before the 1917 October Revolution, were eliminated by the new regime. This difference between the U.S. and Russia changed after World War II. There were no known limitations on accepting Jews to universities in the U.S., and there were very harsh (although not proclaimed officially) limitations or complete refusal of accepting Jews to universities in the Soviet Union, especially in the 1950s.

The history of Jews in the U.S. is thoroughly analyzed in the recently published book by Beth S. Wenger, *The Jewish American*.[13] According to this publication, the attitude of American society toward Jews dramatically changed during the war. About one half million Jews served as soldiers in the war against Germany. Jews have been making significant contributions to modernization of industry, trade, medicine, science, art, music, literature, sports, and movie making, and some have reached high positions in government.

A story about Henry Morgenthau, Secretary of Treasury from 1934–1945, is of special interest. In 1943 he submitted to President Roosevelt a personal report with a complaint that some officials at the State Department failed to implement measures of saving European Jews; he even accused these individuals of being "indifferent, callous, and perhaps even hostile." A large number of highly educated German Jews (among them Albert Einstein) emigrated to the U.S. in the late thirties, bringing with them expertise in science, modern technology, business, culture, and a clear understanding of the situation in the world. Morgenthau convinced President Roosevelt to establish the War Refugee Board, which resulted in rescuing about 200,000 Jews, mostly from Hungary. Before writing his personal report to President Roosevelt with concerns of saving the European Jews from Hitler's atrocities, Morgenthau went through a period of hesitation when he thought it might not be appropriate for him, as a Jew, to become a representative of other Jews in communication with his friend, President Roosevelt.

The position taken by another prominent American Jew, Supreme Court Justice Felix Frankfurter, was dramatically different from Morgenthau. In 1943, the justice was approached by a Polish Catholic, Jan Karski, who had succeeded in escaping from German extermination camps and came to the United States. At that time, knowledge of Hitler's atrocities against Jews was not well-known, and most of the Western press, including the *New York Times,* buried a few minor articles on the back pages. When the escapee from Poland described to Frankfurter all the horror of the extermination camp, Frankfurter replied, "I know that you believe what you are telling me is the truth, but I cannot believe it." Alan Dershowitz described this incident in detail in his book, *Chutzpah.*[14] He gave an interpretation of it as Frankfurter's fear that the president would perceive this story as the bias of a Jew defending other Jews. He never told his close friend President Roosevelt the story by the Polish man.

A historian, Gerold Auerbach, said about Frankfurter (quoted by Alan Dershowitz), "He concerned himself with affairs in India,

Australia, and Vichy France. Yet Frankfurter would not utilize his position and contacts, or his irrepressible energy, in the service of Jewish needs during the most desperate years of Jewish history...nothing was more characteristic of American Jews like Frankfurter than their acquiescence in Roosevelt's abandonment of the Jews of Europe." As Dershowitz wrote, "No American Jew today wants his or her epitaph to read—as Felix Frankfurter's must always read in Jewish history 'he could have helped, but didn't, he could have believed, but would not, he placed his own interest before those of his fellow Jews.'"

Frankfurter was not alone in remaining silent about the danger of extermination that Jews faced in Europe. Similar attitudes of Rabbi Stephen Wise, Joseph Proskauer, and even Justice Louis Brandeis, described in Dershowitz's book, often illustrate the controversy for some prominent American Jews between being highly visible and being a Jew. Roosevelt's abandonment of the European Jews is well-documented in history records, but the roles of Jewish personalities like Frankfurter, Wise, and Proskauer have left a far more shameful record in history. They failed both the Jewish people and President Roosevelt by being afraid of making a bad impression on the president.

The attitude of some other presidents and political leaders toward Jewish immigration to the U.S. was quite different from Roosevelt's. According to the report by the Associated Press (*International Herald Tribune*, May 28, 2008 and Lenny Ben-David in the *Jerusalem Post*, September 9, 2008) the recently released Oval Office recordings during the Johnson presidency (1963–1969) indicated that Lyndon Baines Johnson (LBJ) was extremely pro-active on behalf of Jewish people and the state of Israel. His activities go back long before he became the president of the United States. In 1938–1939, LBJ used his status as a congressman to rescue hundreds of Jews from Poland and Lithuania by arranging visas for them with subsequent entry to Texas through the port of Galveston. As a senator in 1956, he blocked the Eisenhower administration's attempts of sanctions against Israel after the Sinai War. He also defeated other anti-Israel initiatives, such as by the Chairman of the Foreign Relations Committee Democrat William Fulbright, or in 1967 by the head of the State Department Dean

Rusk. Following the policy started by John Kennedy, decisions by LBJ became instrumental in approving the massive sale of arms to Israel in 1967, particularly after France stopped sales to Israel.

Critical comments about Frankfurter and other prominent American Jews brought back my memories about the shameful behavior of some Russian Jews under circumstances that were beyond any comparison with those faced by the American Jews. One example is related to the events of the 1930s when a group of Jewish intellectuals formed a special unit within the Central Committee of the Communist Party with the goal of fighting any religious attitudes or practices among the Russian Jews.

Another episode was related to the situation in the 1950s just before Stalin's death. At the time of preparation for the infamous trial against the Jewish physicians, a plan was being developed to expel the Jews from all major cities to Siberia. KGB spread a rumor about anticipated mass violence by Russian people angry against the Jews. On behalf of the most prominent Jewish writers, musicians, scientists, and other highly visible individuals, the KGB prepared a letter to Stalin asking for "relocation" of Jewish people to Siberia, to save them from the anticipated violence. Under pressure from the KGB, many prominent Jews signed the letter, and only a few were brave enough to refuse. American Jews never faced such a situation, and anything they did, good or bad, was of their own free will.

After World War II, the anti-Semitism in the Soviet Union resurged. At the same time, the anti-Semitism in the U.S. significantly declined. In 1947, two Hollywood films, *Crossfire* and *Gentlemen's Agreement,* greatly contributed to the confrontation against anti-Semitism. Universities began to eliminate Jewish quotas and the concept of the Judeo-Christian tradition began to emerge. The creation of Israel in 1948 promoted a positive attitude in American society toward Israel and Jewish communities in the United States. Holocaust consciousness in the 1960s enhanced the sympathy of American society toward the plight of Jews in Russia, which resulted in a mass emigration of Russian Jews to Israel and the U.S.

After World War II, the American Jews became very active, not only in defending their rights but also in the forefront during the

Civil Rights movement in the 1960s and 1970s; liberalism became a predominant expression of Jewish identity. Prominent Jewish leaders and activists participated in such events as the 1963–64 Selma marches in Alabama and the 1964 Freedom Summer in Mississippi and symbolized the commitment of the majority of American Jews to the fight for blacks' equal rights and against discrimination. This commitment and sacrifice by the Jews has not been fully appreciated by African Americans.

Decline of anti-Semitism, along with the perception of continuing racism, convinced many American blacks that the joined fight against discrimination benefited only Jews, and that continuing racial division remains the predominant issue and is more important than any other difference. Anti-white sentiment became quite popular among some black leaders, with a cowardly tendency of focusing on Jews as being representatives of white people. It is ironic that today it has become popular among the leading African American figures, such as Farrakhan, Jackson, or Sharpton, to spread and promote anti-Semitic ideas. What is the reason for such an ideological bent? These individuals are playing dangerous political games that have only one evident purpose: to elevate themselves as leaders of their people. This is not a new phenomenon, and its success requires a negative target, a target of hate. Are these well-known figures in any way different from historical leaders such as Hitler or Mussolini? In both cases, selecting Jews as a target of hate appeared to be convenient and successful. Another interesting point to remember: the German word for leader is *fürer*.

Perhaps black's anti-Semitism is also a reflection of a phenomenon called "the liberal betrayal of the Jews." A widely spread idea among liberals is that Jews must be held responsible for any anti-Semitic actions against them, including the wars staged by the Arab countries against Israel. As Ruth R. Wisse wrote in *If I Am Not for Myself*, "Given the asymmetry between the hunter and his prey, it is easier to resent the Jews than to oppose the anti-Semites."[15] In spite of this continuing development many Jews remain attached to liberalism, which became another Jewish tradition, and often just because of this new tradition the majority of Jews remain supporters and members of the Democratic Party, rather than the Republican Party, often contrary to their business interests and despite the strong support of Israel by many prominent leaders of the Republican Party.

When I am trying to convince some of these individuals to change their attitude, they give me a number of arguments. As an indication of anti-Semitism among the leadership of the Republican Party, some quote James Baker, Secretary of State in 1992, as saying, "Fuck the Jews…they won't vote for us anyway." Of course, they are trying to forget the anti-Semitic rhetoric of Jackson or Farrakhan. Others refer to the events and actions against the establishment of Israel described in a book by John Loftus and Mark Aarons, *The Secret War Against the Jews*.[16] They forget that many of the people in this book belonged to different parties, and the major motivation of their activity was not anti-Semitism but strong strategic and economic interests of a number of countries involved. The most serious arguments of the liberal Democrat Jews against the Republican Party are connected to the strong affiliation of this party with the Christian fundamentalists and their centuries-old, traditional anti-Semitism.

It is well-recognized that, historically, the main source of anti-Semitism was the predominate teachings of the Christian churches. For example, the extreme anti-Semitism of the Orthodox Church in Russia originated in Byzantia, where Christianity as a new religion had to compete with Judaism for new souls among the pagan population at the time when the number of Jews and Christians in the world was about the same. The main point of the church's traditional teaching about the Jews and Judaism was the claim that Jewish people rejected and crucified Jesus, along with denial of both Jesus' Jewish identity and Christianity's Jewish roots. Christian anti-Semitism was behind the atrocities of the Catholic Church starting in the fourth century, extreme violence in eleventh and twelfth centuries during the Crusades, and reaching a peak during the Inquisition in the fifteenth century. Christian anti-Semitism was also behind the expulsion of Jews from a number of European countries, as well as behind the Holocaust. Therefore, it is not surprising that many Jews and Jewish organizations in Europe and in the U.S. developed over the years a cautious attitude toward Christian churches, even if they see a friendly interaction from some of the Christian denominations.

The attitude of some Christian denominations toward Jews, at least in the U.S., has changed dramatically during the last decades. After the Israeli Air Force destroyed an Iraqi nuclear reactor at Osirak in 1981, the whole world, including the U.S. government, condemned Israel for this action, which in modern day judgments would appear to be fully justified. At that time, a single but powerful protest against condemnation of Israel came from the evangelical pastor John Hagee of San Antonio, Texas. With this event, Hagee started a powerful campaign for Christian support of Israel and against anti-Semitism in America.

Throughout the centuries and millennia Jews did not have significant friends or allies. The situation in the U.S. is changing now through the initiative of John Hagee. Evangelical Christians, led by Reverend Hagee, have become a powerful ally of American Jews in their support of Israel. The recently published book by David Brog, *Standing with Israel,* describes in detail the growing Christian support in the U.S. of Israel and of Jewish people in general. Pastor Hagee speaks of a Christian "debt of gratitude" to the Jewish people and, "If you take away the Jewish contribution to Christianity there would be no Christianity" (quoted after Brog).[17]

The new theology developed by Hagee is gaining success in the U.S., although not all Christian denominations have accepted it, and some keep expressing rather negative attitudes toward Jews. Anti-Semitism in many European countries is becoming more openly expressed, mostly among non-religious groups, but often within the tradition of the old-fashioned Christian anti-Semitism. In 1965 the Catholic Church issued an important document *(Nostra Aetate)* absolving the Jews of collective guilt for the killing of Jesus, which remarkably improved Jewish-Catholic relationships. Nevertheless, along with this progress, Pope Benedict XVI most recently restored an ancient prayer for the conversion of Jews, which is viewed by Jews as either anti-Jewish or at least controversial, because the Vatican failed to provide an interpretation that this action does not endorse active proselytizing. The recently released film by Oren Jacoby, *Constantine's Sword,* based on the book by James Carroll, addresses in detail some issues of the roots of Christian, particularly Catholic, anti-Semitism. It stresses Carroll's view that the revival of the old Latin Mass on conversion of Jews is a radical departure from *Nostra Aetate* with a return to "triumphant exclusivism" and is "a formula for intolerance and ultimately for violence."[18]

On the background of these and other similar events, the cautious attitude of American Jewry to the ongoing changes in the Christian world is fully understandable. On the other hand, the current attitude of the Evangelical Christians in the U.S. is dramatically different from anything that took place in the Christian world before. For many years, Pastor Hagee explicitly demonstrated his rejection of proselytizing. It is just not a part of his theology; the organization, established by him, "Christians United for Israel," provides unconditional support for Israel, spiritually and financially. They call themselves Christian Zionists.

Unfortunately many American Jews have not noticed the changes occurring in the American Christian world and are rather reluctant to join forces with Evangelical Christians. This insufficient, or often misrepresented information, is related to the continuing political alliance of the majority of American Jews with the Democratic Party. While I was writing this segment, the news came out about the affiliation of 2008 Democratic presidential candidate Barack Obama with Rev. Louis Farrakhan through the pastor of his church, Jeremiah Wright, and his personal friendship with Pastor Wright, who has delivered explicit anti-American and racist (anti-white, including anti-Israeli) statements in his sermons. So far, these revelations have not bothered liberal Democrats, including Jewish Democrats. Perhaps they have forgotten the old saying, "Tell me who your friends are, and I will tell you who you are." It is very likely that Obama, this highly charismatic and energetic man, will become president of the U.S., but it is questionable whether he will support Israel and confront anti-Semitism in the world. It is very likely that, regardless of Obama's position on these issues, most of the American Jews will vote for him just because he is a Democrat.

Rabbi Eric Yoffie, the president of the Union for Reform Judaism, stated an attack against religious intolerance in his public speech of April 2, 2008. Good! But contrary to possible expectations, he did not attack any of the anti-Semitic personalities mentioned above. He did not attack Jeremiah Wright for his clearly expressed intolerance and hate. No! He attacked Reverend John Hagee, accusing him of religious intolerance... against Catholics and Muslims! These accusations alone appeared completely unjustified and were rejected by Hagee. The remarkable point of this episode is the elevated concern of a Jewish rabbi about the possibility that someone may have said something disrespectful about Catholics and Muslims, not about Jews. The question is, who is really intolerant? Reverend Hagee or Rabbi Yoffie?

Perhaps, the actual reason behind Rabbi Yoffie's attack is the fact that John Hagee endorsed U.S. Senator John McCain, the Republican presidential nominee. It is very sad if this suggestion is correct—that one of the prominent Jewish leaders was motivated by his political affiliation with the Democratic Party and is rejecting (so far) a genuine offer of friendship and collaboration, so much needed today by the American Jewish community in the struggle for the very survival of Israel as a Jewish state. It is remarkable that John McCain subsequently turned down Hagee's endorsement. Perhaps, motivation behind this decision is purely political—an attempt to win votes from some liberals, either Democratic or Independent voters. The excuse for McCain's disassociation was a questionable interpretation of the Holocaust made by Hagee ten years ago. In fact, the religious explanation of the reasons for the Holocaust by Hagee (as God's will) is not different from that by a number of Jewish religious scholars, and according to many expert opinions, it was not anti-Semitic or anti-Jewish at all. One of these experts, Dennis Prager, stated that criticism of Hagee is motivated by politics rather than by truth. He stressed that "Hagee is one of the most pro-Jewish Christians alive..." and "To accuse such a man of anything anti-Jewish renders both truth and anti-Semitism meaningless..."[19]

Some Jewish leaders, while accepting and positively responding to Rev. Hagee's attitude, still express caution that Hagee may have a self-serving agenda in building friendship with Jewish organizations. Not all Evangelical groups are exact followers of Hagee's theology; some of their activities may raise questions. It is remarkable that a growing number of Evangelical communities are celebrating the Passover Seders, but they do it in their own way, combining the Jewish ritual with a Christian worship. It stirs controversy within the Jewish community when Jews are invited to such Seders, as happened in the small town of Huntsville, Alabama—to accept or reject such an invitation? At the same time, with a similar theology to John Hagee, other Evangelical leaders also reject any attempts of Jewish conversion or any attempt of blending together Judaism and Christianity. For example, Rev. Robert Somerville of Huntsville also stressed that Christians owe a debt of gratitude to the Jewish people, as the forebears of Christianity and for the long history of Christian anti-Semitism.

Perhaps it is the right time for the American Jewish religious leaders to build interfaith relationships, and many of them are doing just that. One such leader, Rabbi Arthur Schneier, recently attracted public attention in connection with the visit of Pope Benedict XVI to the U.S. Rabbi Schneier, an immigrant from Europe, was known for his diplomatic skills and connections in the past, and played an instrumental role in forcing the Soviet authorities to allow the Jewish emigration from Russia. This time, he arranged the Pope's visit to his Park East Synagogue in Manhattan, which was viewed by many as a historic event in Jewish history. What a contrast with the past, remembering the Vatican's indifference to the Holocaust during World War II or the sponsorship of the Nazis' escape from Germany to South America after the war!

In 1985 the Republican Jewish Coalition was established to express the views of many American Jews who understand the changing U.S. political climate, particularly the ongoing shift of support for Israel from the Democrat Party to the Republican Party. Many Jewish immigrants from Russia perceive the rhetoric of some Democratic leaders in recent years as quite similar to that of the Soviet demagogues, particularly when they promise "everything to everybody." In this regard, some of them sound like pupils of Vladimir Lenin. The Republican Jewish Coalition has forty-four chapters throughout the U.S., and the proportion of Jews voting for Republican candidates is growing.

Senator Joe Lieberman, a member of the Democratic Party and an orthodox Jew, participated on July 22, 2008 in the "Night to Honor Israel," the most recent event in a series initiated by Reverend Hagee since 1980. At the convention of the Christians

United for Israel, with three thousand participants waving the American and Israeli flags, Lieberman explicitly expressed his appreciation for the Evangelical's support of Israel and the strong stand against anti-Semitism. He stressed his firm support for John Hagee and true friends of Jewish people. It is not the first time this brave American patriot has gone "against the stream"; principles and truth are much more important to him than cheap popularity. This time he said that he is ignoring a plea not to support Rev. Hagee expressed in a petition addressed to him and entitled "Don't Go Joe," which was organized by a group of liberal left-wing Jews with 42,000 signatures.[20] One can only hope that more Jews will follow examples set by Joe Lieberman, Rabbi Arieh Scheinberg, David Brog, Israeli Ambassador Dan Gillerman, and others to openly express their views on the issue of a possible alliance with our Christian friends.

Most recently, Joe Lieberman demonstrated again his courage and honesty. In addition to his previous endorsement of John McCain, he participated in the Republican National Convention and delivered a fiery speech with an appeal to both parties to overcome the divisions between them for the interest of the country. He said, "This year, when you vote for the President, vote for the person you believe is best for the country, not for the party you happen to belong to." It is most reasonable to address this appeal to the American Jews as well.

The most important issue is not whether the Jews are voting for Republican or Democratic candidates, but the fact that they have freedom of choice based on their political convictions, like all other American citizens! It is inevitable that there are some anti-Semites around, but under provisions of free expression, they are known, and can and should be confronted. Unlike in some European countries, American society in general is overwhelmingly friendly toward Jews. It is of paramount importance that the Jews are able to recognize not only enemies but also real friends as well and treat them appropriately. The overall impression by most of the immigrants coming to the U.S. from Russia or, in fact, from any other country, is that the social, economical, and political climate in the U.S. appears to be more favorable to Jews than in any other country throughout the centuries of Jewish history. In fact, it is the only country in the world where Jews not only have equal rights with other citizens but also are treated as equals, with all the opportunities that this great country provides to her citizens. We did have grievances of unfair treatment in the past, as did all other minority groups in the U.S., but we should oppose the tendency of some political leaders to divide the American people by reviving old historical grievances that emphasize the differences between various ethnic and religious groups rather than their common goals. It is most important today, for Jews as well as for all other minorities in the U.S., to look forward and make all possible efforts to be unified for the overall sake and success of the American people and this great country.

2. Commissars in America (Déjà vu)

It is only natural for new immigrants to compare their homeland with the U.S. Our primary concern was the situation in the workplace. One immediate contrast was seeing a broad democracy in the general society but a peculiar lack of democracy in the workplace. It was explained that corporate America would become dysfunctional if, for example, the CEOs were chosen by election. This non-democratic workplace did not appear to be a problem for employees, since many government and public agencies watch for violations of established rules concerning employees' fair treatment, safety, protection from discrimination, and so forth. Nevertheless, there was one similarity with the Soviet system—the ascendance of bureaucracy.

Bureaucracy in the Soviet Union had specific historic roots related to the early development of the state; it was found throughout the civilian and military settings. Before World War II the structure of the Red Army, as the Soviet military was called, reflected the leadership's distrust of the professional military caste (a distrust that extended to nearly all professional groups). They devised a system in which two individuals were in charge of every military unit—a military commander and a political commissar, the latter an appointee of the Communist Party to monitor the commander. When the war started and the German Army began its rapid advance, crucial decisions were often paralyzed by tension between commanders and commissars. For example, when the military commander saw the need to retreat to save the troops, the commissar, bound by the party line against retreats ("Not a step back!") would refuse to sign the order. That all changed early in 1943. The commissars then became "political assistants" and the commanders had their full combat authority restored. The course of the war started to change in favor of the Red Army, and the restored powers of the military professionals greatly contributed to the victorious path.

The term commissar denoted a politically motivated person with excessive administrative power. After the war it became a word of the past, but no lessons were learned from the tragic war experience about the role of commissars. The Communist Party control became a fact of life, even more so than it was before or during the war.

In the early years of the Soviet Union, the term commissar was widely used to emphasize the difference between the new system and the old. For example, instead of "minister," the great positions were Peoples' Commissar of Industry, Peoples' Commissar of Health Care, Peoples Commissar of Foreign Affairs, and such. Decades later, when the term commissar became unpopular, it became minister again. During the time of the commissars, the control of every activity by the Communist Party was enhanced. Every ministry, factory, university, high school, hospital, and scientific institution had a Communist Party Bureau; the head of the bureau, called the Secretary or PartOrg (Party Organizer), had the same power as the commissar in the army at the beginning of the war. Decisions could not be made without joint approval by the director of the institution and the party secretary. All documents required signatures by both, even a modest letter of commendation for an employee. In whispers, people called these party representatives commissars.

The party secretary of any department reported to the next level secretary, who in turn reported to the secretary of the district or the city bureau, all the way up to the General Secretary who was either above the Soviet Prime Minister or occupied both posts. Even the General Secretary, (also called Secretary of the Central Committee of the Communist Party) did not have to be a professional, and his expertise in any field was attributed to his high political wisdom. Stalin, Khrushchev, and Brezhnev all held this position during their rule. Not only did they lack professional education, but several were nearly illiterate. This suffocating dominance by the Party caused stagnation in the economy and failure in nearly all fields of endeavor and finally resulted in the disintegration of the Soviet Union in 1991!

It was a big surprise for me to learn that parallel management also exists in the U.S., especially in nonprofit organizations. Here too, similar to the Soviet Union, this bureaucracy grew out of mistrust of professionals by administrative leaders. The role played by the commissar is assigned to managers in the U.S. These managers oversee the professionals (research scientists, for example) handling the financial aspects of their work, the hiring and firing of their employees, and other administrative tasks. It's not unusual for a laboratory director (generally a professor with a Ph.D.) to be reporting to an administrative person with the title of manager or department director. This individual, usually lacking in most of the professional expertise, reports to an administrative executive rather than to the senior scientist.

A personal story about one of the managers may be useful for understanding the nature of the American "commissars" phenomenon. The story was recounted by Dr. Ben Halevy, an American physician who came from Russia and was astonished by the similarity of bureaucratic patterns in the two countries. (*The individuals in this story are fictional, as well as the places and institutions; any similarity with anyone or any place is simply coincidental.*)

The place is the cafeteria of the Mount Sinai Jewish Hospital in Comfree, New Jersey. A tall man wearing a black shirt accented with a prominent cross approached the table at which an older gentleman was having lunch and said, "Sorry for the intrusion, but you seem familiar and I think we've met before. I think it was in Coldwater, Idaho, which is my hometown. By chance, were you visiting there in the early 1980s?" Because of the large cross around his neck one might have thought the man was from the clergy. Instead, he was James Dillinger, recently hired as manager of clinical laboratories at the Office of Technological Support at Mount Sinai. Dr. Halevy confirmed that he had, in fact, visited Mr.

Dillinger's hometown and recalled having met him.

The story then goes back to 1982 when Dr. Halevy, now a staff physician at Mount Sinai, came to the U.S. from Russia and was traveling around the country with his wife to become more acquainted with their new homeland. Being interested in small towns and rural areas, they stopped to rest in Coldwater, a town of about ten thousand. It was Sunday, and as they went for lunch at the pleasant restaurant in their small hotel they found the place beginning to fill with families who had just come from church.

The waitress overheard the couple speaking in a foreign language and couldn't resist asking where they were from. She was excited to learn that they were from Russia, a country she knew little about, and the news of the Russian visitors spread quickly throughout the restaurant. This prompted a surprising burst of hospitality from several people who came to the table to welcome the newcomers, offer drinks, and ask many questions. Some were intrigued to learn that these Russians were also Jews who had spent years overcoming difficult and hazardous political obstacles to escape from Russia. The Russians also had many things to ask about this place, which had the look of a typical American small town. James Dillinger, just home from college, was among the curious group who wanted to ask about Russia. Since his majors in college included medical technology and business administration, he wanted to hear about Russian medical practice, the state of their technology, and how healthcare worked in the Soviet Union. James's family had been deeply rooted in this tightly knit community of Coldwater. It was almost exclusively white and deeply attached to the local church where nearly all attended. There were a few black families in town, but no Jews or Hispanics or Asians. There was a touch of xenophobia in Coldwater. They were suspicious of different races and cultures, and, in particular, non Christians. The cultural environment at James's college was not very different from that of Coldwater.

Moving to the East Coast after graduation, James experienced a rather different environment and some awkward moments as he searched for a new job. He got his first position as a medical technologist at Saint Luke's Hospital and found himself in the midst of people of all races and religions. It wasn't easy for James to overcome his prejudice toward some coworkers, but he did find solace in learning that most of them were Christians, albeit mainly Catholic. He didn't like the job and therefore was not there for very long. He wanted to be in charge rather than a subordinate, and he started looking for a position in management. He eventually found one at Mount Sinai Jewish Hospital. It was there that he faced a more serious challenge in a strange new cultural environment. The workforce was diverse in race, culture, and religion, including many Jews.

James was not entirely comfortable working for an institution with a Jewish name and significantly Jewish medical staff. He started wearing a large silver cross, which served to instantly alert anyone who might have taken him for a Jew. The workplace was friendly and James' management skills were appreciated by the administration; however, shortly after he started, his director, a Catholic, advised him that as a manager in a nonsectarian institution, wearing a cross was quite inappropriate.

With some effort, James made a reasonable transition to the mainly secular culture of the hospital, and then began to shift his concentration toward obtaining a promotion. He was glad he had majored in business administration, which was the best path to a position of some authority and dominance.

James realized quickly that to succeed with his superiors he needed to become the man who could implement many of their desires. He also learned not to question or quibble with orders that were given to him, even when they seemed unreasonable or counterproductive. It was clear to him that he should avoid presenting new ideas as his own, but attribute them to those in higher authority. Thus, he became a successful middleman in the management chain by his agreeable "yes, sir" or "right away" attitude.

The 1980s in the U.S. could be characterized as having a general business philosophy (in the nonprofit sector as well as the corporate) that managers with business degrees and business skills should be in charge, aiming to make the organization more productive and cost-effective. To meet these needs many colleges increased their programs in business administration, and it gained popularity. Graduates in business administration could often find higher-paying jobs. So it was with James, who had not really succeeded as a medical technologist, but progressed nicely as a department manager and was soon promoted to Director of Clinical Laboratories. Concurrently, the former director, a Ph.D. with expertise in several fields of laboratory work (and affiliated with the medical school as a Professor of Microbiology) was reassigned as the Medical Director of the Laboratory Department, a position with no administrative power, mostly a figurehead needed to sign certificates and lend some scientific credence to the department.

The general idea of advancing people with a business administration degree was that they could run any operation, even without specific knowledge in the field. The formal reason for James's promotion to director was that he had the advantage over other individuals who became managers in that he was familiar with the subject of management (although not a very good medical technologist).

James realized that to impress his superiors and to justify his job he had to be visible day to day. This meant attending meetings at all levels of administration. This became a priority in his time schedule, even at moments when the department needed his attention. To show the department's productivity ("his work") to his superiors, James devoted much of his time presenting documents and slide shows on his plans for future development, with an emphasis on anticipated revenue. One could often see James running through the institution from one meeting to another with his portfolio of proposals.

He was a man who lived in the present but seemed to belong in the past, somewhere in the 1950s. He subtly projected the bad boy image reminiscent of the film *Blackboard Jungle,* in which teenage boys derisively referred to the teacher as "teach" or "daddy-o." The boys' attitudes were sullen, and they were always spoiling for a rumble. As a manager, James maintained the proper decorum, yet he still displayed some "bad boy" characteristics. His primary goal was to intimidate people around him, which he managed to do in a variety of ways. For example, to make everyone aware that he was around, he would walk with a swagger, hitting the cleats on his loafers loud enough for all to hear. He would sit on a table with his feet on a chair or he'd perch on the back of the chair to be elevated above the rest of the group.

The laboratories conducted their work and implemented new technologies in the emerging market with or without James's presence; however, he managed to take credit for much of the progress. To elevate his position he started building a group of leaders under his authority, including an assistant director, a marketing director, a business consultant, a manager, and his secretary. It was called department administration. Counting on strong support from higher management, James sometimes departed from accepted protocol and asserted his authority with demeaning reprimands at the lab directors—those with Ph.D. degrees.

His secretary, Beatrice, an attractive blond in her mid-twenties, fell in love with James and succeeded in entering what she called a friendship. Beatrice was married and had a two-year-old child but very soon divorced her husband. She was lazy and often came in late, sometimes by an hour or more. James, who was strict on prompt arrivals (he would reprimand staff for being fifteen minutes late) actually covered up for her by opening her office, turning on her computer and lights, making it appear as if she had stepped out for a moment.

He introduced a system where any administrative action in the Clinical Laboratories Department required his signature, while the lab directors and supervisors lost their administrative authority. This included such actions as posting of new positions and hiring the technicians, preparing an annual budget, acquiring new equipment, and such. Most important, he monopolized all communications with the personnel and finance departments.

For proper management of his patients, Dr. Halevy depended on a variety of laboratory tests, which placed him in a close communication loop with clinical laboratories. He had the opportunity to observe, with some amusement, that the administrative people, such as James, had little bio-medical knowledge yet were placed above the real professionals. It reminded him of the life he had left behind in the Soviet Union. Nevertheless, Dr. Halevy could still interact with the lab people directly to order the testing for his patients, and so far there had been no serious interference from James. He could also pick up information about the political climate in laboratories.

One of the labs had the status of a Reference Clinical Laboratory because it serviced a large number of medical institutions outside the hospital. The director, Dr. B., complained that he couldn't make any decisions about the use of extra income for additional equipment or technical support. These were subject to approval by layers of administrative managers without pertinent bio-medical expertise, and several were not healthcare professionals at all. Dr. B. complained to Dr. Halevy, "The volume of work and revenue in my laboratory is growing, and I need an additional technologist to meet the production demand and for development of new procedures. I'm not trusted to make decisions or to even calculate and financially justify a new position. I have to go to James, not to the Medical Director, and James submits his requests to the vice president, whose background is only in business administration. But he makes the decisions. Moreover, any decision, such as posting a position, salary arrangement, recruiting a selected candidate, must go through a series of administrative signatures, all the way up to the VP. Most of these approvals are done without any understanding of the professional bio-medical issues but rather on personal mood, whim, or whether they like the lab director who originated the request."

There is a tendency by bureaucrats to take control over the professionals. It is not rare to hear the commissars say that they can quickly learn the specifics of any professional scientific operation, and make appropriate business decisions without requiring any input from the professionals in the field. This attitude is nothing new. Vladimir Lenin, the founder of the Soviet Union, said. "With the new (Soviet) regime we will replace all the 'experts' inherited from the capitalist system with workers, and the housewives will run our country." And so they did. The final result of this came to pass in 1991 when the country disintegrated. All commissars, either in the Soviet Union or the managers in the U.S., who follow their bureaucratic method, at various ranks throughout the hierarchy, are able to create frustration and dysfunction. Sometimes the ego-driven actions of low-ranking commissars can be particularly damaging.

The question is, what would happen to such fields as science, medical care, and the industrial economy in the U.S. if these important areas of our lives continue to be dominated by the modern-day commissars?

Fortunately, America was not fertile ground for the commissar phenomenon. Dr. Halevy's fear that the commissars would institute the same destructive role as they did in the Soviet Union was not justified. One of the important differences in the American environment from the rigid system of the Soviet Union is the high level of adaptability demonstrated throughout the history of the U.S., which is based on general principles of democracy and free exchange of opinions. The ideas developed and expressed in industry, technology, private enterprises, medicine, and academia led to an overwhelming opinion that commanding positions in these and other fields should be in the hands of individuals with a higher level of education and professional experience rather than managers with a degree in business administration or lawyers.

It is peculiar that a similar conclusion was made in the former Soviet Union, and high-ranking officials with a lower education started preparing to obtain their Ph.D. degrees, which helped them to secure their jobs and to receive promotions. Nevertheless, having a Ph.D. did not make these individuals experts in the field because they did not conduct any research; other individuals, real scientists at research institutions, were subordinates to these commissars and consequently prepared Ph.D. dissertations for them.

Such corruption is virtually impossible in the U.S., and a completely different phenomenon is taking place now. Many highly educated Americans with Ph.D. or MD degrees and abundant experience in research and/or development in their professional field realized their capability in administrative activities and decided to make a switch in the middle of their careers to high-ranking administrative positions, such as CEOs in academic institutions, or division chairmen of departments in research institutions, etc. This phenomenon will guarantee that managerial activities will be in the hands of qualified professionals.

3. Back to Russia: Visiting Russian "Weapons Scientists"
For more than twenty years after my departure from Russia I had

no inclination to return or even to know what events were taking place there. The idea of ever going back to Russia was unthinkable. Leaving Russia was rather like the end of a bitter divorce. I closed my mind to everything that was a reminder of the past. Assimilating into the American way of life was paramount.

Then the once-unthinkable happened. I found myself making travel plans to visit Russia! Filled with many conflicting emotions, I was heading back to that country. I had determined that three separate issues propelled me to revisit: time had softened my heart and mind; my curiosity was aroused about the country and how it had changed since the fall of the Soviet Union in 1991; and finally, one of the U.S. nongovernment organizations and the U.S. State Department were interested in possible collaboration with Russian scientists in the field of tuberculosis.

After the fall of the Soviet Empire, dramatic changes took place in the political, economical, and social arenas. The veil of secrecy surrounding the epidemic of tuberculosis was lifted. To the great surprise of the world health community, Russia was suddenly on the radar as one of the countries with the highest prevalence of tuberculosis, which represented a threat of spreading the infection to other countries.

For a long period of time, tuberculosis was among the most neglected world health problems. The problem was not even recognized, and the general assumption in the world health community (including in the U.S.) was that it was a problem of the past. In the 1980s the situation started to change, particularly after a number of outbreaks of tuberculosis in the U.S. were characterized by very high mortality rates. The severity of the problem of tuberculosis became apparent and could no longer be ignored. The World Health Organization (WHO) was compelled to address the issue. They developed a strategy that would not require tremendous resources and, thus, would become appealing to the governments of developing countries with a high prevalence of tuberculosis. In response to the appeal from the WHO, the U.S. government committed substantial funds to fighting tuberculosis, malaria, and AIDS in countries with a high prevalence of these diseases. Funds were given to a number of nongovernmental organizations to implement measures needed to combat these dreaded diseases in a large number of countries. One of these organizations was Euro-Asian Medical Educational Program (EMEP) at the Institute for Health Policy Analyses, directed by Dr. Edward Burger. Two faculty members of the National Jewish Medical Research Center in Denver, Dr. Michael Iseman and I, were invited by EMEP to consult with the medical community in one of the largest districts of Siberia called Sverdlovsk Oblast, with its capital called now Yekaterinburg (formerly Sverdlovsk), for consultation aimed at enhancing the TB control program there. Dr. Iseman and I visited this area in 2001. We investigated the situation, gave a series of lectures, and participated in the development of a new program. Four microbiologists from Sverdlovsk came to Denver to receive four weeks of training in my TB laboratory. Subsequently in 2002, with similar goals, I visited another large area in Siberia called Novosibirsk Oblast, and over a period of a few years I have lectured at several scientific TB conferences, mostly in Moscow.

During my first few visits to Russia I was concerned that I would not be welcomed, particularly by some of my former acquaintances. Contrary to my preconceived notion that I might be viewed negatively, I was warmly greeted personally, and my lectures were well received. A possible explanation of this friendly approach is because the whole atmosphere in the medical and scientific community of Russia has changed, and most people did not carry the past Soviet sentiments into the present. Another reason for the friendly approach was the desire of many Russian scientists and institutions to collaborate with me, now a representative of the American scientific community. I kept receiving multiple invitations to visit conferences in Russia. I even felt that some leading Russian medical authorities had a preferential approach toward me compared with other foreign scientists, which may have had an additional important explanation: My visits to Russia coincided with a conflicting situation in regard to the TB control programs between Russia, on one hand, and the WHO and associated groups on the other hand. This was related to the attempt of WHO to force the Russian medical community to accept and implement the WHO strategy to control tuberculosis around the world.

The new strategy proposed by the WHO for implementation in all countries was called DOTS (Directly Observed Therapy Short course). The main idea is directly observed therapy to ensure that patients comply with the prescribed treatment to guarantee a good outcome of it. There were no arguments against this main principle; its importance has been known for a long time and even practiced in Russia to treat patients usually hospitalized according to the Russian standards. Reluctance of the Russian specialists and administration to implement the DOTS strategy was related to a few elements of this strategy viewed as not appropriate for Russian conditions.

One of these elements was a requirement that treatment of the TB patients should be done in an ambulatory setting without hospitalization. Second, all newly diagnosed patients would receive a standard combination of antimicrobial drugs, without any individualization. Third, diagnosis of TB and the criterion of recovery was to be based on microscopic sputum smear examination only, without an attempt to cultivate the tubercle bacilli and without a determination of drug susceptibility of the patients' bacterial isolates. The Russian position was based on the reference to their many years of experience and that WHO could not recognize specific conditions in Russia requiring standards different than DOTS; this was viewed by the Russians as more appropriate to the underdeveloped countries, not to such an advanced country like Russia.

Most of the foreign experts coming to Russia automatically agreed with the WHO position even before coming to Russia and before learning about the situation there. Therefore, they were facing negative, mostly hidden, but sometimes even openly negative reactions in the medical community. I knew well about the sensitivity of Russian people at any level of society in regard to national pride. Also, I was familiar with the abundant experience of Russian medical professionals in dealing with TB. Based on this knowledge from my past, I developed a balanced approach. One of the points was to earn trust through building personal, friendly relationships with the leading figures. I also advised the people working at the WHO office in Moscow to consider this approach. Over the years, this principle became the basis of a better relationship between WHO and the Russian authorities, at least by appearance.

The Russians officially accepted the DOTS strategy, which provided WHO with an opportunity to make a checkmark in the records on the number of countries that joined the WHO strategy. For the purpose of demonstrating the advantage of the WHO approach over traditional Russian practices, a few field trials were conducted in some areas. At the same time, in the rest of the country, and even in the areas of the field trials, the events continued as usual. Most of the TB patients were hospitalized, and attempts to use a full scale of bacteriological methods continued. Since these methods were not recommended by the WHO, no attempts for their improvement were made, either by the Russian professionals or by the foreign experts visiting Russia. The archaic bacteriological methods used in most of the Russian laboratories could not provide results in a timely manner and, therefore, appeared useless in the adjustment of the patient's treatment regimen. Therefore many patients were treated with drugs to which their bacteria were resistant, and they continued to be a source of infection for new cases with drug-resistant TB.

Under support from EMEP, we implemented a development project in the Sverdlovsk Oblast in Siberia, including training four of the most experienced microbiologists in my laboratory. We also proposed a new bacteriology support program that included implementation of new technology and revision of the laboratory services system. In the rest of the country, with few exceptions, insufficient bacteriological support resulted in a growing number of patients with drug-resistant tuberculosis.

Under pressure by similar developments in other countries, recently the WHO modified its strategy by recognizing that the microscopic smear examination has limited value. The importance of modern bacteriological methods (by culture) is fully recognized now for complete detection of all TB patients in the community and especially for timely detection of patients with drug-resistant TB. The problem now is how to achieve this goal. The obstacle is not insufficient funding: The U.S. and other countries have contributed large sums, and some countries (as in Russia) have enough of their own resources, just not focused on TB control. The problem is driven by local and international bureaucracy attempts to create universal rules and to be credited for such development, and that is along with unreasonable, and sometimes corrupted, distribution of funds. Tuberculosis has always been a political problem, and it is not surprising that in our time the political issues surrounding this major health problem heavily dominate over decisions on the programs to control TB epidemics.

In my publications, as well as in many presentations, I keep emphasizing that the key element in preventing and diminishing the epidemics of drug-resistant TB is proper laboratory services, which can be the least expensive element of the TB control program. Only proper bacteriological examination of all new TB patients provides detection of individuals who carry drug-resistant bacteria. Such testing, if the results are available within short period of time, not only ensures more efficient treatment of patients with drug-resistant bacteria (by making adjustments in the initial standard treatment regimen) but also helps to alleviate the spread of drug-resistant strains of tubercle bacilli. One of the obstacles for this approach is the tendency to have a network of small laboratories ("close to the patients") or, as this approach is labeled, a decentralized laboratory system with many microscopy stations or other so-called seeding stations. Under these conditions none of the small laboratories can afford any modern equipment or even proper biosafety protection. I am trying (not very successfully) to convince my colleagues that only a centralized system with direct delivery of sputum specimens to large, well-equipped laboratories that have highly qualified personnel will resolve the problem of obtaining results within the shortest possible time. This also guarantees high-quality testing, and is much less costly than a decentralized system. Most of the Russian professionals and administrators are sympathetic to the idea of centralized laboratory services, contrary to different views by some international experts. Currently in Russia they have only a few well-equipped laboratories providing direct laboratory services to a large number of patients. At the same time, even the best laboratories don't have proper biosafety standards, and in some places the laboratories have become a source of infection for laboratory workers. It is known that prevalence of TB among the laboratory workers is about ten-fold higher than in the general Russian population. There is a need to create model TB laboratories to demonstrate their cost efficiency and productivity, but also as educational facilities for TB microbiologists from around the country.

In May of 2002 a call from Moscow by Edward (Ed) S. came on behalf of the International Science and Technology Center (ISTC) office. He asked whether I would be able to meet with him in Washington, D.C. to discuss a possible collaboration with some Russian scientists in the field of tuberculosis. I learned at that time that the ISTC was established in 1992 as an international nonproliferation program with the purpose of engaging former weapons scientists from Russia and other former Soviet Republics in a productive international partnership. I met Ed in June in Washington during the Fourth International Congress on Tuberculosis. He was interested in whether I would be willing to become an American partner in tuberculosis research with Russian scientists who were formerly involved in the Soviet bacteriological warfare program. After receiving my positive answer, Ed took me to the Office for Nonproliferation at the State Department, where I met Anne Harrington and a group of her associates. The discussion with this charming and most intelligent lady was detailed and interesting. She said, "I know that you published a scientific paper on nanoparticles as a vehicle for TB drug delivery. We are interested in the research by some Russian former weapon scientists who are now using nanoparticle technology for other medications. Would you be able to host four of them at your institution in Denver to discuss possible collaboration?" I responded positively, and, literally, the following week, (to the surprise of the administration at the National Jewish Medical and Research Center) four Russians— three scientists and an administrative assistant—arrived in Denver and gave interesting presentations (in perfect English) at a seminar that I had hastily organized.

Within a few days in Denver, and with my help, they prepared a grant application on possible use of nanoparticles for administration of TB drugs, and left for Washington to present this application. The research was subsequently approved and funded by the Biotechnology Engagement Program (BTEP) through the ISTC office in Moscow. I submitted a parallel application to NIH and received a similar grant as a basis for our collaboration. An interesting and productive relationship ensued. The individuals who came to Denver were well-known former weapons scientists from the Russian Research Institute for Molecular Diagnostics and Therapy (RIMDT)—V.I. Kiselev, P.G. Sweshnikov, and S.E. Gelperina. Later I became aware of the reason for the interest of the Department for Nonproliferation of the State Department in nanoparticles. In fact, "nanoparticles" was a buzz-word; they were used to "weaponize" bacteriological warfare agents by creating a stable presence of toxins or bacteria in the air. In well-known episodes of anthrax bacteria in the Senate offices in 2001 the spores of anthrax bacilli were incorporated into nanoparticles, resulting in a stable aerosol.

The Russians appeared to be experts in the incorporation of various materials into nanoparticles. The idea of our collaboration was to incorporate anti-TB drugs into nanoparticles, so they could be administered to patients with less frequency (perhaps only twice a week) than the free drugs administered daily. These expectations were based on the potential of nanoparticles to create a drug depot in the system with subsequent slow release into the body.

I visited some institutions in Moscow that used to be off-limits because of the secrecy of research related to the bacteriological warfare program. I was now impressed by the advanced technology and equipment they had and by the high level of education and skill of the people they employed. Collaboration with the Russian scientists was a very good start and produced very important results, particularly with regard to the possibility of improvement of the anti-tuberculosis therapy by using nanotechnology.

The U.S. Civilian Research and Development Foundation (CRDF) is a charitable foundation established by the National Science Foundation (NSF) in 1995. It was authorized by Congress to develop collaboration between the U.S. and former defense-oriented scientists in Russia and other former Soviet Republics to transfer their skills to productive civilian science. In August 2004, encouraged by CRDF, and with additional support from Becton-Dickinson, I organized a conference in Denver to discuss collaboration plans for coordinated TB research between the U.S. and Russian scientists. The four-day conference was a great success. In attendance were seven leading Russian scientists, a group of leading American TB experts, representatives from CRDF, representatives from the CDC, and Anne Harrington and two of her colleagues from the State Department. We discussed current progress in collaborative research and formulated specific projects for which grant applications to CRDF and BTEP were recommended. The main Russian partners were scientists from the Russian Research Center for Molecular Diagnostics and Therapy, with whom we already had some working relationships. Encouraged by the recommendations of this conference, both Russian and American sites began collecting preliminary data and submitted several grant applications.

Subsequently CRDF became involved in sponsoring a number of very promising projects that are now being implemented; however, after Anne Harrington left the Office of Nonproliferation, the attitude of the State Department changed dramatically for unexplainable reasons. First, some Russian scientists told me that someone from the State Department visiting Moscow had informed them that TB research would not be sponsored by the State Department (through BTEP and ISTC). An authoritative representative from the Office of Nonproliferation denied this news as unjustified rumors. Nevertheless, the funding for TB research from the State Department through BTEP has significantly diminished. Regardless of the score, some very promising projects recommended at the 2004 conference were rejected, and one of them that had received a highest score and had already been funded (BTEP #120) was recalled by BTEP because of "changes in policy." It seems that investments in time and energy and the cost of establishing productive collaboration with the former Russian weapons scientists was wasted because of such mysterious changes in policy (without details or explanations).

Collaboration with the aim of redirecting the goals of research by the former weapon scientists can be based exclusively on the development of mutual trust. Dramatic changes in unexplained policies appeared to be most damaging to such trust, as I was told by some leading Russian scientists. My perception of the situation (from what I have learned during the last few years) is that the attitude toward the problem has not been based on the scientific analyses of experienced American scientists but rather was made by bureaucrats appointed to various offices; those professionals who happened to be government employees had only limited involvement. Are these administrators making decisions about collaboration with Russian scientists another rendition of modern-day commissars?

In countries like Russia, where tuberculosis represents a major national health problem, effective control of this illness cannot be achieved without qualified diagnostic TB laboratories. During 2003–2005, when I visited many medical institutions in Russia, I could not find a single TB laboratory that had implemented modern biosafety standards. (I witnessed the same situation later, in 2007.) Without such standards in place, these laboratories often become a source of dangerous infection not only to the lab personnel but to the surrounding environment as well. It became clear that a number of U.S.-Russia projects, already funded by the State Department in millions of dollars, could not be effectively implemented in such conditions.

Initially encouraged by the Office for Nonproliferation, with very enthusiastic support by the Russian high-ranking medical authorities, I developed a relatively inexpensive project for a model TB laboratory in Moscow. It was planned that a number of joined TB projects that had already been funded would be conducted in this laboratory. Various Russian agencies approved the plan, along with expenses for space renovation. The project was submitted to the Office for Nonproliferation at the State Department for some additional funding for laboratory equipment and supplies.

Suddenly the situation was dramatically reversed. An unusual letter from Mr. R., representative of the Office for Nonproliferation at the State Department, was sent to Dr. Mikhail Paltsev, the president of the Sechenov's Moscow Medical Academy who was in charge of the project and one of the most influential individuals in Russian medical administration. The letter stated that the State Department policy did not support development of "Biosafety Level 3 (BSL-3) facilities outside of the U.S." Neither the Russians nor I knew about such a policy. I had made a terrible mistake. Instead of simply listing the measures needed for the safe operation of a TB laboratory, I unwisely inscribed the forbidden acronym "BSL-3" on the floor plan of the laboratory. Mr. R. then stated that it was against policy, although he understood the need for safe conditions to work with tuberculosis. At the same time, he stressed that compliance with policy was a priority. Eventually I learned that the basis for this so-called policy was the fear that the Russians would use the BSL-3 facility for illicit purposes. In fact, no such policy at the State Department ever existed.

As a result of this lapse, engagement of most of the skilled Russian scientists in TB projects has dramatically diminished. It is a loss for them, but also for us. The plan for technology transfer of nanoparticle methodology that I have nurtured will not be implemented. The Russians will not sit idle, and they may find partners in other countries (China? Iran? North Korea?) who, unlike our policymakers at the State Department, don't have a tendency to cut the branch on which they are sitting. Recent conduct of the Office for Nonproliferation of the State Department has not enhanced its reputation among Russian medical leadership, whose views have reached all the way up to Putin's office, in line with the leadership's concern with tuberculosis in Russia. Collaboration between Russian and U.S. professionals in the field of tuberculosis would not only bear fruit for essential progress in this field, but also could serve as an avenue for building better relationships between the two countries. All this is possible if the power of bureaucrats is replaced with a professional attitude, and when professionals are given authority to make professional (and administrative) decisions.

My last trip to Russia in June 2007, sponsored by EMEP, was particularly educational. Coming via Seoul, I entered Russia at the city of Khabarovsk in the Russian Far East. From Khabarovsk I traveled by train with Dr. Burger to the city of Blagoveshchensk. We traveled to several universities, ending at the All-Russia TB conference in Moscow. I was pleased that my lectures were very successful. The local medical authorities, particularly in Irkutsk, asked for specific recommendations to improve their program to control the epidemics of TB and AIDS there. They expressed an interest in reorganizing the TB laboratory services on a basis of the centralized services principle. There is hope that Irkutsk may become a model site for an effective TB/HIV control program.

During our fifteen-hour train trip from Khabarovsk to

Blagoveshchensk, we had an opportunity to interact with some Russian professors from the medical school who accompanied us, as well as some other Russian passengers in the same car. The atmosphere was relaxed, particularly because of a traditional Russian custom of having small vodka drinks while traveling on a train. Not surprisingly, we were the center of attention, but at the same time we had ample opportunity for relatively free conversations with Russians on their views regarding the current problems in the country and predictions for the future. These discussions continued in the cities of Blagoveshchensk and Irkutsk, mostly with the faculty members of the medical schools and the physicians.

One of the great concerns among those living in Siberia and the Far East of Russia is the perception that China may capture the whole East of Russia up to the Ural Mountains. They gave us a number of reasons for their fear. One reason is the fact that many Russians are moving from the Far East to the European part of the country, and the population of ethnic Russians in Siberia is declining. At the same time, there is a population explosion in the part of China that borders Russia, mostly because of population relocation from other parts of China. There is a visible movement, legally and illegally, of Chinese nationals across the border, to settle in Siberia, mostly in rural areas. We saw a substantial number of Chinese individuals when visiting the open market in Khabarovsk. Most often they engage in a cooperative arrangement with the Russian citizens, who now have legal rights to own parcels of quite fertile land in this area (the Chinese cannot), on which the Chinese newcomers (legal and illegal) work very hard with superior productivity.

By an invitation from a Chinese young man who was a graduate of the Blagoveshchensk Medical School, we had an opportunity, in the company of the dean of the school, to spend one day in the new Chinese city of Heihe, located on the bank of Amur River opposite Blagoveshchensk. It was a shocking contrast to the old and mostly dilapidated Blagoveshchensk; Heihe is a new and growing modern city with many construction cranes around, modern tower buildings, large shopping centers, hotels, and crowds of people everywhere. We were told that there is an airport near the city and roads connecting it with the rest of China. Signs in shops, restaurants, and other public places were in two languages: Chinese and Russian. People in the streets could converse in Russian and some even in English. People are friendly and welcome Russians to their city. They even offer Russians an opportunity to buy condominiums for reasonable prices, much more reasonable than back in Blagoveshchensk.

We witnessed unusual trade cooperation between Russians and Chinese. A group of about thirty to forty Russians, mostly women, boarded the steamboat to cross the river from Blagoveshchnsk to Heihe, which took about forty minutes. After expedited passage through the Chinese customs, the Russians boarded two large buses that were waiting for them. After our visit to Heihe at the end of the day, we met the same group going back to Blagoveshchensk. This time each person had a large sealed bag, which we were told weighed not more than thirty kilo. This allowed the individual to pass both Chinese and Russian customs without any delay. There seems to be a simple explanation to this mystery. The Russians served, for a fee significant to them, as "mules" transporting goods from Heihe to a Chinese trader in Blagoveshchensk. From Blagoveshchenck these goods were distributed throughout Russia, with a steady price increase at each transfer, but still more affordable (and of better quality) than the Russian-manufactured goods, particularly textiles.

We also learned that there is a division among the Russians in Blagoveshchensk in regard to their attitude toward the Chinese. Most Russians are, at least, neutral, but there is a growing influence of extreme nationalists who promote intolerance and violence toward Chinese visitors to Blagoveshchensk area.

One former high-ranking Russian military man told me that China has a huge concentration of military troops and installations on the border with Russia, and, in case of a Chinese invasion, Russians will not have any significant ground forces to withstand such an invasion. Along with these widely spread rumors, we did not come across any official statements or media reports regarding a possible confrontation between Russia and China. Current media reports on various levels of cooperation between Russia and China are indicative of unjustified Russian fear of Chinese invasion, at least in the foreseeable future.

Another subject we broached during our frank conversations, particularly with the Russian professors, was their perception of the current post-Soviet development of the country. Although most of them were pleased with it, some were nostalgic for the past, when, in their perception, everything was "in order" and more predictable than today. Generally, most middle-class, well-educated professionals we met expressed much less concern about human rights (as viewed by Western and a number of Russian journalists) as with simple family economy, even within this social group, which is much better off than the general population. They had very negative feelings about the new non-government private corporations and about any wealth accumulation in private groups such as the so-called New Russians (a new class of super-rich individuals).

These points became particularly clear when Dr. Burger asked about the Russian view of Mikhail Khodorkovsky, who owned a large and growing oil company (Yukos) and is now imprisoned for tax evasion. It was clear to any objective observer that with the generally relaxed and loosely enforced tax laws in Russia, the tax issue was just a good excuse to go after Khodorkovsky. The real reason for his imprisonment was the success of his company and that it was not under any government control. Currently, most segments of the oil and gas industry in Russia are placed under direct or indirect government control, most likely with much less efficiency than the previous private enterprise. The professors' immediate response to Dr. Burger's question was condemnation of Khodorkovsky with a reference to the tax problem but with an obvious idea of unfair distribution of wealth. One of them said, "After all, oil belongs to the people of the country and the profits from its sale should be distributed among all citizens, just as it is done in Saudi Arabia, instead of going into the pockets of few." Beyond the professors' ignorance about the economy (quite common among the Russian intellectuals, and not only Russian...), these views are widely spread within any social group and are used by some political manipulators for pointing the blame to some enterprises and individuals for the low standard of living. Although ultra-rich people in Russia represent a substantial class of people, political criticism is targeting only a few of them, by coincidence or not, especially those of Jewish descent. Among these criticized individuals particularly mentioned by our professor was even Mr. Abramovitch, a quite efficient and popular governor of Kamchatka, who not only brought prosperity to his large district, but also developed personal wealth. One could find no condemnation, either in the press or by individuals such as the professors mentioned above, of a large number of very wealthy individuals having high-ranking positions in the country, such as the mayor of Moscow and even Putin himself. It seems that ideas about inequality and fair distribution of wealth that in the last century led to the establishment of the Soviet Union are still alive in Russia.

The country is suffering from three epidemics interacting in a synergistic manner: drug addiction; HIV/AIDS; and TB, including multiple drug-resistant TB. Drug addiction leads to the increasing IV transmission of the HIV virus and to crimes associated with the needs for money to buy the drugs. Overcrowded with these criminals, prisons become a common place where the spread of tuberculosis is occurring, especially to the HIV-infected individuals having a diminished level of immunity. When the individuals, newly infected with TB, are released from the prisons they settle among the local population and spread the infection further. Neither the WHO strategy nor the traditional Russian practice will resolve the growing problem. New approaches, tailored for specific conditions in each area of Russia, are needed. New approaches, without common politics involved, can be developed by close cooperation of independent, nongovernmental, international groups of experts with local medical professionals.

At the end of my fifteen-day journey around the globe, I attended the 8th All-Russian TB Congress in Moscow on June 7–8, 2007 to give my presentation; I was invited by the WHO office in Moscow. I found full understanding of the ideas mentioned above, including specific projects (such as for Irkutsk mentioned above), as well as a general desire for collaboration. Unfortunately, there are too many obstacles on the way to such collaboration. So far, only personal contacts still exist on the way to it. Members of the Russian top medical leadership (directors of various TB institutes) and the WHO representatives greeted me enthusiastically. At the picture taken at the banquet after the Conference are (left to right): Deputy Director of the Novosibirsk TB Institute, head of the WHO office in Moscow Dr. Wieslaw Jakubowiak, Deputy Director of the Moscow TB Institute Dr. V. A. Aksenova, myself, Chief TB Pulmonologist of the Russian Federation Dr. M. I. Perelman, and Director of the Novosibirsk TB Institute Dr. V. A. Krasnov; at the table, Dr. I. V. Bogadelnikova.

4. Lessons from the Past, Survival Tips

To be successful and to survive in a research position is not easy. It is not enough to be talanted and to have a good education. The most important element for being hired to such a job is to gradua-te from a prestigious school or to have a record of training (and recommendation) from a prominent, well-established scientist. There are two groups of scientists who must struggle for their sur-vival in a research institution. One of these groups is the young beginners, who have to acquire grant support and be able to publish the results of their studies in well-recognized journals. Often they have to overcome a vicious cycle: To receive a grant, one needs to have experience, but to obtain this experience (with publications), one needs finacial support in the form of grants. The other group of scientists facing the problem of survival at the sci-entific institutions are those in the aging group. No matter how successful one has been throughout his/ her scientific life, people of a younger generation may look for an opportunity to take over the already-established laboratory or group and push out the older person. I have experienced both situations: first, as a beginner when I came to the U.S. (at the age of fifty-three); and second, as an established scientist after receiving a large number of grants and becoming a director of one of the largest and successful TB diagnostic laboratories. Perhaps, based on this extended experien-ce of survival for a period of almost thirty years now, I will be able to provide others with some tips for survival at a scientific institu-tion.

In my past experience in Russia, one of the important tools for survival (in a general and broad sense) was to have a network of good friends. Immigrants from the Soviet Union brought with them to the U.S. a unique set of survival experience skills. Are they needed here in the free world? Are they applicable here? Does friendship play the same role in the U.S. in survival and prosperity as it did in the Soviet Union? The answer is both yes and no. It is yes in regard to prosperity, because the networking and connections are important elements anywhere for building one's career, developing business, marketing, etc. At the same time, there is no need for connections for survival and to satisfy basic needs, so this type of selected friendship is not essential. Therefore, relationships between friends and the meaning of friendship in the U.S. are not the same as in the Soviet Union. In most cases the terms friendship and friend are used more loosely and pertain primarily to having a good time together. On one hand, it is not bad that survival in a free society does not rely on the help of others; on the other hand, the social environment in the free world is causing in some people an extremely damaging individualistic mentality, and, in others, a sense of alienation and futility. This safe environment in the U.S. is a reason for many people to search for a group to which they can belong. No ideal social environment can be found in the world, but with all the "pros and contras," there is not a place in the world where an individual can feel safer, and there is no other country that provides so many choices for a happy life.

Many of my new American friends kept asking me whether my children and I experienced any nostalgia for Russia. My answer was simple and truthful. We had no nostalgia for Russia or our lives there, and the only nostalgia we experienced was for our good friends. The harsh and dangerous conditions in Russia gave rise to absolute and undeniable friendships. Under the conditions of the opressive regime, one had to be very careful in selecting friends, and years of experience were needed to make sure that the person next to you was not a police informer. But people needed mutual support to survive, and life in the Soviet Union required interdependence: help in finding jobs, obtaining an education, housing, and permission to reside in large cities, as well as in every small item of everyday life, such as getting food not available in stores, tickets to popular shows, etc, etc. People had to have connections to have what they needed, and complex networks arose to meet those needs. In the most serious matters, networking and friendships were crucial elements for survival in the very literal sense.

I believe that one can be happy and successful in the U.S. without any Russian experience and its paranoia. Nevertheless, there are enough American-born individuals who blame society and government for their failures. It is those people who need to have an experience of surviving in the Soviet Union or in another country with a opressive regime. Maybe these people with subnormal mentality should learn about such experiences as part of a prescribed psychotherapy. These groups of Americans are very small, although often boisterous (some are celebrities), and some may be dangerous, particularly those who are playing their anti-American statements into the hands of our enemies. Fortunately, the majority of American people appreciate what they have in this unique, free society, and the vast majority of immigrants from Russia join them in invoking *God Bless America!*

5. Not "Russian" Anymore

The aforementioned criticism of the growing bureaucracy in the U.S. is by no means a reflection of my Russian past. Rather, it arises from my concerns as an American for the future of the U.S., and it is inspired by my positive feelings and love for this country. I stress that after almost thirty years of work at the National Jewish Medical and Research Center in Denver, longer than I worked anywhere, I feel that these years represent the best period of both my professional and personal life. My criticism of that or any other place of employment is only a reflection of sadness about events that could and should have been avoided in the great American institutions such as National Jewish in Denver, which provides superior patient care, has great physicians and scientists, and makes important contributions to medical research, despite problems with bureaucracy. My critical comments about the State Department regarding the deals with the Russian former weapons scientists should be viewed in the same manner. In other words, all my critical comments should be viewed as those of a caring person proud to be an American citizen and an American professional. Yes, I belong here and nowhere else. I love this country, but I have fear, based on my Russian experience, that bureaucracy may destroy this great and unique country.

Back in Russia I was labeled Jewish on my internal passport and in all other official documents and questionnaires. Identifying myself in official documents as Russian would have been a punishable misrepresentation. But here, after almost thirty years in the U.S., some people continue to refer to me as Russian, notwithstanding my U.S. citizenship, ability to speak and write in English, and my devotion to this country. I cannot make them forget about my origin. I keep telling them that I may have a Russian accent, but my thoughts are without any accent and purely American—more precisely, conservative American. It seems that nobody here refers to me as Jewish, simply because, unlike in Russia, this term connotes not the ethnic origin but religion.

In the past six years I have travelled to Russia to collaborate with Russian scientists. During these trips I delivered lectures and scientific presentations, always in Russian, and interacted with many people. Despite the fact that my Russian is still correct, people have frequently identified me as an American because I don't make use of the anglicisms that fill contemporary Russian expression. In Russia I am now an American who speaks Russian.

So, who am I?

I am an American; I am not Russian anymore! Not Russian! *American*!

END NOTES

1. Paul de Kruif, *Microbe Hunters* (New York, NY: Harcourt, Brace & Co., 1932).
2. *Bolshevik magazine in Russian,* (Moscow, Russia: Politizdat, 1943).
3. Amur Weiner in Crimes of War: Guilt and Denial in the Twentieth Century, edited by O. Bartow, A. Grossman and M. Nolan (New York, NY: New Press, 2002) p. 2002-2030.
4. Jan T. Gross, *Fear* (New York, NY: Random House, 2006).
5. Phillip E. Johnson, *Darwin on Trial* (Lanham, MD: Regnery Gateway, 1991).
6. Anne Appelbaum, *Gulag: A History* (New York, NY: Doubleday, 2003).
7. Tolengen Kazymbekov, Slomaniy Metch (Broken Sword) Frunze: Kygyzstan Publishing House, 1973.
8. T.M. Pollock, ed., *Trials of Prophylactic Agents for the Control of Communicable Diseases* (Geneva: World Health Organization, Monograph Series No. 52, 1966).
9. Lev Feodorov ed, Bulletin (Union of Chemical Security Press, 1999). Distributed electronically by lefed@glasnet.ru.
10. Ken Alibek with Stephen Handelman, *Biohazard* (New York, NY: Dell, 2000).
11. Jeanne Abrams, *Blazing the Tuberculosis Trail* (Denver, CO: Colorado Historical Society, Monograph # 6, 1990).

12. Beth S. Wegner, *The Jewish Americans* (New York, NY: Doubleday, 2007).

13. Alan Dershowitz, *Chutzpah* (Boston, MA: Little, Brown & Co., 1991).

14. Ruth R. Wisse, *If I Am Not for Myself* (New York, NY: Free Press, 1992).

15. John Loftus and Mark Aarons, *The Secret War Against the Jews: How Western Espionage Betrayed the Jewish People* (New York, NY: St. Martin's Press, 1994).

16. David Brog, *Standing with Israel* (Lake Mary, FL: FrontLine, 2006).

17. James Carroll, *Constantine's Sword* (Boston, Ma: Houghton Miflin, 2001).

18. Dennis Prager, *Intermountain Jewish News*, May 30, 2008.

19. *Intermountain Jewish News*, August 1, 2008.